P9-DXH-030

ORCHARD HOUSE

. . .

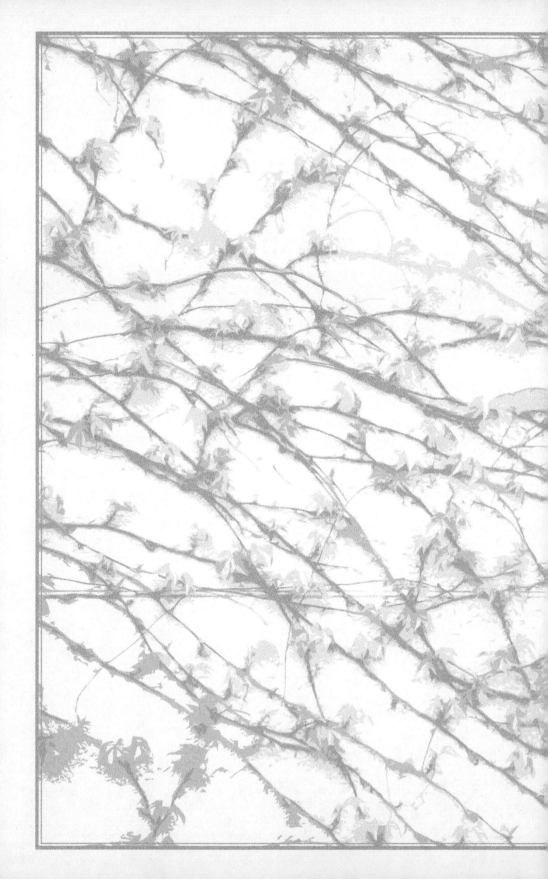

ORCHARD HOUSE

*How a Neglected Garden Taught
One Family to Grow*

. . .

TARA AUSTEN WEAVER

BALLANTINE BOOKS · NEW YORK

Published in the United States by Ballantine Books, an imprint of Random House, a
division of Random House LLC, a Penguin Random House Company, New York.

BALLANTINE and the HOUSE colophon are registered trademarks of
Random House LLC.

LIBRARY OF CONGRESS CATALOGING-IN-PUBLICATION DATA
Weaver, Tara Austen.
Orchard House : How a Neglected Garden Taught One Family to Grow /
Tara Austen Weaver.
pages cm
ISBN 978-0-345-54807-8 (hardcover : alk. paper)—ISBN 978-0-345-54808-5 (eBook)
1. Gardening. 2. Personal narratives. I. Title.
SB455.W42 2015
635—dc23
2014039547

Printed in the United States of America on acid-free paper

www.ballantinebooks.com

2 4 6 8 9 7 5 3 1

First Edition

Book design by Susan Turner

For my family

Oh! the things which happened in that garden! If you have never had a garden you cannot understand, and if you have had a garden you will know that it would take a whole book to describe all that came to pass there.

—Frances Hodgson Burnett, *The Secret Garden*

. . .

To bury grief, plant a seed.

—German proverb

AUTHOR'S NOTE

. . .

If the garden has taught me anything, it's that you cannot hurry time. A seed will sprout and flower and fruit all on its own schedule (greenhouses notwithstanding). A story, however, must sometimes be condensed—as this one has been. The timeline has been shortened, and, in some cases, names have been changed.

A memoir is, at heart, a work of memory—and memory is subjective. No two people experiencing the same event will remember it the same. This story is true to my memory, but anyone else who was there would tell it differently. This is what I experienced, this is how it was for me.

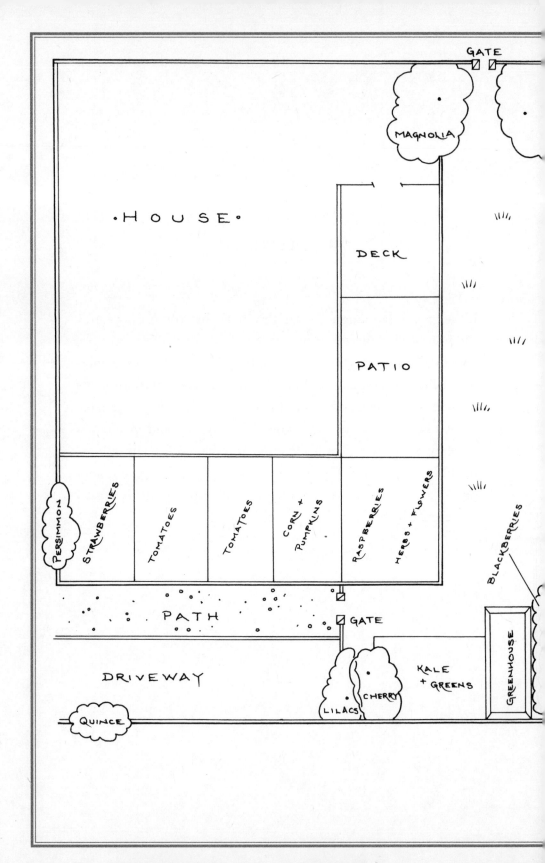

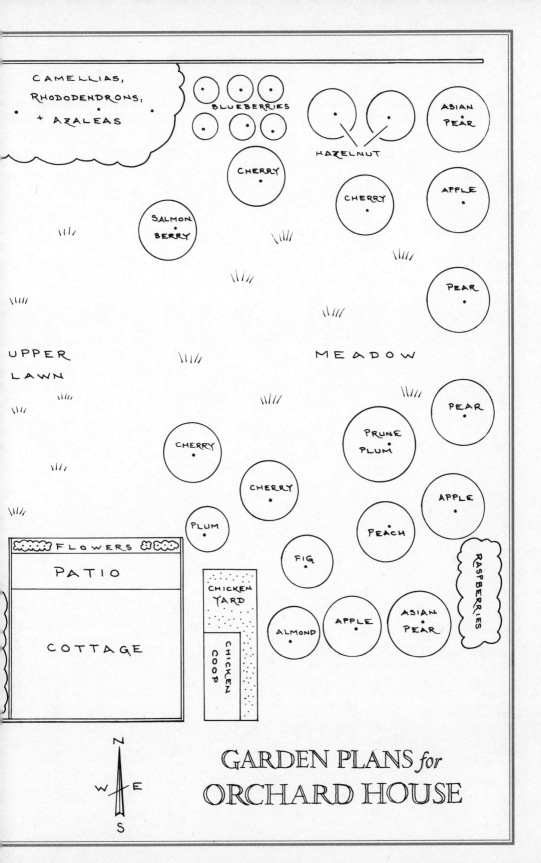

CAMELLIAS, RHODODENDRONS, + AZALEAS

BLUEBERRIES

ASIAN PEAR

CHERRY

HAZELNUT

CHERRY

APPLE

SALMON BERRY

PEAR

UPPER LAWN

MEADOW

PEAR

CHERRY

PRUNE PLUM

APPLE

CHERRY

PLUM

PEACH

FIG

RASPBERRIES

FLOWERS

PATIO

CHICKEN YARD

COTTAGE

CHICKEN COOP

ALMOND

APPLE

ASIAN PEAR

N
W   E
S

GARDEN PLANS *for*
ORCHARD HOUSE

A PLACE TO GROW

I HADN'T EXPECTED MUCH from the house. Looking back now, the details run together: ugly brown-and-orange carpet, windows turned cloudy where seals had failed. The stains on the wood floors, we were told, came from pet urine. Each room rolled out, one after another, a parade of awfulness. But it wasn't the house that I wanted to see.

It was the garden—half an acre, sloping long and narrow down the hill to a high wall of blackberries in the distance. We burst out of the dank house into generous sunlight, my nieces running ahead, past a small cottage locked up tight.

Time seemed to stop. Thorny vines snaked over rhododendrons towering tall above our heads. It was so quiet. The workday world lay elsewhere, far from this neglected garden. The grown-ups laughed in delight at this secret place we had discovered, improbable and unexpected.

The girls, small, blond creatures in sundresses, ran down the hill, their shouts ringing out. When they returned their faces were streaked purple from berry juice, arms filled with ripe Asian pears. *"Look,"* they cried. *"Look what we found."*

I did look—at sun-dried grass crunchy underfoot, at fruit trees drowning in vines and weed-strewn flower beds. Years of neglect had backed up on this place, overcome it like a wave, wiping out any order. Nature was reclaiming what had always been hers.

And yet, it felt magical. As the sun beat down on my shoulders, as my nieces' laughter floated up to the house that crouched atop the hill, I smiled. This, I thought, would be a good place to grow.

PART ONE

. . .

PLAN

1

. . .

STOLEN BERRIES

THE DAY AFTER WE saw the house with the real estate agent, my mother convinced me to go back, to break into the garden to pick those luscious blackberries. There was a solid stripe on the dry lawn where the berries were falling to the ground and staining the grass purple, unpicked and uneaten.

"What if someone catches us?" I was nervous. The house was on the market; it was a weekend; we would, technically, be stealing. My mother was unmoved. She has always been bolder than me.

"No one is going to catch us—and those berries are just going to waste."

If there is one thing my mother hates, it's wasted food. Her childhood taught her there is always someone who is hungry. We grabbed six large plastic containers and a bag to carry them in and made our way to the garden.

The house had been on the market for a year, uninhabited all that time. Large PRIVATE PROPERTY NO TRESPASSING signs hung on each of the tall wooden gates. The first we tried wouldn't open. Through the slats of the fence, I glimpsed the heavy padlock keeping it shut. For a moment it seemed our expedition would fail.

This would have been more comfortable for me—no risk of discovery, no getting in trouble, but also no berries. Peering on tiptoes over the tall wooden fence at the weedy backyard, I could see laden vines in the distance.

The second gate, on the south side of the house, was unlocked. Trying to ignore the angry red letters of the warning sign, I swung the sturdy door open, and we entered the garden.

The grass, mowed short and dry from the late summer sun, stretched from the house down the hill. On either side of the lawn, blackberries hung on vines that had engulfed whatever lay beneath them. The slightest shake or tug and they tumbled into our outstretched hands. The house was uninhabited, the garden fenced; no one had been there to pick. My mother and I looked at each other and grinned.

In a lifetime of picking blackberries, these were the largest I had ever seen. They plunked into our containers with a deep and satisfying thud, tasting like childhood, like summer condensed and made sweet. The sun warmed our backs as we fell into the slow rhythmic pace of picking.

"Do you really think you'll buy this place?" For me the property was equal parts enchantment and horror. I suspected the only way to redeem the house was to tear it down and start over, but I knew my mother wouldn't see it that way.

"I don't know," she said, picking steadily, always in motion. As long as my mother is busy, as long as something is being accomplished, we can talk. Otherwise she is off and running, and I am left trying to keep up.

"Do you really want to move back to Seattle?" It was the question I kept asking. *"Are you sure?"*

"I'm not sure about anything," she said, "but I *am* moving."

My mother had tried moving to Seattle once already. It hadn't worked.

Five years earlier, when my brother and sister-in-law were expecting their first child, my mother had bought a house on an island in Puget Sound, just off the Seattle coast, with a view of Mount Rainier. She settled in and prepared to play grandmother. It seemed a good idea at the time.

This baby was the first of a new generation: anticipated with such excitement, loved long before she arrived, so many hopes and dreams embodied in this small creature. When she was born, on a gray day in late January, we all rejoiced.

An unexpected reality quickly descended. The baby had been injured during the birth. There were complications, doctor's appointments, medical decisions no one was prepared for. Differences of opinion between new grandmother and daughter-in-law soon emerged, strife no one knew how to fix. I was hundreds of miles away, still living in San Francisco then, the recipient of anguished phone calls. I sat there, unable to make things better, listening to the sound of a family coming undone.

After a year my mother packed her things and fled back to California, to the home there that she had never gotten around to renting out. She didn't like Seattle, she said. The weather was gloomy, the island isolating; the mystical mountain that was her view rarely appeared. But I knew the real reason lay deeper. It seemed we were better at being a family from a distance.

Now, five years later, I was living in Seattle, and she wanted to move back.

I thought of my mother in California, in the house surrounded by the leafy yard where I had spent my teen years. The distance made things between us easier, smoother. We were kinder to each other on the phone than we ever were in person.

And yet, in some ways, it would be good to have her close. She was getting older. It was hard for me to reconcile the woman

who had always been the solid cornerstone of my world with the
idea of frailty, but when I hugged her now, she felt smaller in my
arms, less steady. Like a bird that might easily be crushed. Already there had been times when I couldn't reach her on the
phone and I had worried she might have fallen and been unable
to get up. She had few friends and no family in California, no
one to check up on her. In some ways it would be a relief to have
her in Seattle, especially as time passed.

"Is it locked?" I stopped picking and rattled the doorknob of
the cottage that stood halfway down the garden. It was a small
two-room thing, set atop a cracked patio and painted brown
with decoratively carved white trim. Moss grew on the roof,
and the windows were marked with strips of tape arranged in a
diamond pattern. It looked like something out of Bavaria, out of
"Hansel and Gretel," an enchanted garden cottage.

"The agent didn't know where the key was," my mother
said, peering through the dusty windows at empty rooms with
faded beige carpet.

"What would you use it for?" Already I was imagining her
living there.

"It could be my office," she replied. For most of my life, my
mother had seen her private practice therapy clients in an office
on the lower level of our home, with my brother and me on
orders to tiptoe around creaky floorboards and ignore any crying we might hear.

"You could use it as a writing studio," she suggested, looking
at me as I squinted through the windows. There was electricity
in the cottage; I could see baseboard heaters and light switches.
I could bring my laptop here to work surrounded by leafy green.

"The girls would love it." I imagined handmade DO NOT
DISTURB signs posted on the front door, no grown-ups allowed,
the walls soaked through with laughter and whispered secrets.
They'd be old enough for things like that in a few years.

"There's a sleeping loft," my mom pointed out. A tall ladder led to an open platform under slanting ceilings. I imagined them having sleepovers there, the proud and important feeling, as a child, of having a small corner of the world to claim as your own.

The garden was honeycombed with leafy bowers formed under towering rhododendrons, plenty of places to hide, and enough fruit to eat so you wouldn't have to stop for lunch. It reminded me of the semi-wild country yard I had grown up in, where apples off the tree and wild blackberries had fueled escapades of fort building and water-skeeter catching and where there was always a tree to climb to escape and read a book. This would be a wonderful place to be a child.

"Did you see the greenhouse?" my mother asked. This was what I had been most excited about: a greenhouse.

It was not an elegant greenhouse. Instead of glass, this greenhouse was made of corrugated plastic. It hadn't been well maintained either. Paving stones failed to suppress weeds now tall and yellowing in the summer sun. It didn't matter; I was thrilled.

A greenhouse would allow me to get a jump on the growing season, to sprout seeds in January or February and coddle them through the cold, wet spring. Peering into the plastic structure, looking at shelves and a venting system, I felt a bit giddy.

Beyond the greenhouse lay a long field. The blackberries were growing high there, hedges fifteen feet tall and loaded with fruit. Through a gap I could see the neighbor's yard, where chickens were running around, a rooster crowing triumphantly.

"Look, a fig tree." My mother was standing next to a tree slightly shorter than her five-foot frame. She reached out to touch the tiny fists of green. "They're not ripe yet," she said, disappointment in her voice. In California, a towering purple fig tree kept her in fruit through the late summer and into fall.

Beyond the fig was an Asian pear, the tree my nieces had found the day before. The fruit here had fallen to the ground, as if waiting for us to arrive and gather it.

Crunching on a juicy pear, tasting the clean, clear notes of approaching autumn, I was reminded of Japan, the far-off country where my mother used to live and where my family had all spent time. There these pears were served peeled and cut in wedges, a surprising juxtaposition of grainy texture with sweet juice. One bite and I could almost hear the creak of feet on tatami-mat floors. It made me feel oddly at home.

"Look at this." At the sound of my mother's voice, I turned to where she was standing, facing the tall, impenetrable hedge of blackberry brambles. There, suspended among the berry vines, hung a single red apple. If the apple was attached to a tree, we could see no sign of it.

I looked at the wall of berries, at least a decade's worth of growth. The vines were thick, jagged leaves on stems swollen and woody with age. "Are there *fruit trees* under all of that?"

"Who knows what's under there?" my mom said. There could have been anything—old garden sheds or rusty cars. Yet there hung an apple, glinting in the sun, tempting us to pick it.

It was late afternoon as we rounded the end of the yard and made our way up the south side. Large stands of pine and cedar in a neighboring yard cast shadows, and we had picked nearly six quarts of berries. Yet the garden still held a few more surprises for us.

"Is this an arbutus?" I ran my hand up the trunk of a medium-sized tree, the cinnamon-colored bark peeling away under my fingers. The more common name for these trees is madrone, but in my family we refer to them as they do in Canada: *arbutus*.

My mother looked up at me, surprised; then she smiled.

Arbutus grow on the small Canadian island where my family once lived, when I was a baby and my father hadn't yet left us. My mother loved the way the bark peeled off in sheets like writing paper. To see one here felt like a bit of serendipity, like it might have been planted just for us. As with the Asian pear, it was a sign of our past, of where we had come from, a reminder of home. My mother reached out to touch the tree.

"Will you look at that?" she said, a slight bit of wonder in her voice.

My attention had already been drawn to a larger tree behind it, the largest tree in the garden. I couldn't believe I hadn't noticed it. I hesitated before I said anything. I knew my words had the potential to change everything.

"I think that's a tulip tree," I said slowly.

This was the name we used for magnolias, their flowers like tulips, like saucers of pale, milky pink. These were the trees my mother sighed over.

Every spring she called me from California with her annual announcement: "The tulip tree in Larkspur is blooming."

Each year her words transported me back to when I was a little girl with knobby knees and shoelaces that wouldn't stay tied, when my mother took pictures of me and my brother under the outstretched branches of the old magnolia tree that grew on the main road into the town of Larkspur. It wasn't our tree, but we thought of it as our own. I remember looking up into a sky filled with petals, pink and soft like damp velvet. For a moment it felt as if the tree might reach down and hug me. For a moment I wished it would.

My mother stood there and surveyed the garden, gazing down the long, sloping yard, a hand on her hip. I saw what she saw: dry grass, berry vines, ramshackle cottage, fruit trees. I also saw what wasn't visible: *potential, promise, hope.*

"I guess that does it," she said, and sighed.

In the sunshine of that early-September day, my mother found her new home. And with it, my family found our garden.

2

. . .

GIDDY

THE IDEA THAT MY family might garden together was somewhat absurd. We weren't a teamwork family, the sort that does things together. We didn't have Sunday dinners, we didn't go on family trips or hold reunions—we didn't even barbecue. We gathered dutifully for birthdays and muddled through holidays as best we could. It's not that we didn't love each other. I'm just not sure we knew what to do next.

I always hoped we could be more—but I didn't know how to make that happen. If there was an instruction manual on family unity, we hadn't received ours. Instead we were stuck making it up as we went along.

My mother left Seattle the day after our berry excursion and arrived in California the following afternoon. She then walked across the street to her neighbor, who was a real estate agent, and put her house on the market. "I don't want to fix it up," she told him. "I don't want to do anything. I just want to sell it."

A week later, at the broker's open house, she did just that. This left her thirty days to pack up the entire house and be gone.

Two weeks later I was in California, surrounded by boxes and the rubble of my childhood. There was a yawning dumpster in the driveway and a series of moving pods that were slowly being filled with my mother's belongings. The life that had been lived in this house for the past twenty-four years was being systematically dismantled.

Everywhere I looked there were memories: the Chinese carpet where my brother and I had staged renditions of Broadway musicals; the bushes out front where I used to hide the ugly bike helmet my mother made me wear to school. I could still navigate the downstairs hallway without need of a light. My hips swiveled to avoid the corner of the washing machine, my foot naturally stepped wide on the creaky stair. My relationship with this place defied words. Every object, every corner made me stop and sigh. I was drowning in memories and nostalgia. My mother was much more businesslike.

"Do you think you could go any faster?" She had found me stalled over an elementary school knitting project I'd unearthed in a basket in the garage: a mitten, only half-done, abandoned and forgotten years ago.

"I can't believe you still have all this."

The garage still had everything. There was the printing set that had been used to make my baby announcements, a kendo uniform from my brother's brief stint in martial arts, racing tires for a bicycle that had once belonged to me. There were also things in the garage that predated my memory.

"Are these yours, Mom?" I was sorting through a musty cardboard box I'd never seen before.

The box was full of gardening books. There was a paperback copy of the original organic gardening encyclopedia by J. I. Rodale. The collection included *The City People's Book of Raising Food* and hand-lettered pamphlets out of Berkeley on how to make compost. Digging below, I felt newsprint and pulled up a copy of the *Whole Earth Catalog*. As I fingered the fragile pages, a thought occurred to me.

"Hey, Mom. Were you a back-to-the-lander?"

I had heard of the back-to-the-land movement. In the late sixties and the seventies, across America, thousands of young people moved to the country to grow their own food. Some had become disillusioned with modern life; others were spurred by the energy crisis or the environmental movement. I had friends who grew up on a farm their parents had carved out of the Idaho wilderness, but I had never thought it had anything to do with us.

She glanced over at the books I was holding. "What do you mean?"

"You know—back-to-the-land. Is that why we moved to the country?"

"You mean the hippies? I was never a hippie, you know that."

"Not hippies—farms and communes and growing your own food. There was a whole movement."

My mother shrugged. "I don't know anything about that."

"Then why did we move out of the city?"

She sighed, brushing back strands of wavy gray hair that had worked their way loose and now framed her face, wiping her hands on a worn sweatshirt that might once, many years ago, have belonged to me.

"I wanted you kids to grow up in nature," she said, leaning against the doorjamb. "I wanted you to know that carrots came from the ground, not the supermarket, that eggs don't magically appear in Styrofoam cartons." She looked small and tired.

She sighed again, before turning back to her own boxes. "I was never part of a movement. I just wanted you to have a garden."

———

An anthropologist might argue the case differently. Because she moved to the country in the early seventies in order to grow food, my mother might be considered part of the back-to-the-land movement, but there is one key difference. A movement is an effort by a large number of people organized together. It implies cooperation, community. My mother might have ordered her tools from the *Whole Earth Catalog* and bought the books and pamphlets of the era, but she did not organize; she did not commune. My mother did it alone.

Not long after my father left, she moved to the country with two small children. There she chopped wood and fed chickens—and battled the raccoons that tried to attack in the night. She dealt with winter storms and frequent blackouts and a seasonal creek that sometimes overflowed its banks. None of these were things she had grown up with. She was a city girl, though a few years living in remote Big Sur and on a small Canadian island had worn off that sheen. Still, raising two children on your own is hard when you don't have to chop wood and grow your own food. Why make extra work for yourself?

The answer is survival. When my mother bought a third of an acre with room for chickens and fruit trees and a creek running through it, there was peace of mind in knowing, no matter what happened, she would be able to feed her children. The land was her sense of security.

There's a whole different story that could be told about why such security is important to my mother. It might be because of her own poor and difficult childhood, where her mother died early, and she earned her own keep, and food was a commodity not to be taken lightly. Perhaps the answers lie deeper, handed down in genes that remember what it was like to be hungry, to be hunted. My mother shares blood with those who fled the Cossacks, the pogroms, the Nazis. Ownership of land, the ability to raise food, was a shot at a future.

When we found the Seattle garden, it felt like the pendulum

had swung back to where it had been in the late sixties and early seventies: economic woes and environmental fears. People were rethinking their front lawns and considering tomatoes instead. Sales of seeds had skyrocketed; the waiting lists at community gardens were suddenly years long. Local foods were booming. Were we going back to the land again? In precarious times, was the ability to raise food still our best shot at a future?

I took the dusty books off the shelf in the garage that day. The gardening books, their covers wavy with age, the hand-drawn pamphlets—all tools used to spread a message, to usher in a new age, a better way of life. I put them in a new box to take to Seattle, to the new garden.

I took something else from the garage that day, a scrap of fabric from a dress my mother used to wear when I was a little girl. It was a wraparound dress, the sort popular at the time. I still remember the long ties looped around her small waist, how the skirt flared when she turned.

I took the fabric to remember a young woman who moved to the country, alone with two small children. She might not have known what she was in for, but she dug a life for us out of local dirt and her own grit. When I think of it now, I am astounded. How hard it must have been, how we all struggled, how brave she was to even try.

In the midst of that month of packing, my mother flew up to Seattle for the inspection on the house with the garden. After it had sat on the market for a year with little interest, there were multiple offers as soon as my mother showed up. For a while it seemed possible she might have gambled and lost: sold her California house for nothing. In the end, a clever escalation clause got her offer accepted.

We arrived for the inspection on a day that was gray and overcast. The house looked worse than I remembered: small, dingy bedrooms, a kitchen and bathroom that had been cheaply overhauled before the place was put on the market. The house had been added to over the years, resulting in an awkward layout that included a living room jutting into the garden. Here the elderly gentleman who was selling the house had spent the last few years: in bed with a view of azaleas and rhododendrons.

"This is where I am going to live when I can't get out of bed anymore," my mother said as we walked through the empty house, footsteps echoing on wooden floors. "You can all come to pay your respects."

That's the sort of humor my mother has, a dark and sarcastic sensibility shaped by struggle.

I was looking at the house the same way. Were the hallways wide enough to accommodate a wheelchair? At seventy-two my mother was in good health, but this was for the long haul. With the extra bedroom and family room on the lower level, the house was large enough to accommodate a caretaker living there.

"Is your mother worried about resale value?" the real estate agent asked me.

"*She's* not going to be the one selling it," I told him. I knew this would likely be my mother's last home.

Despite the house, the property seemed like a gift—this much land in the city, fruit trees, a greenhouse. It would be a family farm we could work together, a place for my nieces to grow and run wild, a source of security my mother would pass down to me and I would eventually pass on to the girls. No one was thinking of selling.

If the worst came to pass, as economists and environmentalists were forecasting, it would be possible for our entire family to live and grow much of what we needed in this large new house and yard. I suspect other people don't plan for worst-case scenarios like this, but other people didn't grow up in my family.

All through the discussion with the inspector about water

damage and drainage issues, my attention kept shifting to the garden outside the windows. The windows whose seals had failed and would need to be replaced. The house felt like a necessary evil; it was the garden I cared about.

The night after the inspection, we talked about the garden.

"Where would you put the raspberries?" my mother asked as I stood leaning against the doorway of the room she stayed in when she visited. She was in bed already, the reading lamp next to her casting wild shadows against the walls and high ceiling.

"Down along the fence, on the left side." I imagined a wall of raspberries, red and golden, growing in the sunshine of the south end of the yard. Bowlfuls of tender ruby thimbles to be picked on summer days, a crush of tart sweetness in the mouth.

"What fruit trees would you grow?" she asked.

It had been years since my mother had truly gardened. The winter I was eleven a storm had flooded our area, knocking down fences, carrying away picnic tables, and nearly evacuating our town. Houses slid down hillsides as the water-saturated earth gave way, and people canoed the streets on rising floodwaters the sandbags couldn't restrain. Northern California was declared a disaster zone.

When the floodwaters receded, our garden was covered with a fine sandy silt and knee-deep muck. We moved not long after that, partially to be closer to the city where my mother was then working and partially, I think, because she didn't have the heart to rebuild her garden. She tended the fig trees already growing in the leafy yard we moved to, but she hadn't planted a vegetable garden again.

Growing up, I had never liked gardening. I remembered the weeding chores of my childhood, the wait for something to grow and become ripe. Gardening seemed to belong to those more accustomed to the passage of time and less anxious about it. I was too young, too impatient. For years, however, I'd had a sneaking suspicion that gardening was lying dormant in me and would eventually awaken. It was only with my move to Seattle that I had taken up the trowel for real.

It was an odd thing, my mother asking my opinion like this. As the lone grown-up in charge of my childhood, she had been the law. Yet I had recently completed a six-month permaculture training course, and it was possible that I now had more gardening knowledge than she did. It was more recent knowledge, at least.

Still, it was strange to have her defer to me, even in this small way. It made me feel as if the earth were shifting ever so slightly on its axis—nearly imperceptible and yet profound.

I pushed away from the doorway and walked around to the far side of the bed, pulling back the covers and slipping under them next to her. This was not something I usually did. Most of the time I tried to keep my distance with my mother, tried to keep my boundaries.

If my mother noticed, she made no comment.

We planned an orchard lying there in bed. Cherry trees for my mom who loves them, a quince and Italian prune plum for me, a persimmon, which we both like. There was enough land in the garden to dream big, wildly. There would be blueberry bushes, a potato patch, kiwi vines, strawberries. We talked about corn and tomatoes and trellises for green beans and peas. We'd plant zucchini. ("Only one," my mom warned. "You never need more than one zucchini.") There would be seeds to start in the greenhouse early in the year and then move outside. A fragrant and fruitful garden grew in our heads before a single weed had been pulled or speck of soil amended.

"You know we're giddy about this?" my mom said quietly, and she was right. We were both so excited about the idea of this huge garden.

Happy is not a word often associated with my mother—never

giddy. But this garden felt like the beginning of a new chapter for all of us. Perhaps things could be different this time.

The next day my mother took my nieces to the garden, to play in the fall sunshine. The inspection was done, but the house was still not ours; it didn't seem to matter. In every other way, the garden belonged to us.

I met them there later to drive everyone home. I came around the south side of the house, past the weed-strewn side yard and through the wooden gate that still held the NO TRES-PASSING sign.

I heard the laughter before I saw them, the girls' faces again streaked with fruit juice and berry stains, bare feet running across the dry grass, my mother chasing after them as they shouted and giggled.

"Let's roll down the hill!" Abby stretched out on the mild slope of the lawn, flopping over and over again as she rolled away from the house. Her sister came after, a blond ponytail that whipped around and around. Then my mother, my stern and cynical mother, followed, rolling and rolling until she sat up, dizzy, with dry grass in her hair, smiling, laughing. I had never seen her like this before.

That was the moment it all melted away: my resistance to this move, fears about what might happen, discomfort at the idea of my mother living so close.

As she had with my brother and me years before, my mother wanted to give her granddaughters a garden. It was as simple as that.

3

. . .

PLANTING HOPE

SEATTLE IS A CITY of gardeners; I noticed it immediately the first spring I spent there. As I left to go to the farmers' market on a sunny weekend in April, every house on the block buzzed with yard work. After weeks of not seeing my neighbors, I found that they were all outside, weeding, pruning, digging: hearty folk in fleece pullovers and muddy boots. That Wednesday, mine was the only house on the block without a green yard-waste bin at the curb for pickup.

I had arrived in Seattle from San Francisco at the end of March. I was staying in a house meant to be a rental, chosen for minimal maintenance. It had a deck off the back and a postage stamp of a lawn in the front, and wood chips had been laid along the sides, so there was no need even for weeding. It was absolutely the wrong place to try to garden. And yet, there were the raspberries.

I had seen them at a nursery stand at the farmers' market in

San Francisco before I came to Seattle. They were an old heirloom strain, I was told, planted years ago by a Dutch woman in
the town of Sebastopol and passed from gardener to gardener
over the years. They bore small and sweet fruit in the early summer.

I had memories of picking raspberries when I was a child,
when we lived in the country on a rambling third of an acre.
Our raspberry patch was too shady and had never really thrived,
but there were a few small, thimblelike berries to pluck each
year. I remembered the soft crush of flavor in the mouth. I
wanted my nieces to have that same experience.

I bought two half-gallon pots. I couldn't resist.

The raspberries rode up with me to Seattle, nestled in the
footwell of the passenger seat. I felt like those explorers and settlers from history who sailed off to new lives and new worlds,
bringing seeds and cuttings they could only hope would thrive
in the places they were going. I thought about how much trust
and blind faith it takes to uproot and replant oneself on unfamiliar shores.

That was not what I was doing. I wasn't moving to Seattle;
my plan was to come for a few months—through the summer. I
had a book to write, an empty house in which to stay, and I
wanted to help my brother and sister-in-law with the kids, to get
to know my nieces. I never planned to put down roots. Despite
the raspberries, I was not the gardening type.

We'd had a garden when I was a child, of course, but besides
playing in it, I'd had little interest. I didn't like weeding. I didn't
like to be hot. I couldn't understand the long-sleeve shirts my
mother donned to protect herself from the acrid tomato plants.
I never wanted a garden when I grew up.

And yet, there was something appealing about creating
beauty. I was sixteen when my mother bought the house she'd
live in for the next twenty-four years, surrounded by its leafy
yard, and asked if I wanted to help with a neglected portion that

backed up against a large oleander hedge. It might have been an odd thing to entrust to a teenager, but as the oldest child in a single-parent home, I often functioned beyond my age.

I bought gardening books, did research, and discovered not much would grow in the shade of the large hedge. I settled on ferns and rhododendrons, even though I have never liked them, and took my list to a nearby garden store. When I showed the plans to my mother, they came with a cost estimate of nearly three hundred dollars. The rhododendrons I had selected were sixty dollars each.

"Oh, no, sweetie. You don't buy them full-sized," she said. "You go to the starter nursery where you can get them small, for seven dollars."

"But how long will it be before they get big?" I was doubtful.

"Six or seven years."

This was an inconceivable period of time to me—nearly half my life. I didn't have that sort of patience. I wanted things to look pretty now.

Secretly, though, I suspected gardening was a seed that might awaken in me given the right set of circumstances: enough water and light, room to grow.

It might have already tried to emerge the winter before I left San Francisco. That year for my birthday, I had bought a series of window boxes at the hardware store and heavy brackets. I then spent an afternoon hanging out the window, mostly upside down, trying to mount them to the exterior of my third-floor Edwardian dining room.

It was a precarious situation. Getting the correct angle to drill into the building required me to lean so far out the window I worried I might fall. The weight of the power drill made my arm ache, and trying to brace both the bracket and the small screws was a feat in one-handed coordination. If I dropped anything down the air shaft, it would be lost forever.

At one point I looked over to see a neighbor staring at me

quizzically from his side of the space between buildings. I smiled wanly and went back to my task. Those of us who want to grow in a densely populated city have to make our own gardens.

When I was done, the boxes were crooked, uneven, but solid. I felt triumphant as I filled them with potting soil and nestled tender herbs in the earthy mixture. It smelled like a forest, dark and primitive.

All the while I was thinking of the day I would pull open the window to clip sprigs of thyme, oregano, and rosemary. I dreamed of fresh basil to layer with summer tomatoes, minced parsley and chives to sprinkle on goat cheese omelets.

After a week, however, I noticed white spots on the soft, wide leaves of the sage plant. Was it some sort of fungus? I lived on the foggy side of San Francisco; perhaps the moisture and lack of sun had led to an infection.

When I looked closer, the mystery became clear. It wasn't a fungal infection at all. That splattering of white on my sage leaves was pigeon poop, an offering from the neighborhood birds.

I knew then I wouldn't be using any of those herbs. I wouldn't be gardening in the city.

Seattle, however, felt like the sort of city where you could have a garden. In those first weeks and months, I saw many. There were other yards with raspberry canes growing in them. The owners of a house two blocks away had planted their entire front yard with blueberry bushes. And one day, while driving through the Madrona neighborhood, I passed a yard where small goats with floppy ears were eating their way across a steep hillside.

The raspberries thrived. I planted them alongside the house, in one of the few sunny spots, and watched them grow. I hadn't expected fruit that first year, but there were a few small handfuls of tiny berries, sweet and tart. My niece Abby, only two at the time, picked them alongside me, gobbling down the fruit still warm from the sun.

"More," she said, when she was done with the seven or eight berries we had picked that day. Her straw-blond hair was pulled back in a ponytail, wispy bits curling around her face. She held out a small, pudgy hand to show it was empty. *"Want more."*

"Oh, sweetie, we don't have any more today." I knelt down next to her and looked into imploring blue eyes. "We have to wait for the plant to grow more berries, and for the sun to ripen them." I knew this was a foreign concept to a child whose food came entirely from the grocery store, plentiful in season or out. "Maybe there will be more next week."

I braced myself for incomprehension, for tears or tantrums, but there were none. "Grow more berries, plant!" she said encouragingly, and I wondered if perhaps nature is the best teacher of patience at any age.

The raspberries led to herbs, which led to a desire for tomatoes and arugula and to the purchase of two blueberry bushes. At that point you might as well throw in a zucchini and a cucumber. There needed to be basil—enough for batches of pesto—and radishes for their crunch and color. My garden dreams included far more plants than I had room for.

I couldn't disturb the lawn out front, and the back deck overlooked a steep wilderness of blackberry bushes. My only hope lay in the small area alongside the house. It was terraced due to the hill, covered in wood chips, and got only partial sunshine, but it would have to do. Bloom where you're planted, right?

But when I raked back the wood chips, the soil I found was awful—clay dirt mixed with gravel. I wasn't sure anything would grow in such poor conditions, certainly not bloom. My gardening urges were being foiled at every turn.

Replacing the soil seemed the only solution: to dig up each and every one of the terraced beds and fill them instead with a mix of compost and good soil for planting. It was a daunting task but I got my shovel and started digging. Hesitation never grew anyone tomatoes.

When a friend came to visit, I excitedly showed her my "garden" thus far: the series of terraced planter areas, how much soil I had dug and replaced, how much I still had to do.

"Why don't you hire someone to do this?" she asked as we stood in our sandals looking at the partially shady, mostly un-suitable area where I was trying to garden. "Some burly guy could take care of this in a weekend."

I was taken aback. It had never occurred to me to get help—it almost never does. Not even when digging out the poor soil and gravel inflamed my lower back and left me lying on the floor, knees up, waiting for the spasm to pass.

The truth was, I loved the digging. I loved the physicality of it. At the end of an afternoon, I had something to show for my labor: I could point to what I had accomplished. There was very little of this in my job as a writer and editor, where I often felt like I was spinning my wheels. After an afternoon of work, my in-box was only slightly less full than when I started. There was rarely any sense of achievement, little pride.

There was something deeper as well. Perhaps it was my childhood in the country, or perhaps it was the legacy of our own agricultural past, but when I placed my shovel in the dirt and used the strength of my leg to drive it deep, *it felt right*. My body knew the motions. As if, in some primitive way, this was exactly what I should be doing.

I could have hired someone else, but I didn't want to. When my neighbor caught me outside one day, still digging and put-tering as the sun went down and the sky grew dark, she laughed. "You've become a Seattleite!" she shouted across the small lawn between our houses.

Even though I had told everyone I was only going to Seattle for the season, I could feel myself falling for the slower pace of life and a city that seemed to float on water. Summer there was glorious, filled with early-morning lake swims and evenings that lingered, light shimmering endlessly on bays, islands, and mountains. Though I needed to go back to San Francisco for work in the fall, I was already wondering if I could come back the next spring, if perhaps this watery city where people planted their front yards with blueberry bushes could be home.

It was June of that first summer in Seattle when I went to the Ballard Farmers Market with a friend. We were sitting on the low curb of the sidewalk, eating quesadillas we had bought from a vendor and watching the crowd go by, their shopping bags stuffed with strawberries and lettuce, fresh eggs and flowers. There were kids and dogs and a carnival atmosphere as my friend let slip the news I had been expecting. Expecting and dreading.

I had been in love in San Francisco, a relationship that had felt comfortable and comforting, unlike any I had known before. Over time, however, things had begun to warp into bouts of drinking and self-destruction. I had never loved anyone who struggled with addiction before, and I hadn't known how to deal with it. Or how to deal with the long periods between the drinking when everything seemed good, seemed wonderful. In those periods it was easy to pretend there was nothing wrong, until it all fell apart again.

I was not blameless in the situation. I had been scared, unable to commit, unable to walk away. I couldn't understand how this connection that felt like home could, at the same time, feel so unstable, so scary. Perhaps I did not remember how unstable my own home had been. I learned early to deal with crisis: I coped, I white-knuckled it. How do you walk away when the person you love is drowning?

The eventual dissolution left me dizzy with grief and guilt. I *had* walked away, but not because I wanted to. The end had damaged us both beyond repair. I found myself blinking in disbelief at an open blue sky. How was it possible we wouldn't grow old together?

I had been replaced, immediately—a new relationship to plug the gaping wound left by the old—but even there lines were not drawn clearly. There were late-night drunken messages left on my phone, offers of forgiveness, second chances if I wanted to come back. Things lingered on, erupting at unexpected moments.

In the back of my head, even I thought it might still work out—at some distant time in the future when we were both more healed. If it's meant to be, I told myself, maybe it still will be. It was what I needed to believe.

That day, sitting on a Seattle street corner, I heard the news: They were expecting a baby, due in the fall. The life we had talked about would now be lived with someone else.

It didn't hit me until later in the afternoon, as I was standing amid racks of plants at a local nursery. I didn't know what to do with this grief, this thing that made me question all my decisions. Surely they must all have been wrong to bring me to this place of sadness and loss. I put sunglasses on to hide my tears. I longed for exhaustion, to sleep like the dead, anything not to feel the roil of my own emotions.

Instead I bought plants. I loaded my cart with three different types of tomatoes, basil, arugula, and chard. I took them home and planted them as the day grew gray and it began to rain. I stomped my shovel into the earth and piled the dirt high, worms burrowing to get away from the disturbance. Then I settled the plants in with a grim face, patting the soil around them until I dropped my trowel and sat on the stairs and wept.

The shock of it made me feel like I was drowning in cold water, like it was hard to breathe. I cried into my gardening gloves and smeared dirt on my face. The future I had held on to would not be mine, and I was left wondering what the shape of my life would be. Suddenly the slate felt blank and foreboding; the only thing I could focus on was the plants.

My tomatoes would not cure the pain or make me feel less lost, but it was the best I could do on a dark day when the Seattle skies cried along with me. Putting a plant in the ground is an investment in the future—even if that future is only tomato season a few months away. You are saying you think you'll be around to water those plants, to eat their yield, to enjoy what they may produce. In the midst of uncertainty, it is an act of faith.

That day I planted hope, tender and green.

4

. . .

A CITY OF GARDENS

I HADN'T HEARD OF the Boeing Bust until I moved to Seattle, but I soon learned the details. In the late sixties, with government spending on the Vietnam War and the Apollo space program drying up, Boeing found itself heavily leveraged. The aerospace company was the largest employer in the area, and the resulting layoffs devastated the local economy, leaving Seattle with the highest unemployment rate in the country. Tens of thousands lost their jobs; so many people fled the city that local U-Haul dealerships ran out of trailers. A billboard was put up near the airport that read WILL THE LAST PERSON LEAVING SEATTLE TURN OUT THE LIGHTS. Dark humor for darker times.

This was also the era of the back-to-the-land movement, across the country. These two forces inspired a young student at the University of Washington to action. In the midst of economic woes and environmental concerns, Darlyn Rundberg Del

Boca decided to plant a garden. Like my mother, she thought it important that kids know where their food came from. She also wanted to grow vegetables for Neighbors in Need, a precursor to the local food banks. Jobs and paychecks in Seattle were vanishing overnight; people were hungry.

In the months that followed, Del Boca convinced the Picardo family, owners of a truck farm in northeast Seattle, to let her use one of their fields. The city agreed to pay taxes on the property, and the teachers and students at a nearby school volunteered to tend the land. Families who helped were given small plots for themselves around the perimeter. It was the beginning of what would become the city's community gardening program.

I had heard about these gardens even before I moved to Seattle. They were called P-Patches in homage to the Picardo family. While I was still living in San Francisco, I'd read newspaper articles about how so many people in Seattle wanted to garden that there were waiting lists for community garden plots. It seemed hard to believe at the time.

By my second spring in Seattle, still living there only part-time, I considered myself one of those people. I had reached capacity with my tiny side garden and had begun casting my eyes at the embankment below the deck. It got only morning sun, but buttercups grew there, thick and lush. If there was enough sun for weeds, surely there was enough for vegetables.

Emboldened by my success the summer before, I carved out a strip of earth from the hillside using a pitchfork and shovel. The soil was rich and dark, and I got giddy with the possibilities. I would plant broccoli! Cauliflower! Kale! Leeks! All things are possible at the beginning of a gardening season.

At the nursery the next day, I bought the season's first vegetable starts. The leeks were threadlike, fetal versions of the vegetables they would grow to become. The kale and cauliflower were sturdier, textured leaves spouting upward. I nestled them into the dark soil, planting their plastic tags beside them, though clearly the leaves of the cauliflower looked nothing like those of the kale.

Then I went out of town. It was March but I wasn't worried—the vegetables would be watered by the rain. I couldn't wait to see how much bigger they would be when I returned. All things are possible at the beginning of a gardening season.

I came home from my two-week trip late at night, but by first light I was outside, still in pajamas, scrambling down the steep and muddy slope to check my vegetables at the bottom. How big had they grown?

Vegetables? *What vegetables?* I couldn't find them.

I searched along the strip of soil I had cleared but saw nothing. The plastic tags were still there, but the sprouting starts had vanished. All that was left were a few nubbins of stem. Any tender leaves had been nibbled into oblivion.

This is how I learned that buttercup makes excellent slug habitat—and that slugs have a taste for kale. I couldn't believe the destruction. The hillside belonged to the slimy creatures. I had to come up with another solution.

The back deck that overlooked the buttercup hill also overlooked a house down below. I didn't know those neighbors, but in winter when the trees lost their leaves, I could see into their yard. There was a deck, a path, and four raised garden beds just sitting there. *Four raised garden beds.*

It was more space than I had ever dreamed of, and I itched to plant them with peas and radishes and tender lettuces. The things I could grow with four whole garden beds! The Commandments warn us not to covet our neighbors' wives; they make no mention of their raised garden beds.

Would it be weird to ask if they were going to use them?

Maybe they had installed them in a fit of ambition but had later grown tired of gardening. Maybe the beds had been there when they bought the house and had never been used. Desperation makes us concoct all sorts of crazy schemes—and this was my first taste of gardener desperation. I could offer to rent their beds from them, or share what I grew. There had to be something that could be done.

I pondered my plan for a few days, until I woke up on a Saturday to the sound of digging. I ran out on the balcony and saw a man wearing a straw hat spading up the beds I had dreamed of working myself. As the day went by, I watched him weed and plant and do all the things I wanted to do.

I moped for a week or two, looking balefully at my small gardening area. It seemed such a disappointment after I'd envisioned flat land and full sun. What had given me great happiness the summer before, what had seemed like such an upgrade over my crooked window boxes in San Francisco, no longer satisfied me. I wanted more.

Something needed to be done.

The year before I had taken myself on a tour of the P-Patches. There was a waiting list for plots, and I'd wanted to apply early, to be ready. Before I sent in my application, I decided to survey the scene.

There was a steep bit of hillside on Phinney Ridge, with a view of snowcapped mountains, that had been terraced into cascading garden beds—I could only imagine the work it had taken to build on such a slope. There was a sunny plot attached to a pocket park near Green Lake, and a tidy spot in Ballard that featured a demonstration garden. I took my toddler niece with me on that last visit. We looked curiously at ruby-colored stalks of rainbow chard and the lacy fronds of carrots.

The garden I liked the best, however, the one I could imagine myself part of, was the original Picardo Farm in the northeast section of the city. It was large—more than two hundred plots. The year-round gardens featured berry bushes, grape trellises, and other perennial plantings. The summer plots offered a seasonal lease, after which time the gardens were dismantled,

plowed, and sown with a cover crop to enrich the soil. Because
of the size, I assumed it would have a decent turnover. In the
smaller gardens, I suspected that someone would need to move
away or die before you could get a plot.

In the midst of my garden frustration, a postcard arrived
welcoming me as a new member of the P-Patch program, assigned to Picardo Farm. My planning had paid off.

One Saturday in April I attended the orientation for new
gardeners. I looked curiously at my fellow newbies: families
with small children, a few older folks, some young. Though we
spanned the age range and a few ethnicities, everyone had the
hearty look of a Seattleite, dressed in rain slickers and fleece. I
wondered about the other thing we all shared—whatever mysterious thing made us want to grow food.

There were other people at the orientation, returning gardeners who had been at Picardo for years. There were benches
dedicated in memory of gardeners who had passed on. I'd heard
of three Picardo marriages: relationships that had started over a
row of peas or chard. I was charmed by a place where such things
might happen. I was still new to Seattle, still trying to find where
I might fit in, still deciding if this was my place. A garden seemed
like a good spot to find community, or to grow it.

What was harder to find that first day was my Picardo plot.
I stood on the sidewalk overlooking the farm and tried to align
the map I had been given with the grid in the garden below.
Picardo Farm was set below street level and took up the better
part of a block. I wondered if people driving by had any idea of
the small garden city down below.

The side of the garden that held the seasonal plots looked
like a gold rush boomtown that April morning. String and poles
measured out paths on bare earth: Here were the trails. Here
were the garden plots. This was your land to tend. We all had a
claim to stake that early-spring day.

Returning gardeners were already at work, building trellises, marking paths. Some of the more ambitious had decorated with flags or banners—though this might have been to help them find their plots again in the maze. All the plots looked the same: flat brown soil newly turned up. Each had that rich smell of good earth, like a forest floor, primal and fecund. I looked at the ten-by-twenty-foot plot that was now mine.

The emptiness was daunting. Always before, I had gardened around obstacles: poor sunlight, a sloping hillside, other plants already in place. Restrictions made decisions for you; they narrowed options. The idea of a flat and sunny plot, a blank slate, was overwhelming. It was intimidating. Where to begin? I had no idea how to start a garden.

I should have known what I was doing. I had watched my mother garden for most of my childhood. But when I close my eyes, I see cherry tomatoes, cornstalks, green beans, a plum tree laden with fruit. There must have been early-spring days full of seed packets and mud, but I don't remember them.

I looked at the returning gardeners, already working their plots. Some were covering the soil with black plastic—presumably to kill weeds, though perhaps also to warm things up. I imagined the black plastic would attract the heat of the sun. April in Seattle is still too cold to plant many things.

Other people were even more industrious. A few were working with wooden frames spread with coarse mesh, using them to sift out lumps and rocks from their plots. The resulting soil looked like fine powder, but what a hassle! I couldn't imagine sifting through two hundred square feet of what was already better soil than I had ever gardened in.

I couldn't imagine much. Should I plant seeds? Should I buy starts? Should I build a trellis? And what to plant? Too many questions; I didn't have answers.

Instead, I did the only thing that made sense to me in the moment. I looked around, tried to orient my plot so I could find it again, and I fled the scene.

Earlier that year, before I had been assigned to my P-Patch, I had attended a presentation on permaculture, though I didn't really know what that word meant. I went because I was new to the city and attending a lot of things, casting my net wide. I was idly curious but not serious. I assumed it was a type of gardening: organic, biodynamic, permaculture.

As I sat listening, my interest was sparked. Permaculture was about gardening, but not only that. It was a methodology for creating sustainable human development—it dealt with growing food, of course, but also water issues, waste management, building homes, creating energy. Instead of depleting our resources— as most human activity does to some extent—we could design systems that were truly sustainable and even regenerative. People were already doing this around the world.

Using a mixture of age-old wisdom, the study of nature, and new science, permaculturalists were creating perennial gardens and food forests with nearly unimaginable yields. They were designing systems that allowed food to grow in desert areas with almost no rainfall. They were building houses that reused water and barely needed heating. Growing up in the environmental movement, I had been told all my life that we were on a course bound for certain devastation. Permaculture was the first thing I'd heard of that sounded promising, seemed hopeful. I left that day, my mind abuzz, and soon signed up for a six-month training course in this methodology I barely understood.

Permaculture would teach me how to plan and plant a garden, I was sure of it. But on that April day at Picardo, I'd only had one class; I still didn't know anything.

As spring rolled into summer, however, I began to learn. In my weekend classes, we studied how to start seeds, to plant in "guilds" so each plant was compatible with its neighbor and would grow strong. I learned how to landscape in a way that channeled rainwater where it would be most useful. We built trellises and dug a pond and calculated the amount of rainwater that could be harvested off the roof of a house.

My garden was a reflection of these early lessons. Instead of square beds, I made curving paths to maximize my planting area. Instead of rows, I planted more naturalistically, with strawberries tucked along the edges, lettuces behind, and chard to the rear where it could grow tall. I scribbled everything down in a notebook, for fear I might forget what I had put where. There were few straight lines in permaculture. It was a wilder, less obvious system.

As my gardening knowledge grew, so did my P-Patch. I was always amazed at what had taken place since my last visit. Pea shoots unfurled and began to climb the tepees of bamboo poles I had built (two of them, so my nieces could each have one to hide in). Purslane sprouted, and strawberries flowered, and an unidentified tomatolike plant that had volunteered began to thrive. When it sprouted flowers and small, round green fruit, I assumed it was some sort of Thai eggplant, but the fruit was bitter and never seemed to ripen. This is how I learned that potato plants produce fruit above ground as well as spuds down below.

There were disappointments as well. The tender arugula I started from seed was nibbled into lacy patterns by something called a flea beetle. The basil refused to sprout, the beans were similarly reluctant. But one day I harvested a handful of radishes, another handful of peas, and three whole strawberries and felt triumphant. I had planted a garden!

All around me the plots were growing. There was a field of basil across the path and the most beautiful kale I'd ever seen one block over. Pole beans twisted up trellises, and tufts of corn stood guard in straight rows. There were green pumpkins that would turn orange, papery husks of tomatillos, long green cucumbers, fat purple eggplants. It was a feast of colors and scents in the garden that summer. That grid of bare earth had become

a patchwork quilt of food and flowers, all reaching upward toward the sun.

After a day spent staring at a computer, I loved going to the
garden. It was a relief to push my chair back and head outside. I
kept tools and garden gloves in the car, and no matter how challenging the day, my spirits perked up as I walked down the
Picardo path. On hot days it was cooler there, with the scent of
warm earth and herbs, a low, persistent hum from the bees kept
in a hive. I often stayed until sundown, hoeing, weeding, soaking up the place. Time moves slower in a garden, the hours unfold gently, generously. There is a deep quiet that can only be
described as peace. The soft breeze, the sun on my back, the
colors of cascading flowers, the feel of warm soil, the satisfaction
of tools in my hands and work made visible. Most days I didn't
want to leave.

I thought a large garden like Picardo would provide plenty
of people to get to know, but it didn't work that way. There
were almost always other gardeners there when I was, but they
were often on the other side of the field. Because there were so
many of us, there was no expectation for you to know everyone.
I always waved, but conversation rarely ensued.

I saw the man who had the plot next to me only once that
summer. When he noticed I was growing Japanese vegetables, he
mentioned he had been there on leave from Vietnam. The neighbor on the other side I also saw only once. When I asked about
the straw covering her garden, she explained it kept in moisture
and suppressed weeds. We agreed to water each other's plots if
the plants looked particularly droopy. I never saw her again.

The woman across the path was there more frequently.
When she heard this was my first proper garden, she compli-
mented the spacing of my plants. "So many people get that
wrong in the beginning," she said. Her name was Heather. She
lived in the neighborhood and came to the garden often.

"Lucky for you to live so close." It was a fifteen-minute drive from my house to Picardo, longer if traffic was bad.

"I had the garden plot before I had the house," she explained. "But I was coming here all the time, and eventually I saw a For Rent sign. That's how it works—everything starts revolving around your garden."

Months later I would wonder if I should have taken this as a warning.

I was happy to meet someone friendly—happier when she offered to water my plot while I took my nieces to Canada that August. I had planned to ask my brother, but when Heather offered I was glad not to. I couldn't imagine him in the garden, coming straight from work in his pin-striped shirt, dragging the hose down a dusty path in Italian leather shoes.

I saw Heather only one time after that, the day I got back from Canada. I brought her a jar of peach jam as a thank-you. She reciprocated with a bouquet of her dahlias, picking each flower with care, bundling them together before handing them to me with quiet pride.

"You just can't buy flowers like this," she said.

I sank my face into their soft petals, all the colors of a sunset there in my hands. *No, you cannot buy this.*

I had come back to a late-summer garden. Suddenly everything was ripe, and I took home handfuls of cherry tomatoes and bunches of basil every time I visited. The volunteer plant yielded potatoes: yellow, red, and an unexpected purple-fleshed variety. There were broccoli and beans and plenty of chard, and I was surprised to discover I had grown enough food to make a meal: an entire dinner from my own little garden plot.

On an otherwise ordinary Thursday evening, I sautéed the new potatoes with fresh herbs. I cooked broccoli and tossed cherry tomatoes with basil for a salad. Only the olive oil and salt were not raised by my own hand.

Sitting down to this meal felt momentous. It felt like something to be proud of. I had brought it into being, with the help of the sunlight and water and soil. All this was my own doing. This meal would not have existed without me.

When my mother came through Seattle at the end of the summer, I was eager to show her my garden, the first proper one I'd ever had. She was in town for only a day or so, spending most of her time with the kids, but that afternoon I drove her to Picardo, parking on the street and leading her down the worn dirt path and along the checkerboard of plants and flowers that made up the community plots. I thought she would like the garden. Sunflowers were rising high; scarlet runner beans had overcome their trellises and were reaching up to the sky; bees and butterflies flitted everywhere. It was a glorious afternoon in the garden as I led her to my plot and stood there with quiet pride.

My mother looked at my garden, at the bean-covered tepees in the back, at the staggered chard plants and purslane and strawberries. The garden was shaped like a giant *S,* with two half paths that didn't go all the way through. It maximized the planting area and the edge that permaculturalists love. There was nary a grid or straight line in sight.

My mother looked at my plot, beautiful in its glorious profusion, and was silent a moment.

"Well," she said at last, "I guess you like messy gardens."

As August rolled into September, October's deadline loomed: the end of the season, the date by which everything needed to be dismantled in the garden.

My deadline was even earlier. I had to be in California by mid-September. My garden needed to be taken down before I left. Everything needed to be gone, the earth returned to its naked state.

Down came the bamboo tepees, the beans stripped from them still flowering. The strawberries were transplanted to my house. The root crops were all dug up—potatoes I hadn't even planted and the tiny carrots I had. My nieces had helped plant the carrots, and I wanted them to have the fun of pulling them up, but their schedule was too busy for my sister-in-law to bring them by the garden. I yanked the carrots out myself and stuck them in a bag I hoped my brother would give the girls: Sad little thin carrots the length of my thumb, they needed the end of summer to size up.

The most painful was the chard. I had bought a pack of starts early in the season—forty small sprouts with roots tinged pink and yellow. They all thrived, producing ruby and gold stalks with lushly textured greens, far more than I knew what to do with. I was grateful for the program that took P-Patch produce to food banks and other support organizations. P-Patch gardeners were encouraged to "grow a row" for charity, and more than twenty thousand pounds of vegetables were donated annually. That summer some of those pounds were chard from my little plot.

Pulling the chard felt cruel and wasteful—left alone, the plants would produce all winter and into spring. After spending months encouraging them to grow, watering and weeding them, how could I rip out these plants and toss them on the compost heap? It felt *wrong*.

I sent an email to my permaculture class. Did anyone want chard plants? I got a few replies, and one night I stood under the covered entrance to my front door passing off rainbow chard in the shadowy dark. I felt like a dealer, trafficking in something illicit, but I was happy my plants were going to good homes. I hadn't known how gutting it would feel to raze a garden in mid-bloom, to undo months of work and care. I salvaged as much as

I could, composted the rest, and left town in the late days of summer. It was all far harder than I expected.

It was November before I returned to Seattle. By then leaves had fallen off trees, the city turned gray and brown, the days short, dark. I drove up to Picardo and stood on the sidewalk overlooking the garden. The year-round plots had been put to bed but were still recognizable. The seasonal side was not. Paths and plots were gone. The stands of sunflowers and dahlias, towers of pole beans, fragrant basil, rows of corn: It was all gone. Only dirt remained. Summer had packed up and gone home like the circus. It made me want to cry.

When I received a postcard in the mail that winter asking if I wanted to renew my garden plot at Picardo for another year, I checked the box that said "no." That autumn my mother had bought the house with the large, overgrown garden. Come spring we would both be gardening there. There would be no ripping up plants at the end of a season. This was for the long haul. Together we might be able to grow something that would last.

PART TWO

. . .

PLANT

5

HOW TO PLANT AN ORCHARD

MY SISTER-IN-LAW LIKED TO name things: houses, cars, boats. My favorite was the car she had when the girls were first born: a silver vehicle she called Jane Honda.

My family had never done anything like that. Once, long ago, my brother and I tried to name our mother's faded Volvo Big Blue, after a whale in a children's book. But not even that stuck for long. It felt a little silly.

Our houses were never named either—they were called by the names of the streets they stood on: Creamery Road, Pine Hill, Longfellow, Montford. My 1910 flat in San Francisco was Seventh Avenue.

But perhaps my sister-in-law was rubbing off on us, because we did call the house I lived in when I first moved to Seattle The Treehouse. It was tall and narrow and surrounded by the green trees of the Arboretum. But mostly we called it that because Twenty-sixth Avenue East doesn't have much of a ring to it.

With this new house, however, my mother wanted a name. Although she had one in mind already, she asked the girls. "What should we call it?" They paused to consider, small foreheads furrowing in concentration.

"We could call it Fruit House," said Abby, who remembered the first day we spent there, eating juicy Asian pears and picking blackberries.

My mother smiled, then offered her choice.

"How about Orchard House?"

We all liked the ring of that.

I'd read somewhere that an orchard can be made up of as few as five trees—by that definition we had one. When the blackberries were finally cleared, they revealed twelve fruit trees. I imagined them like people imprisoned too long, now blinking up at unexpected light, stretching branches, luxuriating in the feeling of sun on their leaves at long last.

When the final tally was made, we had three apple trees, two pears, two Asian pears, two plums, one fig, and two trees whose identity we weren't sure of. I was hoping for a sour cherry.

Of course we wanted to plant more. Part of the allure of the garden was a chance to grow on a large scale. I wanted a peach and an apricot, an Italian prune plum, persimmon, and quince. My mother wanted cherries, dark and sweet—as many as we had room for.

We had room for quite a lot. The yard stretched out long and narrow. Most of the existing fruit trees were arranged in a border along the back fence and up the sunny south side. The rest of the yard was open space—former lawn now beginning to grow wild. My mother had a thing against mowing.

It was still winter, a season that lingers in the Northwest, and my mother had been in Seattle five months. The city was wet and mossy, the trees not yet leafed out. It was the time of year most charitably described as the season of mud. It wasn't time to plant a garden yet. It was, however, a good time to plant trees.

In permaculture, when you buy a piece of land, it is recommended you do nothing for the first year. Just observe. This way you can learn how the sun moves across the property in all seasons, where the shadows fall. You can see the flow of wind: where the protected spaces are, what gets buffeted. You learn about water, where it puddles, where it drains.

This way when you plant, you won't put tomatoes in a spot that gets afternoon shade; you won't plant corn where it is windy; you won't place your bulbs in a wet bog—the moisture there will rot them, and come spring you'll have nothing to show for it.

How many people have the time and patience to do this? We certainly did not.

"Start with trees," my permaculture teacher Jenny had said. "It's pretty easy to figure out where the trees should be."

But planting a tree is serious business. Unlike with tomatoes, you can't just rip out a tree at the end of the season if you've discovered it's not in a good spot. Fruit trees can bear for more than a hundred years. If the trees flourished and the property stayed in the family, it was possible the niecelets' future children and grandchildren could eat applesauce made from the fruit of these trees. It's not something you want to get wrong.

Because trees are such serious business, we decided to bring in Jenny, to make sure our overall plan was a good one. When she's not teaching, Jenny Pell designs and consults on permaculture installations all over the world. And in the slow season, early in the spring, she was offering a discount on her consultation rate.

Jenny was lead instructor for the six-month permaculture course I had taken the previous year. One weekend out of the month our group gathered to learn about rainwater harvesting, sheet mulching, and how to construct a proper compost pile. We built a pond, planned a productive cottage garden, experimented with grafting fruit trees, and set up a shiitake-mushroom-growing operation. We also learned about food forests.

These ancient agricultural systems walk the line between wild and cultivated. The plants are selected to thrive together but minimally maintained. It's a complex system with overstory canopy trees to provide fruit or nuts, smaller trees and fruit-bearing bushes, perennial vegetables, ground cover, and even a layer under the soil of roots and tubers that may also be edible. To look at it is to see a forest, but one capable of providing food for a family or community.

Looking at the back of the yard, the wild meadow that was sprouting, the trees that were already there, I imagined a food forest. Or at least an orchard that would provide more than just fruit from trees. There could be greens and herbs growing among them. We could have multiple harvests. It just came down to the right plan.

Because I had only ever seen commercial orchards, that was how I planned it: trees planted in rows. I figured three rows of three across the meadow—nine more trees to add to the collection for a total of twenty-one.

"Oh, no," Jenny said when she saw my carefully drawn plans. "You don't want to do that."

This was exactly what I needed—a teacher to check my work. I may have been given a certificate in permaculture design when I finished the class, but that didn't mean I knew what I was doing.

Jenny looked at the aerial-view drawing I had made of the backyard and erased the trees I had planned in rows. "Before you decide on trees, think about the paths," she explained. "But don't plan—just think about where you walk naturally. That's where the paths should be."

My mother and I drew the routes we tended to take—from the downstairs door to the greenhouse. From the greenhouse to the compost pile. As we traced our patterns through the landscape, a structure of paths emerged.

"Then you want to plant the trees in a circle." Jenny looked at the established fruit trees, at hard angles along the rear of the property. She took the pencil and marked a series of trees that would soften the angle, surrounding the meadow in a semicircular embrace. Rather than rows cutting straight across, her plan encompassed what was already there and brought it into balance.

"Hey," I said, looking at the new map. "It looks like a person."

The trees around the meadow now resembled a head; the main path that led to the house served as body and legs. The north–south route from greenhouse to compost pile formed arms.

Jenny smiled. "It's like that in permaculture," she said. "The plans always end up looking like people."

This was not the first time my family had planted fruit trees. Years ago, in the countryside of Northern California, my mom had wanted fruit in her garden. The old house I grew up in had come with apple trees large enough to climb, a few tall walnuts, and two plums—one yellow, one red—whose tiny fruit ended up all over the ground. One of my most hated childhood summer chores had been collecting gushy plums, sticky warm and starting to ferment in the sun.

My mother had wanted more: pears, cherries, a peach. She ordered them from a garden catalog sent from some far-off and slightly mysterious location.

I remember the day we got the call that the trees had arrived. We walked two blocks down the road to our small-town post office. It was next to the restaurant that catered to city folks out exploring the country, the only other business in town.

When she saw us coming, the postmistress heaved a large

parcel wrapped in brown construction paper onto the counter. It was a bumpy, fat cylinder, taller than I was and far wider. We carried it back to the house and into the backyard—my brother and me trying to help, our small hands barely able to grasp the fat package, so excited to unwrap the trees. We were not expecting what happened next.

My mother stood there looking blankly at the spindly saplings, a bunch of twigs bundled together. "I'm not sure which end is the roots and which is the branches," she said.

We looked at the long, dark twig-trees. It really was hard to tell. There were no arrows pointing: *This way up.*

"I think they go this way," my mother said, propping them upright. "No." She frowned and turned them around. "Maybe this way."

We tried one side, then another, until we got it right. At least we hoped we had it right. Only time would tell.

Time did tell, and the trees did grow. The cherry and peach never flourished—it was a yearly battle with peach leaf curl and a yearly battle with the birds who got most of the sour cherries, despite our cloaking the tree in black netting each summer.

But the pear trees took root and thrived: through the severe drought of the seventies, when they were watered with runoff from our bathwater and washing machine; through the flood of the early eighties that led to our move away from the country. Each fall we had pears. I was too young to know about fruit varieties; it would be years before I heard the names Bartlett, Bosc, and d'Anjou. I thought of them only as brown pears and golden pears. I liked the juicy golden ones the best.

When I think of those pears now, I think of my mother undertaking that life in the country—though clearly she did not have the knowledge required. She learned along the way; she taught herself, and she taught us, through trial and error. It wasn't a madcap adventure either. We weren't playing farmer. My father had left us with nothing, contributed nothing toward our support, and there were no other resources. My mother could not have afforded to buy those pears at the market, but she could plant a tree and tend it and, with effort and patience, she could feed her children sweet fruit each fall.

The last time I saw those trees, their tops had grown level with the second-floor window. It's been years since I've been back, but I imagine the pear trees my mother planted are still going strong. Golden pears and brown pears each fall, to feed the children who live there now.

There was no trouble telling branches from roots on the trees my mother bought the first spring she was in Seattle. They came, still spindly and twiglike, but with their bases bundled in burlap. Some came from the nursery, some from a nearby plant sale. It was hard not to buy fruit trees that spring—and hard to stop once we'd started. Who wouldn't want a mess of peaches, plums, cherries, quince? A fruit tree is an investment in happiness, in sweetness, in jam. Every time I considered the potential, I couldn't say no.

When our spring buying spree was over, we had four cherry trees, one peach, a pluot, a quince, a persimmon, an Italian prune plum—and one final pear, to make sure we would have both golden and brown fruit in the fall. Orchard House, indeed.

Jenny may have guided our design plan, but it was still daunting to place the trees in the ground. You had to look at this stick of a sapling and imagine it big, imagine it in ten years, in fifty. This is the challenge of gardening: to see what is there now and to allow for what will grow. It is an exercise in imagination, in hope, in faith.

My mother was not very good at it. Hope and faith have never been her gig.

"Oh, no—that's not the right spot." I had arrived at the garden, after a day of work at home, to find my mom had planted the peach tree. "It's too close to the pear—see how it throws off the whole circle? It needs to be planted here." I strode a couple of yards to the left.

"I thought we would put the cherry there."

"The cherry should go here." I paced out a few more yards to the side and stood there. "This way, when it grows, the canopy won't run into that apple tree."

When I closed my eyes, I could see it—the trees bigger, the open meadow ringed by leafy green, shade where now there was just sun.

My mother couldn't see it—she has never been one to gamble on what was not already there. She deals in absolutes: bills, deadlines, hard work. But here, at least, she trusted me.

She shrugged. "Okay, we'll move it."

Neither of us was digging the holes for the fruit trees. That task fell to Don, a man my mother had hired to do some odd jobs around the house and yard. He was the one who had to dig yet another large hole—about four feet across—to move the peach tree into. When he heard the news, he shrugged; he was being paid by the hour.

My mother had done some renovations to the house when she moved in. The hardwood floors were refinished, the downstairs wet bar taken out, and new carpeting and flooring laid throughout. The upstairs layout would always be odd, but the one eyesore that remained was the bathroom.

I suggested gutting the narrow upstairs bath and putting in a Japanese soaking tub, but that was another idea my mother couldn't quite envision. Instead she had the boxy cabinet ripped out and replaced with a pedestal sink, an attempt to give the narrow room more space. Don was doing the installation.

That's what was happening when we heard shouts in the upstairs bathroom and came running. Something had gone wrong and water was pouring out from under the bathroom door, into the hallway, headed for the stairs. I grabbed a large bath towel from the top of the laundry hamper and was about to lay it down to stop the flow.

"No!" my mom exclaimed. *"Wait."*

She dashed around the corner and opened the linen closet door, grabbing a mesh bag and turning it upside down, dumping the contents onto the stream of water.

What came out of the bag was my childhood: a cascade of pieces of cloth, each bringing back memories. There was my brother's old pillowcase with chunky trains printed on it, a faded tea towel that had hung in our kitchen in the country, a bit of yellow-flowered sheet I had stained as a child, a favorite red scarf, the remnant of a work dress my mother used to wear.

This was my mother's ragbag—I hadn't known such a thing existed. It was another reminder that she came from a time and a set of circumstances in which resources were valued. Even old T-shirts were not thrown away. I felt a flicker of guilt at the clothes I had consigned to the garbage can. Anything wearable went to charity shops, but stained T-shirts and ripped pajama pants I threw away. What else was I supposed to do with them?

Here my mother was, squirreling them away to use when needed. Not for the first time, I wondered if a large part of our problems in the modern age stems from the fact that we've been given so much we no longer see the value in a thing; we no longer know its worth.

In a hardware store a few weeks later, I saw a bag of "T-shirt rags." They were scraps of new cotton fabric marketed as the perfect thing to clean or wipe up mess.

The two-pound bag cost $16.50.

My mother's ragbag came from the same era, the same mentality, as having an orchard. You can't eat the yield of an orchard by yourself—even a single fruit tree can produce too much for some families. Backyard fruit trees come from an era of home food

preservation, of putting up the harvest, of canning and freezing
and making applesauce. These days we buy the fruit we need for
our lunches and the occasional fruit salad or pie. Most of us are
not prepared for a harvest.

I was in a good position to deal with such abundance. I might
not have had a ragbag, but I knew how to can and make jam. I
had learned the basics long ago, from a babysitter who lived with
us for several years. Lorraine had taken the gushy plums that fell
on the ground—the sticky ones about to ferment—and made
jam with them. Plum jam, from our trees: It tasted like summer.

Later, in high school, I taught myself to make canned treats
as holiday gifts, nestling jars of chocolate sauce and jalapeño
pepper jelly in decorative baskets. It must have been odd to receive such a housewife-like gift from a teenager, but I had been
cooking for the family for years. The kitchen was more my do-
main than my mother's.

Then I forgot about canning for a decade or so. College and
starting a career left no room for putting up the harvest. Life was
busy and full. I scarcely noticed it was harvest until Halloween
pumpkins started showing up. My city apartment did not come
with a plum tree in the backyard.

Then, while living in San Francisco, I started canning again.
The urge came from the same place as the urge to grow herbs—a
desire for something tangible, rooted, made by my own hand. I
remember the first batch of Meyer lemon marmalade, the afternoon spent over a pot of simmering fruit and sugar waiting for
it to firm up enough to jell. It took time, a slow, can't-rush-the-
clock sort of time. It took standing in the kitchen and smelling
the citrus and stirring and some lazy daydreaming as well, but by
the end I had twelve jars of jam, lined up and gleaming golden
in the light.

That night I went to a literary event at a local bar. As I
looked around the crowd of people in designer glasses and hip
clothing I had an odd thought: *None of you made food today.* I felt

proud and productive in a way I hadn't in a long time. Like winter might come and the winds might howl, but I had made jam for my people, and whatever happened we would be all right.

I knew each of these trees in my mother's orchard would provide for many. It might just be jam, or applesauce, or canned pears, but the winter could come, and even if the power went out and the roads were snowed under, I would have food for my people. We would be all right.

One by one, the trees were all planted, though my mother and I rarely agreed on a location. Don was forced to re-dig more than a few holes, until one day my mother called on the phone.

"Can you come up here? Don refuses to dig any more tree holes until you make sure it's in the right place." I was still trying to envision the big picture, to see what the orchard would grow into.

When I truly stepped back and tried to see the big picture, however, it didn't always make sense. I may have yearned for a harvest, but my mother was in her seventies. By all rights she should have been slowing down, having a smaller and simpler life. Instead she was taking on a huge garden project, living alone in a house larger than any she had lived in before. I understood her urge to give the girls a garden, but surely a small and manageable yard filled with flowers and vegetables would do the same job. Did we really need an orchard? I confessed these concerns to my permaculture teacher.

"Your mom is in the legacy phase of her life," Jenny said. And maybe she was right.

Maybe this whole garden was about what we leave behind, how we are remembered. My mother would not live to see the fruit trees we were planting come to full maturity. She would not see the leafy canopy they would eventually develop; she would never see these small cherry saplings covered in fruit.

And still, she planted them. It reminded me of a Martin Luther quote I'd once heard: "Even if I knew that tomorrow the world would go to pieces, I would still plant my apple tree."

My mother knew all this too. The final tree we planted was a persimmon, an unusual choice for a backyard fruit tree, perhaps, but we both love them from our time spent in Asia. There persimmons are common, shiny, green-leafed trees hung with bright orange fruit like small lanterns. In the fall the fruit is dried to make a popular snack. It is not uncommon to walk through the streets in Japan and Korea and see strings of orange persimmons hung from upstairs windows, drying in the autumn sun.

There were always a few old persimmon trees that went unharvested—deep in the countryside where farmhouses had sometimes been abandoned. I loved to see them after the season's first snow. The dark branches threw a stark relief against the white, and the brilliant orange fruit floated among them, often with a tiny cap of snow.

We planted our persimmon at the top of the side yard, in a spot that had held a dead cherry tree. It seemed right to put it there. I knew that when the fruit grew, we would pick it long before the first snow of winter fell in Seattle, but still, it made me feel happy and nostalgic for Japan.

Persimmon trees take years to bear. Unlike the cherry and plum and peach we planted, which had a good chance of producing small crops within a few years, the persimmon would take at least five years before it flowered or fruited, maybe seven.

"Well," my mom said when we had patted the last shovelful of soil around the base of the small sapling and stood back looking at the twiggy tree. "*I* may never get to taste any of these persimmons—but you better enjoy them for me."

I put my arm around her, surprised as always by how small she was becoming—fragile, in need of protection.

"I will, Mom," I said, drawing her close. "I promise."

6

. . .

A STRONG FLAVOR

WHEN I WAS BORN, my mother thought I had Down syndrome. I was beautiful, she said, but she worried there was something wrong with me. She asked the nurses; she asked the doctors. Finally a specialist came and sat down with her. He said he understood her concern, but the baby was fine. I didn't have Down syndrome.

"*Why* would she *tell* you that?" my friend Lianne asked when I told her this story.

I shrugged. "I don't know. I've never thought about it."

The story was part of my history—I knew it the way I knew that my parents first met at a party, introduced by a mutual acquaintance, drawn together because they had both lived in Asia, and that had I been a boy they would have named me Adam. I never questioned these things.

My friend was outraged. "Every baby deserves to be seen by their parents as perfect," she said. "Your mother looked at you and saw something wrong—*something that wasn't even there*—and she *told* you about it?"

My mother often told me things that would be better left unsaid; she had a blunt and uncensored tongue. In this case, however, I knew things were more complicated.

When my mother was born, her own mother nearly died. There was hemorrhaging, blood loss. The complications that would kill my grandmother three years later, in childbirth with her second daughter, had made themselves known. The doctor pulled the baby out and rushed to save the mother. My mother's birth was not a celebration, it was a close call. Nobody was rejoicing and declaring her perfect. Perfection is something we have little experience of in my family. My mother had no role model for joy.

I once asked her why she thought I had Down syndrome. Newborn babies are often funny looking—wrinkled little guppies or wise old men, they sometimes look alien or amphibious. But for the most part, no matter their oddness, their parents find them beautiful.

"You were a C-section," my mother told me. "Your head was perfectly round—even the nurses commented on it. But there was an almond slant to your eyes. Nobody else noticed it, but it made me think you might have Down syndrome."

My mother is a worrier, prone to concerns large and small, perennially convinced the worst will happen. Her assumption didn't surprise me. People talk of those who see the glass as half-empty or half-full, but I've long known for my mother it is neither.

For her the glass is cracked, the water has seeped out and dripped off the table, now the floorboards are warping. Eventually the house will fall down.

This is the way things have always been. No amount of hope, happiness, or optimism on my part has ever made a difference.

Bringing back a long-neglected patch of earth is no easy feat. On the days I came to Orchard House, I never knew where to start. The scale of all that needed to be done was overwhelming; it was tempting to just stand there and gawk. My urge was always to run away, or to take a nap. In the face of the insurmountable, my instinct is to not even try.

My mother is built of sterner stuff. Because she expects the worst, perhaps, she jumps in swinging. Every time I came to the garden, she was in the back, knee-deep in weeds, hacking at blackberries. Each week she asked me to roll around the large yard-waste bin so it could be put out on the street for garbage day pickup. "It's hard for me to do it by myself," she said apologetically the first time.

"That's because it weighs more than you do," I said, struggling to pull the tall container forward. "How did you get so much packed in here?"

"I filled it up and climbed in to stomp it all down," she said. "Then I added more."

When my mother wasn't pulling weeds, she was focused on removing rocks from what she planned to be her vegetable garden. When we had seen the garden the summer before, the beds had been overgrown with tall wild grasses, an occasional straggly dahlia peeking through: flowers left by the man who had gardened here long ago.

The selling agent had sent us pictures of the house from the seventies or eighties, when the garden had been a well-tended thing. The grass, now pockmarked with dandelions, had been mowed to a velvet nap, perfectly straight lines running the length of the yard, like in a baseball field. There had been tall trees, maples and cedars that towered over the back, making the yard shadier, more northwestern. Only the stump of the maple remained. There had been entire flower beds of dahlias. The few bulbs we dug up here and there were the survivors.

"I just don't know why there are so many rocks," my mother said, kneeling in the flower bed. The stones were midsized and rounded, like those from a riverbed. "I wonder if he put them here on purpose. Maybe to break up the soil, or improve drainage."

By "he," she meant the Korean man who had, from what we knew, tended this garden. He had lived here with his companion, the Japanese gentleman, now quite old, from whom my mother had bought the house. Lee and Kaito were becoming characters in our imagination. Lee had been married before and had children. It was his son who had been in charge of selling the house when Kaito could no longer live on his own.

This story amazed me. It would have been unusual to have that sort of intercultural relationship in the seventies and eighties, but to be living together, raising children? This sleepy off-the-beaten-path neighborhood held more complexity than it might have seemed to at first glance. Perhaps all families do.

I wondered about these men. Had the two-room cottage been built for the children? Was the Japanese garden out front a gift from Lee to Kaito? Had it reminded him of home? Suddenly the Asian pear trees made more sense, and the ornamental maples. The weeping cherry tree, now dead, must have been a nostalgic sight each spring.

There were deeper mysteries in the story as well. It was said that Lee killed himself, maybe by hanging. We didn't know the details. Apparently even this lovely garden, even the banks of dahlias and towering maples and the perfectly straight mower lines on the velvet lawn, had not been enough. Maybe a garden cannot overcome the ways in which we are broken. Perhaps flowers and vegetables and hopeful things poking out of the soil cannot heal all wounds.

I was hoping that wasn't true. I was betting on it.

The first person outside my family to see the garden was my friend Knox. In the few years I had known him, Knox had taken a bare plot of land behind his house and turned it into an enchanting spot. You entered by a gate in a picket fence and felt as though you had been transported, perhaps to the south of France. There were flowering borders, a tidy vegetable plot, artichokes galore, apples and quince in the fall. On my computer I kept a picture of the mounds of bare soil it had started out as, a reminder of what is possible with vision and hard work.

I had barely brought the car to a stop in the driveway before Knox jumped out and started poking around the front yard, its sculpted evergreens and large, carefully placed boulders.

"It was obviously laid out as a Japanese garden," he said. "But then there's that viburnum and dogwood. What are they doing there? Maybe they were added later."

"That's not what I want to show you," I said, shutting my car door and beckoning him around the side of the house.

I took Knox past the weedy side garden, through the NO TRESPASSING gate, and into the back. "*This* is what I wanted you to see." I gestured to the long, wild yard sloping down the hill.

I expected Knox to be ecstatic. He is an enthusiastic person, a devoted gardener. I thought he would be as giddy as I was. *Look at all that is possible.*

He wasn't excited. He was silent.

He started wandering around, still not speaking, an expression on his face I couldn't read.

Knox wandered a full ten minutes without a word. He looked into the greenhouse. He looked at the fruit trees. Eventually he made his way back to where I was standing.

"So," he said gravely. "What is your plan?"

"There's no plan—are we supposed to have a plan?"

"Yes, you need a plan." He looked over at the garden. "You *really* need a plan."

The garden was huge, Knox said. Gigantic. I might have thought this wonderful, full of promise and potential, but Knox was more practical. Or perhaps just more experienced. He knew what we were getting into.

"The only way I see this working is if you divide the garden," he explained. "If you put a picket fence across the middle, then you can have an upper garden that is tended and tidy and let the field go wild. But you need something to mark it."

I knew my mother would never agree to a fence. My mother liked the long sweep of the property; she liked the wild.

"It's great, but it's a lot of work." Knox looked at the garden again, then turned and looked at me. "You know my garden killed my freelance career."

Knox had spent three years getting his garden in shape—three years of neglecting work in favor of weeding and pruning. That glorious patch of flowers and herbs that felt like the south of France had come at a cost.

I had a freelance career too, and already I was feeling the pinch. I wanted to be in the garden; it was just hard to find the time. I worked long hours, often on deadline. When I had my community garden plot, there had been periods when my attention was required elsewhere and the weeds started to rise. That's the way life was.

But now I had someone to remind me I was falling behind. I had my mother on the other end of the telephone.

"When are you going to come up here and work in the garden?" she called to query. "I need your help tying up the wisteria, and what are you going to do about the side yard?"

I looked doubtfully at my schedule. I didn't have time for it. My work rarely fit in a forty-hour week. But it was hard to say no to my mother.

"I *think* I can come this afternoon."

"*What time* this afternoon?" My mother did not mess around.

"I'm going to aim for three." I never knew when I would be able to get away. Three often turned into four or four-thirty, sometimes five. I was always later than I said I would be. By the time I got to the garden, my mother was annoyed.

"You're late," she said by way of a greeting.

"I'm sorry—I just couldn't get away."

It was true too. I would rather have been gardening than working. I had been looking forward to coming—up until the very moment I got there and ran full force into the weight of my mother's disapproval. Then I wanted to be somewhere else. Anywhere else.

This was not a new feeling for me. I often liked the idea of my mother more than the reality. The reality never seemed that happy to see me. The reality pointed out all my flaws.

"We'd better get to it," she said. "There isn't time to do much before it gets dark."

When I try to explain my mother, I have to start in the past. My brother and I were young, we lived in the country, we had baby-sitters who lived with us and did the cooking and cleaning and school pickup. Our babysitters were young too. We had a few good ones over the years, but most were pretty flaky. Our baby-sitters had boyfriends who were always stoned. Sometimes our babysitters were stoned as well.

My mother would come home late at night, tired after a long day of teaching or clients, and look around for what wasn't working. With the final bit of energy she had, she fixed prob-lems. Sometimes she yelled in frustration or anger. There was no time to enjoy what might be going right.

Even today, my mother scans for problems. If something is done there is no acknowledgment, thanks, or praise; done means one less thing to worry about. It's the problems that draw her.

Maybe she just needs to be useful. If something is going right, it's no longer her concern. My mother's spent her life in triage, as if on a battlefield.

It's efficient, but it's a hard way to live. It's almost impossible to live with.

The truth is, there wasn't much going right for my mother back in those early days. Her husband had left, she had no financial or emotional support, no family nearby to be of help. She was working hard to keep her head above water. Maybe life felt like a battlefield. Except she had these children, climbing trees, and making up games and songs, and growing like weeds. I wonder if she allowed herself to enjoy that. To enjoy us.

Perhaps the story starts earlier than that. In Florida, where my grandfather moved with my mother and her newborn sister after their mother had died. The family had wanted to take the children away, to have them raised by one of my grandfather's many siblings. He probably should have let them.

My grandfather quickly remarried to keep the family intact, proposing within months of his first wife's death, but the woman he chose was cruel. When my mother came home from school, her stepmother made her sit on a stool in the yard. She was not allowed to play or come into the house—not even to use the bathroom. She sat on a stool alone, clenching her thighs together to keep from wetting herself. She'd have gotten in even more trouble for that.

When she was ten, my mother tried to run away. She set off out the front gate, and at the end of the block she turned right. At the end of that block, she turned right again. She wasn't allowed to cross the street, so she soon found herself back at her own gate. She couldn't run away because she wouldn't disobey.

She left home at seventeen, bound for New York. "If you ran away at sixteen," she told me, "the cops would come after you. But if you ran away at seventeen, your family had to pay the police to track you down. I knew nobody was going to pay money to get me back."

I could probably go back further still. Back to ancestors who fled from oppression, who hid from armies, who survived on their wits. Perhaps my mother expects the worst because her people so often experienced it. My brother and I are the first generation to know privilege, to have opportunities and advantages. It seems ungrateful to complain.

But what a cross to bear—to expect the worst, to wait for the sky to fall. All my life I had been told it wasn't *if* the world would go to hell, just when. Tomorrow? Next week? It's best to be prepared.

I didn't want to live like that. I wanted grace.

And yet, I owed my existence to the fears that had made my ancestors suspicious. Those who were not scared became complacent. Those who trusted often died. Only the crafty and cynical made it out alive. Who am I to say where the line should be drawn?

The weedy dahlia bank my mother had cleared of rocks was going to be planted with vegetables. There were three planting beds, about ten feet long and five feet wide. Not that either of us had measured them. Preparation may be a family trait; precision is not.

"What are you going to plant?" I asked my mother as she raked in soil amendments: fertilizer, compost, coffee grounds.

"Kale." I knew her one-word answer wasn't meant to be brusque, even though it sounded that way.

"I was thinking of planting raspberries against that back fence. Is that okay?" The fence lay behind the vegetable beds and marked the property line. "It will get nice sun almost all day long."

I planned to take cuttings from those first raspberries I brought from San Francisco, the small and sweet ones. I imagined them grown tall, full of ruby-colored fruit each June. I liked how this bit of California was following me, that the berries my nieces and I had been picking for three years now would be planted here too. We were settlers, bringing the saplings and seeds from our old home to the new one, even if this new home did not require a sea voyage or months in a covered wagon.

"Sure." My mother looked up briefly from her work. She had abandoned the rake for a moment to cut back a tree branch that was leaning over the vegetable bed, blocking the path. We didn't know if the tree in question was viable—it looked like a cherry but had no blossoms that spring. Despite our shared cynical nature, we were holding out hope.

My mother took the heavy loppers and reached over her head to grasp the branch between twin blades. Standing below, she had little leverage, yet she kept trying to bear down with enough force to sever it. Trying and failing.

"Here, let me do that for you." I was taller, stronger, just standing there. Why hadn't she asked for help?

"I can do it," she said gruffly, scissoring the handles again, trying to make the dull blades cut through the branch. Still, nothing.

I put my hand on the loppers. "Really, Mom—I can do it." I stood over her, holding the handle, not letting go.

Finally she released her grip and stepped back. From where I stood on the slight embankment, the branch was level with my shoulder. Bracing one handle against my waist, I pulled the other toward me with both hands and took the branch off with one try.

Not for the first time, I wondered: Did she think we kids didn't know how to do things, or was she just unused to having any help at all?

In the early days of my childhood, my mother went to see a psychic. Or perhaps it was an astrologer or someone who read auras. It's hard to say. The stories I've heard from the days before I can remember have a fantastical feel to them. As if the cloud of incense and marijuana smoke hanging over Northern California in the early seventies resulted in a state of magic realism: Things don't always make sense.

In the story I am with my mother, no more than two years old. My brother had not yet been born. Perhaps it was before my father left—when my mother was pregnant and worried about the stability of her marriage. Or maybe it was afterward, when she was panicked and looking for answers. I don't know.

What I know is what she has told me: that there were books and toys in the corner of the office and I went to play with them.

The woman gestured to the back of my small blond head.

"You know the two of you have been together in many lifetimes," she said.

"Really?" My mother was surprised.

"Oh, yes," the woman continued. "You've spent many incarnations together. Sometimes you were her mother—and sometimes she was yours."

My mother says I was playing in the corner, not paying attention, but the moment the woman said that, I nodded my head. I didn't turn around, I didn't say anything. I just nodded. As if I had known all along.

I don't know what to make of this story. It seems part of that magic realism of my early childhood: reincarnation and enlightenment and free sex and the Summer of Love. That I had been my mother's mother? That we had been linked together for lifetime after lifetime? I'm not sure I believe any of it.

What I do know is this—perhaps the only thing I need to know.

It *feels* true.

———

What I call magic realism other people called freedom. They
called it *following your bliss*. The early seventies were a ferment of
it, particularly in Northern California.

In the case of my father, bliss took the form of a dark-haired
woman who had come to the coast looking for her own freedom. It was said she'd left a husband and children behind. Perhaps, like my father, she hadn't wanted the responsibility of
family.

My mother, already pregnant with my brother, had taken
me to New York. When we flew back, my father met us at the
airport and we set off on the long drive down the rocky coast to
Big Sur, where we lived. I was two years old. My mother says I
sang the entire way home.

When we reached our small house, the three of us walked
in. The house stood behind the lawn where my parents had been
married just a few years before, my father wearing his favorite
leather boots, my mother with flowers in her hair. The smooth
grass sloped toward the sea. My rope swing hung from the euca-
lyptus tree nearby; my little red tricycle stood in the driveway.
My father had attached wooden blocks to the pedals because my
legs weren't yet long enough to reach.

Inside the house there were wine bottles everywhere, the
remnants of two weeks of partying and sex. While we had been
gone, my father had taken this woman into our home and made
it their love nest. A few minutes later my father walked out
alone. Our family was finished. In the ways that really matter,
my childhood was over.

We had to move, quickly. Our small cottage was on the
grounds of the retreat center where my father was on staff, the
housing tied to his job. But he had decided not to be a father; we
couldn't live there any longer.

One day soon after, my mother drove up to San Francisco to
look for a house for us. As we drove back down the winding

coastal highway after a long day of searching, she gripped the steering wheel, white-knuckled with fear for our future and the baby she carried. Trying to keep it together. Trying to keep it in.

I was in a booster seat next to her, just two years old. I don't remember that day, but I've heard the story. As we drove the tortuous coast highway, twisting our way between a rocky cliff face on one side and a sheer drop to the ocean below on the other, my mother says I looked at her.

"Cry, Mommy," I told her. *"Just cry."*

My mother has never subscribed to graceful gardens of flowers; she wanted to grow food. Vegetables. Lots of them.

"I'm going to grow kale all winter long," she said in delight when she first saw Orchard House's run-down greenhouse. "It's going to be my green gold."

That spring, however, she was focused on lettuces: tiny shoots of green and red. My favorite was Flashy Trout Back—a speckled variety—which I loved for the name alone. There were other greens as well: mizuna, pak choi, arugula. It was all about the greens.

My interests lay in food as well, but not in the same way. I wanted flavor. I wanted an abundance of it. I wanted to make grand and generous meals. I wanted to have a garden to cook from.

I had started cooking young, learning from our babysitter Lorraine, who took the squishy plums that fell on the ground and made them into jam. She turned cabbage and cucumbers into pickles. I found it fascinating.

Soon I was reading cookbooks, experimenting with recipes. We moved away from the country when I was eleven. My new school was close enough to ride my bike there, and my mother now had her office in the downstairs of our house, so we no longer needed babysitters. That's when I started cooking for real. My mother worked late, and I liked the feeling of making dinner, of providing for our family in this small way. When I went to sleep at night, I often left a plate of food in the kitchen for her to eat when she was done.

Soon I was giving her shopping lists of things I needed for dinner. Sometimes she gave me money and dropped me off at the grocery store. Once I could drive, I went on my own.

My mother was supportive of my cooking experimentation, but she didn't understand it. For her, food had always been about health and nutrition. It never occurred to her that making dinner could be fun, that sitting down to a meal was pleasurable.

"I don't get cooking," she said. "You put all this effort into making something—and ten minutes later, *poof,* it's gone!"

But food is about pleasure, coming together, sitting down, relaxing; it's about enjoyment and nurturing yourself and others. I'm not surprised my mother does not understand this. None of these words are part of her active vocabulary.

Over the years, however, I learned to cook for her, to tempt her palate. I learned she likes sour and bitter flavors: kalamata olives, radicchio, lemon. I learned to devise dishes that made her smile—just the ghost of a smile, around the corners of her mouth. It might not have been indulgence or community or relaxation, but it was a start.

I learned her palate so well that sometimes, when she was done eating, she ran her fingers around the rim of her plate to wipe up the leftover drips of sauce or dressing. Part of me wanted to tell her to control herself, to have better manners, but I never did. Instead I watched in horrified fascination as she stuck her fingers in her mouth and sucked the very last bit of flavor, hungrily, greedily. Like a child who had never been given enough.

Ever since I was a little girl, I'd been asking my mother what she liked. If only I knew what would make her happy, I could get it for her.

Do you like bubble bath, Mommy? Do you like earrings?

It was years before I realized the sort of sadness my mother had couldn't be taken away by a new scarf or a piece of jewelry. The sadness my mother had was in her bones; it would never be vanquished, no matter how hard I tried to be happy for both of us. There was nothing I could purchase or do or even cook that would change things. Life had fundamentally let her down, it seemed, and the shade of that disappointment colored everything. There was nothing I could do to fix that.

When Mother's Day came that first spring in the garden, however, I knew exactly what she wanted—and it wasn't a scarf or jewelry or bubble bath. My mother wanted a day in the garden.

It may seem odd that she would want to spend her celebratory day weeding and working, as she had most days since moving to Seattle, but I knew she didn't want to do it alone. She wanted me there. Other mothers and daughters might go to brunch or the spa or go shopping; my mother wanted to work. She wanted to get things done.

"I'll come for Mother's Day," I said, "but how about I bring lunch?" I couldn't leave it at just work. There had to be some grace in the day.

"That's fine," my mother allowed.

That morning I assembled my ingredients: bitter radicchio, dark olives that tasted ancient like the sea, peppery radishes, salty sharp cheese. I brought a bottle of olive oil and the season's first asparagus.

Suddenly I was reminded of another Mother's Day, many

years before. Or perhaps it had been my mother's birthday or Valentine's Day. The memories blur together.

On that day my brother and I made breakfast. We must have had help—from a babysitter, perhaps. We had baked a cake the day before and hidden it away: a dense whole wheat thing made from the healthful ingredients in our pantry. I remember we stuck a candle in it—and no small birthday candle either. A red taper off the dining table pierced the middle of our heart-shaped cake and towered over it.

I remember the feeling of anticipation—wanting to see the delight in our mother's eyes, wanting to see her surprise, her happiness. We couldn't sleep: It was like Christmas morning. I was six and my brother was four, and we *could not wait any longer.* Dawn was just beginning to break as we carried the tray in, beaming with a pride far brighter than the huge candle sprouting from the center of our homemade cake.

"Mommy, Mommy—*look what we made you!*"

Our mother looked at us blearily, exhausted, her eyes barely able to focus. She smiled wanly and pulled herself to a seated position as we jumped and danced gaily around her. "Blow out your candle, Mommy. Blow out your candle!"

She blew out the candle and admired our efforts. She let us climb in bed with her, but when we ran to the kitchen and brought back oranges for her to peel, she struggled. She was so tired there was no strength in her hands. She was running on fumes, putting up a brave face. I didn't know it then, but I do now.

If only we had let her sleep!

All we wanted to do was love her, make her happy. All we wanted was to have her delight in us.

She tried; she really did. She just didn't have any more to give us.

———

By the time I carried out the salads I made for our Mother's Day lunch, the fog had burned off and the day turned sunny. It wasn't warm—not the way I was used to from California, where May is summer and everyone wears skirts and sandals. May in Seattle is still firmly spring, summer a month or so away. But the bulbs were blooming—the tulips and irises I remember from my childhood.

We called them San Geronimo irises—named for the small town where I grew up. They were deep purple with a delicate scent and crepelike petals that quivered in the breeze. We had them in our garden in the country, and they had grown in every garden since then. My mother carefully dug up the rhizomes and took them with her when she moved, as families used to do. If something grew well and provided, you took it with you, your seeds and saplings as valuable as money.

"Do you want to eat on the deck?" I called across the wide upper lawn, as my mother sat back on her heels under the magnolia tree.

"No, bring it over here." She stood up, peeling off her garden gloves, and walked over to the cracked patio in front of the cottage. "I've been taking my breaks here. On sunny days the pavement soaks up the heat, and you can actually feel warm for a second."

I hadn't seen my mother take a break, maybe ever, but I held my tongue.

We sat down cross-legged on the patio, and I passed her a bowl full of the flavors I knew she liked: sour, tart, bitter.

"This is *good*," my mother said, fishing red radicchio leaves out of her bowl with the chopsticks she prefers to use.

"A friend made something similar for me. I thought you would like it."

"Yes. It's very good."

"Are you going to see the rest of the family for Mother's Day?" Ever since my brother had kids of his own, Mother's Day had changed. He now spent the day celebrating his wife, which often left me feeling protective of our mother. *"She's still your mom,"* I nagged him on the phone, in a bossy big-sister sort of way. "You have to do something for her."

"Your brother stopped by with flowers early this morning."

"Really?"

She laughed a short, wry laugh. "He took the kids down to Pike Place Market and bought three bouquets—one for me, one for his mother-in-law, one for his wife. I was the second delivery of the day."

"Well. That's better than nothing."

"Yes," she said slowly. "It's better than nothing."

I stretched my legs out on the patio, which was indeed slightly warm, a comforting support on a still-chilly spring day. My mother wiped up the last bits of vinegary dressing before she too put down her bowl and stretched out.

"You know," she said. "Remember how you asked me why I thought you had Down syndrome when you were born?"

That conversation had been months before, but of course I remembered.

"I've been thinking about it—and I don't think it had any-thing to do with you."

"What do you mean?"

My mother moved her legs, rearranged her sitting position next to me, both of us looking up into the clear blue sky.

"It was me," she said plainly.

I glanced over at her—gray hair pulled messily back in a headband, sun on her now-wrinkled face.

"I don't understand."

She sighed long and slow, a sound like air escaping from a tire.

"The reason I thought you had Down syndrome didn't have anything to do with you." She paused, her hand going up to smooth hair back into the headband before she continued, her voice small and sad.

"You were perfect—*I* was the problem. I just couldn't believe anything that came from me wouldn't have something wrong with it."

7

. . .

AS GOOD AS IT GETS

WE ALL SAW DIFFERENT things when we looked at the garden. My mother saw the ability to grow food—a place for her grand-children to run wild, an insurance policy if times got hard. The house was big; the orchard would provide. Having such a garden was about as self-sufficient as one could be in the city. If the worst came to pass, we might all be able to live on apples and kale.

The girls saw play. They saw hills to roll down and pears to pick and the loft of a cottage to climb into. They saw places to hide and seek, berries to gobble, and a sprinkler to run through on hot summer days.

My brother saw obligation. He saw work. "That's a lot of lawn I'm going to have to mow," he said the first time he saw the garden.

My sister-in-law saw leisure. She saw relaxation. "With a yard this big, you could put in a swimming pool," she told my mother. "Wouldn't that be great?"

I saw those things, but I saw something more. I saw possibility.

I hoped this would be a place to bring us together. I saw long Sunday dinners at an outdoor table, churning ice cream together in the summer. I saw us decorating bare winter branches for the birds, with birdseed balls and strings of popcorn, the way my brother and I had when we were kids.

I saw the possibility of us being more to each other, of growing together. I saw a place for us to become a family.

I just wasn't sure how to get there from here. Growing vegetables I understood, but how do you grow a family?

"Why do you think you get along so well?" I once asked my friend Paul's sister. I was making a study of families, trying to see what held them together. My friend Paul's family was high on my list.

Paul is one of three kids. There are two parents, and though I am sure they have their moments, they tease each other and laugh and generally seem to get along. The kids spend time together even without the parents, even when it's not a national holiday or family birthday, even without a guilt trip. Paul likes to hang out with his mom and dad. They genuinely enjoy each other's company.

Other people enjoy their company as well. The door is often opened to friends. I've spent Christmas with them, Easter, the Fourth of July. Paul's dad will make you a drink, and his mom will chat with you about this and that, and before you know it, everyone is sitting in the backyard laughing. Entire afternoons pass with a few good jokes and a lot of gab.

Paul's sister Michelle thought for a moment before answering my question, but not for long.

"It all goes back to when Paul was in his coma," she said. "We realized how easy it would be to lose him and decided not to sweat the small stuff. Life is too short."

She was referring to the day after Thanksgiving, many years ago, when fifteen-year-old Paul and his friends went running down the mountain we both grew up at the base of, a wild and beautiful place. They called it bush crashing—jumping off out-croppings, barreling down meadows, skidding through trees, letting out the pent-up energy of teen boys. A little bit of dan-ger, a whole lot of fun.

At one point Paul jumped off a cornice and landed wrong. His legs buckled beneath him, both ankles broken, and he began to roll down a hill that got steeper and steeper. His body gath-ered momentum with each revolution, faster and faster, until the force flung him off a cliff and he landed in a rocky creek bed.

His friends raced to where his body lay. They were both trained Boy Scouts. One ran to the fire station in a nearby town to get help. The other stayed behind, ripping up his jeans to make splints and bandages, watching over Paul and waiting for grown-ups to come. They got him to the hospital in what is called *the golden hour*—the short period of time after a brain in-jury before the swelling has done too much damage.

At the hospital, doctors put Paul in a medically induced coma. There was talk he might not make it, that he might be mentally compromised. The family was terrified. The hair on Paul's father's head turned gray overnight.

The doctors had a hard time bringing Paul out of the coma. For two weeks his life hung in the balance. Prayer vigils were held at his school and in church. Catholic relics were brought to his hospital room in hopes of a miracle. Then, one day, with his sister sitting by his hospital bed, Paul opened his eyes. From there he made a stunning recovery, returning home in time for Christmas.

"Once we had him back," Michelle said, "we promised not to screw it up."

When I ask Paul, he agrees. "We were falling apart," he says, "always fighting—we'd even started family counseling. We had one session before the accident. But a crisis puts things in perspective. After that we were tight."

Would it take something like that to bring my family together?

When we were growing up, people often assumed my brother and I were twins. We were both lanky, with a coltish look and cowlicks that sent our wispy blond hair in odd directions. We had the same big eyes we hadn't yet grown into. In the early years, it was clear he was younger, but as our size difference evened out, people often asked if we were just siblings or perhaps actually twins.

"No," I would reply, outraged. "I'm *two and a half years* older!"

It wasn't the two and a half years that made the difference, though. We might have looked alike, but we had been born into different worlds. I was the daughter of two parents, planned and anticipated. Two and a half years later, my brother was born into a family in shambles, an uncertain future. He had only one parent—and not even all of her.

And he had me: a sister, not much older, who quickly became his second mother. I was his greatest protector and his biggest bully but never his friend.

I don't remember the moment I first saw my brother. I remember drawing rainbows on construction paper with a babysitter the day my mother was in the hospital having the baby. It is perhaps my earliest memory. The crude lines, the tacky feeling of the wax crayons, the sunlight on our deck that May morning. Beyond that there is nothing.

I don't know how my mother found that house, or how she paid for it, or who hung the swing from the eaves so it dangled over the deck, but we have pictures of me swinging in it not long after my brother was born. In the photos he is wrapped in a blanket that had been knitted for me by my father's mother. Two and a half years later she was dead, my father was gone, and there was no communication or support for us from him or his family.

When I speak of my childhood, I often say we grew up like wild wolves. It is at once a joke and not a joke. How does one explain the collision of needs, anger, deprivation, desire, resentment, and hungry love that all came crashing together in that small house in the country? How does one tell of a mother who had never been mothered, a father who wasn't even a memory, and two children who learned to adapt at all costs? It is a story hard and horrid: We were each our best and worst selves.

Had there been money, community, family—had there been religion, even—it might have been easier. But none of that existed for us. We were on our own, growling and wrestling and marking our territory.

People who knew us then—neighbors, other parents at our school—will tell you that, individually, my brother and I were the most pleasant children. We minded our manners and offered to set and clear the table. We helped with dishes without being asked. They were delighted to have us for sleepovers and invited us on their family vacations; their own children behaved better when we were around.

The dark side of that shiny penny is the way we were with each other, something most people never saw. Some families bind together to survive difficult times—forming a solid unit to defend against what is hard and hopeless. We were not like that. I was hungry for approval and attention and looked outward, not inward. Perhaps I could tell, even then, that the center wouldn't hold. I leaned toward other people; I tried to be what they wanted of me; that was how I got fed. My brother was competition for resources scarce or nonexistent.

"You were so mean to your brother," my mother often says—as if a two-year-old had charge of her emotions. My brother arrived only months after my father left, taking up what little was left of my mother's attention and making me responsible in ways for which I was not prepared. When I took a blanket to cover up the baby, I covered his head as well, as if I could make him disappear entirely.

If I had been older, perhaps I could have done better, been a bigger person. Perhaps then my brother and I would have been on the same team. But I was two when he was born, and my needs were stronger than my maturity. They were an icy cold creature that clawed at me from the inside.

And yet my mother's words haunt me, they sting. The distance my brother keeps, his disinclination toward our family—it feels as though it is my fault. I sometimes wonder if I should apologize to him, if I should tell him how sorry I am for failing him.

My hands were just too small to hold the pieces together.

There was no expectation for my brother to be part of the garden. He could have been, if he wanted—our mother would have been overjoyed. But he was busy with work and his own family and had never shown any interest in digging or weeding. We had both run wild in our childhood garden, plucking asparagus from the dirt to eat raw, climbing trees to pick the new apples that tasted sweet and clean, but my brother felt no need to coax food from the soil.

A good weekend for him was spent with his wife and children on their new boat, or swimming at the country club. My brother worked in high tech and was a natty dresser. He didn't want to get his hands dirty.

My mother made him promise to mow the lawn a few times a year and he reluctantly agreed, but it would be an obligation to him, a resentment perhaps, never a pleasure. We were of the same family, but never on the same team.

His wife did like to garden. In fact she loved it. When I first met my sister-in-law, she was the only person I knew who was my age and interested in growing things. Her knowledge of flower names was impressive.

It was from her that I learned—after years of reading the name in books—what a primrose looked like. I expected such a romantic name to be attached to a more impressive flower and was disappointed to find primroses sturdy and pedestrian, cheerful but uninspiring. I promptly decided to forget this newfound knowledge.

Like my mother, my sister-in-law used the proper names for plants. This too I found disappointing. Why call it *Datura* when you could call it angel's-trumpet or moonflower? I never liked it when accuracy got in the way of romanticism, and the proper names were so often dull.

I suspected I would never make a proper gardener, because the first thought I had when my sister-in-law mentioned the hedge plant *Sarcococca* was: *There has got to be a better name for that.*

Despite its unfortunate name, *Sarcococca* became a favorite of mine (it is also, happily, called sweet box). It was one of those precious plants to the Northwest gardener: the rare few that bloom in winter, a small and select club. Seattle winters are so long and gray, anything to lift the spirits feels like unexpected grace.

One day a few years earlier, my sister-in-law and I had been taking a walk with the girls when I stopped in my tracks. "What is that *smell*?"

It was my first winter in Seattle. I was back from San Francisco, trying to see if I could hack the dark and rainy season, trying to see what there was for me in this unexpected city, trying to decide if I should take it seriously. I wasn't sure.

I was startled to see how much had changed in the few months I had been away. The leafy green I had come to love that summer was gone, the skies were low and overcast, the niecelets had sprouted in my absence. The baby, who had been crawling only three months before, was now toddling on unsteady legs, trying to keep up with her sister.

As I stood with my sister-in-law, watching my young niece bobble unevenly down the sidewalk, I smelled a scent entirely new to me.

"What is that?" I asked her. "Do you smell it? It's lovely."

She looked back to where I had stopped, and a smile appeared on her face.

"Winter-blooming *Daphne,*" she said. "It's one of my favorites, but so expensive." She pointed to tiny pinkish flowers on a low shrub I hadn't noticed. The leaves were green but edged ever so slightly with white, and the whole thing looked unremarkable. I never would have chosen it for a garden—*but, oh, the smell*. It was like citrus blooms and jasmine and tuberoses all tumbled together. Heavenly.

We stood together there for a moment, breathing in as we watched the girls walk away from us with increasingly sturdy strides, and I felt it in my chest—the exquisitely painful passage of time, how it can be both beautiful and gutting.

I wanted to call them back, to reverse the clock, to somehow make up for the few months I had been away. Their progress left me amazed, both exhilarated and helpless at the days that had slipped through my hands. I wanted to tell them, *Don't grow up so soon.*

Instead I breathed the flower scent deeply and tried to fix the moment in my memory: the day the girls walked into their own world.

It wasn't until that first winter in my mother's garden that I noticed it, hidden amid the careful planting of the formal front yard. There, between the Japanese pines and maples and ornamental quince, was the largest winter-blooming *Daphne* I had ever seen. As if it had been selected and placed there especially for us.

All through the bleakness of my mother's first winter in Seattle, all through February, March, and April, I clipped tiny sprigs of *Daphne* to bring home with me. Set in water on a sunny windowsill, they opened and perfumed my house: this unremarkable flower with the intoxicating scent. Unexpected sweetness in the midst of gray days.

It might have seemed natural for my sister-in-law to join us in the garden, but it never worked out that way. Her passion lay in flowers, not food. Her own yard was neat and orderly, with hedges and borders and blooming vines. It was a place of relaxation and recreation, not of productivity. The branches of the neighbor's plum tree that arched slightly over her fence irritated her when they dropped their soft fruit on her stone path. She did not see it the way my mother did. Perhaps she had never been hungry enough.

Instead we fell into a pattern: my sister-in-law dropping off the girls at my mother's house when she wanted some free time. Occasionally I joined them, though usually by coincidence rather than plan. One day I came to do some gardening, and when I walked through the wooden gate, I stopped in my tracks, stunned by what I saw before me.

Blankets were spread on the sloping lawn, books and plates of fruit scattered about. Abby and Cate were wearing flowered dresses from a closet my mother kept stocked with dress-up outfits. Japanese paper umbrellas in bright colors lay blown around the grass. It looked like a graceful scene of bucolic outdoor recreation, an impressionist painting come to life. I was dumbstruck by the beauty, in an aching, wistful way.

Was this scene of wonder and delight my mother's doing?

To me my mother was all necessity and catastrophe; I hadn't imagined she could extend to grace. Maybe it was a fluke. Maybe I had been wrong about her—or maybe this part of her had just been buried so long by worry and fear.

We planted sunflowers that day, digging small holes and showing the girls how to drop in the large gray seeds and mound the earth back in place, to press down gently and water them well. We didn't know that, over the next few days, crows would dig up all the seeds and in the end not a single one would sprout or bloom. It didn't matter. It felt like something else was being planted that day, something that would grow in the girls for the rest of their lives.

When my sister-in-law came to pick them up, she sat on the grass in the sunshine and chatted a bit, as the girls changed back into their regular clothes. She told us what she had bought that day, her plans for the weekend, how happy she was to have such nice weather. But she never picked up a trowel or garden gloves. Even though the lawn she sat on was marred with dandelions, even though there was more than enough work to go around, she never jumped in.

Maybe we didn't make room for her; maybe we never invited her in. Maybe we should have. But then again, she never offered. It's hard to know where the lines are drawn.

Abby had been almost one when my mother left Seattle the first time, after a year of trying to live close to my brother and his new family. After she left she visited frequently, but still she worried her granddaughter wouldn't remember her, that she might die without Abby knowing who she was. When Cate was born, that fear doubled.

This may sound extreme or paranoid, but my mother has only a single memory of her own mother. Everything they shared in the first three years of her life—hugs and lullabies and scraped knees and first teeth and bath time—is lost to the limitations of a child's mind and a death come too soon. My mother didn't want history to repeat itself.

"If I die before they remember me," she often asked in those days, "will you tell them how much I loved them?"

"Of course I will."

"Promise?"

"I promise."

In those days, when my mother visited Seattle to see her grandchildren, she brought books. On the inside cover she always inscribed the same message. It was what she told the girls on the phone from California, whenever they could be persuaded to talk to her: *Grandma loves you all the time.*

As the girls grew, they learned to parrot my mother, they said it together at the end of phone conversations or when she was leaving after a visit. Their high, chirpy voices blended with her own low tones to make a chant, a chorus, a call to arms. She would start and they would join in: "Grandma loves you all the time."

They thought it was a game, a joke. Only I knew the sad, scared place it came from. Only I knew what it really meant: a little girl with a single memory of her own mother. A little girl who did not remember ever being loved.

Even if she is not here, even when you cannot see her, even if she dies, even if you don't remember her: Grandma loves you all the time.

For a number of years, when my brother and I were young, we drove every summer from our home in California to the mountains of Colorado. There was a graduate school just starting up in Boulder; my mother was teaching there.

Mostly what I remember is the drive: long and unending,

my brother and me in the back of my mom's old Volvo. We ate plums along the way, throwing the pits out the almond-shaped rear windows that were held open by a funny little hinge. Our pits made tracks of slime on the outside of the car that stayed there until someone washed them off in Colorado three days later.

We sang in the car too. Once we were out of radio range, we sang songs our mother taught us or that we knew from school. We got so good we could sing three-part rounds, each person staggering their start time and going around and around and around until we were dizzy with the music, our high voices combining sweetly, gracefully. You might have thought there were angels singing in the backseat.

We were angels and we were devils. We sang and we fought. There was a line down the center of the backseat and no war-time border was ever so well defended. The mere hint of a finger straying over the line was grounds for outright attack or wailing.

"Moooommmmm, he's on *my* side!"

But even devils get tired. Eventually my brother grew sleepy. When he did he snuggled up to me, and I let him, temporarily suspending the rules of engagement and allowing him room on my side of the car.

"Make your hands like Mommy," he said, and I gently stroked his hair until he fell asleep. I sat as still as I could as my mother drove late into the night and my brother slept, his golden head in my lap, and together we crossed the desert plains of Nevada and climbed high into the dark mountains, up the spine of a continent and down the other side.

It was my brother who first suggested I move to Seattle. I was still living in Japan at the time, but back for a visit. I had one year left on my contract, and I was thinking about my options. That summer I visited friends in Colorado and Washington, D.C., as well as San Francisco. Everywhere I went I wondered: Could this be my next home?

The one place I never considered was Seattle. I stopped there only to visit my brother—and because it was partway between my mother's house near San Francisco and the island in Canada where she was teaching for the summer.

We hadn't been close growing up. The teen years in particular had been a catfight. Though perhaps it was a catfight all along. I have a scar on my forehead from a spoon my brother threw at me in a fit of childhood anger. It split the skin, and when our mother heard the screams and came running, she found blood coursing down my face. I was eight, he was six; we had only been trying to play cards.

In the year or two before I left Japan, however, there had been a softening, perhaps a warming. My friend Paul had a little to do with it. We were both working in Japan, and when I heard about the great time he'd had when his sister visited him, I blurted out, almost without thinking, "I want my brother to come visit me."

"Invite him," Paul said. And he told me exactly what to say when I called my brother, out of the blue, to ask him to visit me on the other side of the world.

"I'm gonna make you an offer you can't refuse."

My brother did come—our mother quickly offering to pay for his ticket. That trip felt like the beginning of our adult relationship, no longer competing for scarce resources. He met my friends, won over local students ("Leo! Leo!" they cried, thinking he looked like Leonardo DiCaprio). He and Paul both teased me, each of them knowing all too well what buttons to press. Suddenly it felt like I had two brothers.

Still, when he suggested I consider Seattle on my list of possibilities, it surprised me. I thought the reason he had gone off to college and never come home was a desire for distance from family. I thought we were on the same page about that. I had moved to Europe and then to Asia. Distance was a game I was good at.

"Would you *want* me here?"

"I don't think we'd hang out all the time," he said, a bit defensively. "We'd have our own friends—but I think you'd like it here."

In high school my brother had surpassed me. Somehow this small child I used to take care of had picked up a social rhythm I couldn't quite grasp. He was funny, popular, a quick wit with sly humor. I was always a beat or two off, standing alone in the cold.

He could have brought me into this circle, but he didn't. He made fun of me; he shut me out. Perhaps he learned it from me. Hadn't I been first to sell him out?

"Nobody likes you," my brother taunted. It wasn't true, but part of me, the most scared and tender part, feared that it was. That my brother could somehow see through me in a way other people couldn't. That he knew what I really was: a fraud, a failure, destined to be a social outcast. It was years before I realized he wasn't right.

But sometimes my brother surprised me. A few years after he moved to Seattle, I stayed with him on my way down from Canada. I would be arriving late and leaving early and couldn't even tell him for sure when I would show up—ferry lines and border crossings take time. When I arrived, late and tired, I found he had gone across town to my favorite restaurant and picked up an order of the soup that he knew I liked. When I thanked him profusely he shrugged it off, but in those moments I could see the little blond boy who had fallen asleep with his head in my lap.

Now, nearly a decade later, I asked my brother if he was okay with having me in Seattle. I asked several times, just to be clear.

It's one thing to have your sister in your city for the summer, babysitting your kids and dropping off dinner. It's another thing to be stuck with her there, possibly forever.

"You can do whatever you want," he said several times. "It's fine with me."

By then I had some friends in Seattle. I knew my way around. But still. Living in the same city would connect us in ways we never had been as adults. At the time our mother still lived in California and traveled often. If something happened to me, he would be the only relative in proximity. Besides my mother, he was the only family I had in all the world.

This change in geography would force us to be more to each other than ever before. Perhaps that is what I should have asked about. Perhaps I should have spelled it out for him.

Are you prepared to be my family?

Was he willing to take that on? Did I trust him enough to let him?

The first winter I spent in Seattle, I got sick. It started on a Saturday when I had driven north of the city to a large thrift sale. I wandered through buildings filled with everything from sporting equipment to antiques but left early, feeling sick. On my way home, I called my brother and sister-in-law to report on the sale. They had been undecided about making the trek.

"There's good stuff," I told him, "but I feel awful. I have a fever. I'm going back to bed."

"Sorry to hear that," he said. "I'll give a call later to check on you."

He did call to check on me—but not until Tuesday. By then I had spent days in a blazing fugue, feverish and sicker than I had ever been. My sole memory of that weekend is getting out of bed to go to the bathroom and collapsing on the floor, the rough feel of carpet under my cheek. I remember trying to crawl across the room. I remember wondering if I might die there. I woke two days later, in bed, spent and shaken, the sheets twisted around my legs.

By the time my brother called, I was angry. He was the only one who knew I was sick, knew I was alone. How could he have not checked on me? Was I not more important than a trip to Home Depot—or whatever he had been doing that weekend?

But mostly I was scared. I could have died there. Alone.

I was no stranger to being sick on my own. By that point I had been sick all over the world. In my student apartment in Vienna, my roommate had translated the dosage instructions on my medicine and made me garlic soup. In Thailand, kind guesthouse owners took my temperature and offered food from their own kitchen. In China, fellow travelers I had met only the day before ignored my protests and went out to buy soft tofu for me. They told me it was the only thing to eat after food poisoning.

I had been cared for more graciously by strangers than I had by my own brother.

Even in San Francisco I had been better off. There was Chinese takeout across the street. I knew my neighbors; our buildings adjoined. If I were truly dying, I could pound on the floor, and eventually J.L. would come to investigate. I could shout across the air shaft, and George would likely hear, or Mark and Chris upstairs. We might not have been friends, but our lives were unfolding in close proximity. I knew they would help if I needed it.

In San Francisco I had resources. I knew how to protect myself. But in this new city I was stripped bare. The neighborhood I lived in was desired for its proximity to the Arboretum, the university, the bridge that led to technology companies across Lake Washington. The houses were handsome, some stately, but the well-tended blocks were deserted during the day and quiet at night. Everyone had their yard, their space. Money bought isolation as well as privacy.

I could have pounded, I could have shouted, but nobody

would have heard. This cold fact left me more scared than I had ever been.

The one person who was supposed to be my family had let me down.

That Tuesday, when my brother finally called, I insisted he come over. When he did—still in his work clothes, checking his phone—I yelled at him. I shouted. We fought as we had not fought since high school. Since the days when we slammed doors and ripped them open with such ferocity that the knob went through the plaster of the wall behind, leaving a round, gaping hole. A tribute to our rough anger with each other.

"*Why* didn't you check on me?"

"Why didn't you *tell me* how sick you were?"

"I *did* tell you I was sick. I told you Saturday!"

"Why didn't you call to tell me you had gotten worse?"

"I was too sick to call."

Around and around we went, around and around until we were almost dizzy with the accusations. I was angry; he was defensive. He wouldn't apologize, and I refused to let it drop. Instead I raged. I took the horror of feeling so vulnerable, so unprotected, and I unloaded it on him. Perhaps it was unfair of me—it wasn't my brother's fault that I was living alone—but I didn't care. I needed to make him understand, and he seemed determined not to.

I yelled as I had not yelled in years. I yelled like my mother.

In the end I was crying on the couch, and he had still not relented. He took the abuse, but he would not apologize. To him it was a logic problem. *If you had called . . . If I had known . . . It's not my fault.*

It came from his head, not from his heart. He never said what I needed to hear:

I am sorry you were all alone. I am sorry I didn't call. That must have been horrible. It won't ever happen again, I promise.

He sat there stiffly as I wiped tears and pulled myself together. But still, I couldn't let it drop. Where was his compassion? How could the little boy whose head I stroked as he slept in my lap be this cold, this unfeeling? Hadn't I raised him better than this? I tried one last appeal.

"I'm sitting here crying, and you don't even care? You have daughters now. What if I were Abby—what if she were this upset? Would you not put your arm around her and comfort her?"

"Of course I would," he said. "But she's my daughter. You're just my sister."

Without much discussion, my mother and I had begun buying presents for the garden. I mentioned I wanted a croquet set, and she found one before I did. I bought a vintage badminton net and rackets when I saw them at a rummage sale. Later I found bocce balls and added those to our growing collection. I didn't even know how to play bocce.

We were buying things for a life we did not have—some Kennedyesque existence where a boisterous family plays games on a sloping lawn before tromping in for Sunday supper. We had nothing like that.

It reminded me of the first Thanksgiving after my brother and sister-in-law met. They had flown to California to spend the holiday with us in the cabin on the coast my mom rented with friends. It was small and sparsely furnished, awkward for more than two people, but perched on a cliff overlooking the ocean. On a clear day, you could see from San Francisco in the south to Point Reyes in the north, and out to the Farallon Islands far offshore. We fell asleep to the sound of crashing waves and woke to a blazing dawn. If you are the sort of person that my mother is—the sort of person I am—this is worth some discomfort.

The cliff the cabin stood on was mostly wild, but a well-tended lawn lay on the inland side. It belonged to a gray-shingled house with white trim I had always admired. Compared to our tiny cabin, this house looked solid. It looked Cape Cod. I was sure dependable people lived there; none of our wild ways.

That first Thanksgiving with my sister-in-law we walked on the beach, as we always did. For our family the holiday revolved around hanging out together and a long walk. It might be chilly in Northern California in November, but it was always sunny, the dry-grass hills a golden hue.

Walking up from the beach, we saw a touch football game being played on the lawn next to the house on the cliff. The younger members of the family were tossing the ball around while older folks sat on the deck with cocktails; they waved as we walked by. We didn't know these people, but I longed to be one of them. I longed for the friendly ease they had with each other, the rough-and-tumble team spirit.

Around our table things felt wrong. We often bickered. When my brother was around, he would get sleepy, his way of tuning it out. He seemed to prefer to stay distant from it all.

It's not that we didn't want to be a family—we honestly didn't know how to go about it. We were making it all up as we went along. But it didn't feel right; it didn't feel warm. We were awkward and clumsy with each other. Our pieces never quite fit.

It was six years after that Thanksgiving that my mother moved to Seattle and into Orchard House. It still felt like we didn't fit. It felt like we were failing—both ourselves and each other. But we went through the motions: Maybe we could fake it until it felt real.

That first year in Seattle we gathered in the garden to celebrate my mother's late-spring birthday. Seventy-three is a big deal, especially for someone who assumed she would die before thirty. I made a menu I hoped would please everyone. There was a frittata with broccoli I knew the kids would eat; a spring salad of endive and avocado, which my brother and sister-in-law like;

and a fruit pie instead of cake, because that is what my mother prefers.

The day dawned sunny, unexpectedly warm. The flowers were out—the San Geronimo irises, the deep red tulips my mother loves. The rhododendrons were blooming in pink, white, and purple, a carpet of petals on the lawn.

After we ate everyone tromped outside on the grass, and my mother unveiled her latest gift for the garden: an assortment of Hula-Hoops she had found at thrift stores. I had seen their brightly colored rounds leaned up against the house when I had come that week to garden. "I've been practicing," my mother confided.

The children fell upon them with glee, stepping inside and bringing the plastic hoops waist-high, spinning them and swaying back and forth. Everybody clapped and cheered them on.

"You too, Grandma!" Cate called out.

My mother selected one of the larger hoops and began. My seventy-three-year-old mother, hula-hooping. You could see the dancer she had been in her younger years, graceful, flexible. We all laughed and cheered. Grandma was pretty good.

"Mommy, Daddy, come on!" My sister-in-law and brother joined in, able to do only a few rotations before the hoops fell at their feet. The girls were delighted to see their parents fail at something they found so easy.

"You too, Tea-tea," they called to me.

"Just a minute," I said, dashing inside to get my camera.

It was there that I looked out the window and saw it: my family, playing, laughing. My seventy-three-year-old mother and her five-year-old granddaughter were being crowned Hula-Hoop champions among the spring flowers. From a distance I could see what hadn't been clear at close range: *We looked like we were having fun.*

We looked like a family. One you might even want to be part of.

Much later, after my brother and sister-in-law had packed up the kids and all gone home, after my mother and I had cleared the birthday dishes and scrubbed the frittata off the inside of her casserole dish, we went outside to clean up the garden. The brightly colored Hula-Hoops and Frisbees were scattered over the lawn.

"So . . ." I began with some trepidation. "Did you have an okay time?" My mother is not one to mince words. She is not one to pretend. And I would never ask if something had been *good*. Good is more than I ever hope for with my mother.

"I guess it wasn't *too* terrible," she allowed.

In a world of broken glasses, in the world my mother inhabits, this is almost praise.

I thought back on all the laughter, the spring flowers, the hula-hooping, the girls. I didn't know what she was waiting for—*a personal hallelujah chorus*? Couldn't she just be happy for once? There wasn't much time left.

"You might want to try enjoying it," I told her. "This might be as good as it gets."

8

. . .

TO SEE WHAT IS NOT YET THERE

NOTHING PREPARED ME FOR spring in a four-season climate. In Northern California winter brings the rain that coaxes golden-brown hills back to green after the long, dry summer. It causes creeks and rivers to gush. It is a season of life.

In Seattle, winter is the season of bleak. Leaves fall, revealing branches, stark against a lowering sky, with a surprising number of bird's nests abandoned to the cold. The days are short, the sky dark even at noon. Everything feels gray for days, until spring tiptoes in.

Suddenly, after months of waiting, the city erupts in vivid yellow forsythia and purple crocuses. A riotous parade of plum blossoms gives way to blooming cherries, their fallen petals like pink snow blown into drifts on the sidewalk. Daffodils push out of the soil, trees leaf into the palest of green, and strangers smile at each other and strike up conversation. After months of hibernation, people wander around and blink up at a clear blue sky. No one can resist the giddiness of spring in the Northwest.

The first spring in a new garden brings its own delights. There were surprises lying in wait for us. Small white clumps of snowdrops started off the season. Tulip bulbs that had been slumbering, unknown to us, stretched narrow necks and bloomed in shades of magenta and peach. The Indian plum bush we thought was dead unfurled small green leaves and pendulous white blossoms that swayed delicately in the breeze. Each new discovery felt like a gift, left behind by those who had tended this garden in the past.

"What are you looking at?" My mother rounded the corner by the driveway and caught me in what I was calling the *side garden,* a nondescript area to the south of the house that ran from the front yard to the main garden in the rear. This was the area I was beginning to think of as mine.

There was nothing impressive about the side yard. The path bordered a series of cinder blocks that had been set on their side and stacked to form a retaining wall about six feet out from the house. This resulted in what could be seen as a large garden bed—if you were the sort given to gardening. Otherwise you might see it for what it was: a weedy wasteland.

The area had been divided in two sections: An upper bed of thick grass looked like an uncombed mop of hair; a lower bed was longer, filled with poor, sandy soil and sprouting dandelions. A knobby tractor tire leaned against the wooden gate at the bottom that led to the garden. The red NO TRESPASSING sign was still prominently displayed.

"What are you looking at?" my mother asked again, impatient, her hands filled with rusty garden tools from the garage.

"I'm trying to imagine what it might look like—"

"You need to imagine faster," she said as she walked by, a curt tone to her voice. "It's going to rain any minute."

I stood in the side yard, scuffing my clogs in the sandy soil as

Seattle spring drizzle began to dampen my hair and slick my jacket. But I couldn't imagine any faster. Imagining takes time.

Being a gardener requires the ability to see possibility where none may be evident. A real gardener, I was sure, could look at this sad, weedy side yard and see flourishing grapevines and blooming lilac. There could be layers of plants—a ground cover of some sort, annuals and perennials, an overstory of trees. I tried and I tried, but I couldn't see it.

I wasn't much of a gardener yet, but that wasn't the problem.

It is not in my nature to see what is not there. I've never felt like I could create a new reality—I was too busy trying to make the pieces I had been given fit together. It didn't occur to me that I could walk away and start from scratch.

To create takes more than imagination. There is an audacity to creation, whether you are designing a new house, a new life, or a new garden bed. There must be an overriding belief in your own worth—and in a world benevolent enough to make room for your vision. To be able to create, you need to have faith.

I do not come from people who have faith. I come from people who expect to be wiped out in a freak snowstorm in July.

And yet, looking around this bedraggled side yard, I tried to imagine what it might look like. I mustered up all I had, and I began to dream and make plans.

It was the cement foundation that had drawn me to the side garden. Being on the south side of the house, it would get sunlight throughout the day. The foundation would soak up warmth, retain it into the evening, and radiate it back. Permaculture had taught me that this is called a "heat sink." Cement, pavement, metal, and large rocks can all function this way.

Once I knew the concept, I began to notice it in the world. I saw the first ripe blackberries each summer were those growing next to a huge boulder. The stone soaked up the heat and held it, and those berries were purple and sweet while others were still small and hard.

The farm where my permaculture class was held had created a heat sink—taken a sloping hillside and covered it in river stones. This is where they planted the trees that needed warm temperatures, varieties not necessarily suited to the Pacific Northwest: olives, lemons, almonds. They were creating a warmer microclimate. The cement foundation of the house would do the same. I could grow tomatoes here, peppers, egg-plant, possibly melons—all things challenging in an area short on summer. I would be magnifying an asset, all thanks to a rather ugly cement foundation.

Before I planted, however, the soil needed to be amended.

"I think I'm going to sheet mulch the side garden," I told my mom as we drove to my brother's house one early spring eve-ning. The days were still so short it was dark by dinnertime, even an early children's dinnertime, and we drove through streets wet with rain.

"What is sheet mulching?"

"You basically make layers. The bottom layer is cardboard to keep the weeds down. Then you spread compost and soil and straw, one on top of the other. Some people call it a 'lasagna bed.' Over time it all breaks down and improves the soil. It's so sandy over there, I think it needs it."

My mother didn't blink an eye. "Okay. I'll help."

That's when I started showing up at the garden with the back of my station wagon stuffed with cardboard. I had found a framing shop that put out large cardboard boxes for recycling. Every few days I drove past and collected whatever had been stacked up.

I didn't think anyone would mind me taking the cardboard. Permaculture teaches making use of what is available, diverting objects from the waste stream. Later I would learn there is a term for this. Rather than recycling I was *upcycling*.

Even though the cardboard had been put out for disposal—*someone* was going to remove it, and it might as well be me—taking it felt subversive. I did my runs under cover of darkness, spiriting the boxes away in the middle of the night.

Once I told my mother about it, she got into the act, stuffing her small hybrid to the gills, packing the cardboard so tightly she needed help pulling it out once she got home. The piles quickly grew, until the back patio looked like a recycling center, filled with towering stacks of cardboard the size of a refrigerator.

"You need to do something about the sheet mulching," my mom told me on the phone one day. "When are you going to take care of that?"

I hadn't been spending much time in the garden. It had been a long wet winter, and I had been busy. My first book was about to be published, and email had become a full-time job. Messages came in faster than I could dispatch them; I was working frantically just to keep above sea level. I had a lot on my mind. Gardening was the least of it.

"I'll get up there this weekend," I told my mom. I didn't have the time, but it was hard to say no to my mother. I didn't want to be part of the disappointment of her life.

The garden was only fifteen minutes from my house, but it felt like a different world. As I drove north, the city quickly melted into residential neighborhoods, tree-lined streets, small lakes, snowcapped mountains to the east and west. In Seattle the sun rose and set behind a jagged line of peaks cloaked in lacy white. Seeing them always took my breath away.

I'd wanted my mother to have a view of those mountains—that's why I had selected this neighborhood. It was not far from my brother's house, on numbered streets where she was less likely to get lost, with views of water and mountains.

"You know you stuck me in an old person's neighborhood," she said when she first arrived in Seattle.

"It's *not* an old person's neighborhood."

"Haven't you noticed the chairs next to all the bus stops? People here are so old they can't even stand to wait for a bus. Either that or they're just lazy."

I had seen the chairs, a mismatched assortment of plastic lawn chairs someone had set out at the suburban bus stops that lacked a bench. I thought they were sweet.

"Maybe the buses don't come that often."

"Yeah—because *old people* don't have anywhere to go!"

My mother wasn't wrong. This was the sort of neighborhood you would want your aging parent to end up in—quiet, safe, near grandchildren, with stunning views. I liked to think of her reading books, gazing off at the mountains, in a solid and comfortable home, enjoying the security that was the result of years of hard effort. I liked to think of her relaxing at last.

I had been trying to do something nice for her, though she did not see it that way.

But my mother had chosen garden over view. She had chosen work over leisure. She had bought a ramshackle house even though she could afford much better.

Now when I came to the garden, driving over the hill with the stunning views and dropping down to turn onto her mostly viewless street, my heart sank at what could have been. Instead of a view, we were left with potential—but there was so much work to get there. If we wanted grace, we would have to earn it.

The side garden was as I had left it—a large sandy patch punctuated with dandelions. I dragged the pieces of cardboard around from the back patio and began to lay them out, careful to overlap the edges. I weighted each down with large stones.

In truth, I was doing a bad job. The cardboard should have been covered by layers of compost and mulch, inches thick, to smother the weeds. Sheet mulching is not something that should be done in stages. But I didn't have the time—and my mother was impatient—so I did what I could. I half-assed it. By the end of the afternoon, the side garden was a patchwork of different shades of cardboard.

"I'll do the rest when I get back," I told her. It wasn't good; it was simply all I could manage.

My mother said nothing. I could tell she was not impressed.

When I came back from my book tour two weeks later, the side yard was fully mulched with layers of compost and fertilizer and straw. My mother had done it all while I was gone.

"How did you know what to use?" I asked.

"I looked it up on the internet."

"But *what* did you use?" Sheet mulching is an inexact science—there are a variety of soil amendments to choose from. I wasn't sure myself what would have been best. I hadn't had time to do the research.

"I don't remember," she said.

I couldn't deny the work she had done—shoveling compost and mulch, spreading it out on the large bed—not to mention the cost of purchasing materials. Don, the handyman she hired to do odd jobs, had helped. Still, it was a lot of work.

Maybe I should have been grateful; maybe I should have seen it as help when needed, as if we were on the same team, but it never felt that way.

Rather than a gift, her help felt damning. I had let her down again.

One spring, a number of years ago, my friend Jon Rowley wanted to bring strawberries to a wedding, as a gift for the friends who were getting married. Because he is the best sort of obsessive, Jon tasted every variety he could, asked all the growers he met what their favorite berry was. In the end he decided Shuksans were the best around. He arranged to buy flats of them for the wedding, and the guests all exclaimed. People bit into the berries, closed their eyes, and sighed. Years later, they're still talking about those strawberries.

I had never heard of a Shuksan strawberry, but when I heard that story, I wanted some.

Shuksans don't show up in stores. If you see them, you might understand why. They are not a classic, cone-shaped berry. Instead long necks flare into fluted bodies, irregular and craggy; sizes vary wildly. The Shuksan is not going to win any beauty pageants.

Beyond that they are perishable in a time when berries need to be tough. It can take days for berries to travel from the growing fields of California to store shelves around the country. Shuksans need to be eaten the day they're picked. This is why store-bought berries are aesthetically pleasing but white on the inside, with little flavor; they are the ghosts of strawberries past.

These bred-for-the-supermarket berries were what my nieces were eating—tasteless things grown in fields states away. It made me sad. I knew I couldn't undo the industrial food supply chain, but I could make sure my nieces learned the difference. I could grow real berries for them.

This is why, one April day, I stood looking at the thick mop of grass that capped the top section of the side garden. I felt a small pang of grief—it takes a certain steeling of the soul to disturb a plant that is doing well, and the grass was thick and happy. But I focused my mind on the end goal. This patch of grass was destined to be my strawberry bed.

I reached down and grabbed a clump of grass and gave it a firm tug. Nothing happened.

I reached again, grabbing the stalks in an even firmer handhold. I put my body weight into it and pulled hard.

Some of the grass came off in my hand. The rest—and most important, the roots—stayed put. I stared blankly at the green blades in my hand.

What was this stuff?

I'd just had my first introduction to quack grass. Our acquaintance would not be brief.

Quack grass is the Quasimodo of the grass family, monstrous and unwanted. Whereas other grasses send up stalks that put out seed to fall and sprout, quack grass spreads underground via rhizomes—fleshly white roots that can grow up to three hundred feet in a year, so strong they grow through asphalt. You might think you could get rid of quack grass by rototilling, but new plants will sprout from each and every bit of chopped up root. Instead of getting rid of the plants, you will have made thousands more.

This was not a casual weeding project. This was war.

My mother found me not long after my initial encounter with the quack grass, armed with my weapon of choice: a hori-hori shaped like a blade, one edge serrated for cutting. I was furiously attacking the quack grass.

"Here, I'll help you." She knelt down next to where I was weeding and grabbed a handful of grass. The thin green blades came off in her hand. She tossed them in the pile and reached to grab more.

"You can't do it that way. Here, I'll show you." I took my hori-hori and used the serrated edge to saw through the matted, carpetlike grass, prying it out chunk by chunk. Each piece was the size of a brick and nearly that heavy.

"You need to get the roots, or it will just regrow."

My mom made a halfhearted dig with her hori-hori but was too impatient; she yanked the grass again, ripping off blades, leaving roots behind.

"That's not going to work," I told her.

"My way is fine," she said huffily, getting to her feet and looking at the pile of matted grass chunks. "I hope you're not going to put those in the yard waste. There's a lot of good soil in there."

There was a lot of good soil bound up in the roots, but the

only way to separate them was to use the blade of the hori-hori to beat the matted grass into submission, pounding on the clumps over and over again. As I whaled away at the matted grass, I wondered if I could market this as the latest technique in anger management therapy.

Once I removed the clumps of roots, I sifted through the soil. The sandy loam ran through my fingers as I obsessively checked and rechecked for any remaining bit of root or rhizome that might resprout.

At the end of three hours of sawing, prying, sifting, and pummeling, I was exhausted. My wrist ached, my arms were sore, and the fine soil had lodged itself in every crevice of my body. I stood up, shakily, to survey my work. The pile of root clumps was impressive—a mountain of matted grass like carpet. But the square of soil I had reclaimed was a small fraction of the full patch.

I sighed. The war was going to be a long one.

Several times a week I headed to the garden to work on the strawberry bed, excavating, sifting, pounding. I could do only a few hours before my wrist began to complain and my arms grew sore. In the beginning I kept track of my time, but when I hit thirty hours, I gave up. The patch was about six feet squared, but reclaiming it, inch by slow inch, took weeks.

One night, after a day spent sifting through soil and pains-takingly untangling thin roots, I had my first garden dream. In it I was plucking hairs from around my ankles. The hairs came out easily with a firm tug, but each one ended in the same thin dangling roots as the quack grass. In my dream I sat there, slowly pulling ghostly white roots, watching them emerge from my pores as if from soil.

It took nearly a month to finish the strawberry bed. By then my mother had left for the summer—gone to the small Cana-dian island where we used to live and where she now spends summers. She wouldn't be back until September. Until then the garden was mine. My pleasure and my responsibility.

I nestled the strawberry plants in the soil, now entirely cleared of root and rhizome. Eventually I would cover the soil with straw, but for the moment I left it bare. I wanted to be vigilant in case any grass resprouted. I knew there would be future attempts at invasion and recolonization. I had won the battle, but I would be defending my borders forever.

Eventually the strawberries sprouted flowers—delicate white petals around a cheerful yellow center. I'd heard you should pinch off flowers the first year to encourage plant growth, but I didn't have the heart to do it. I pinched off the runners—stems that emerge to form new plants, shooting out and rooting. But the flower buds I left. I wanted some sweetness for all my labor. To the victors should go the spoils. Or at least the strawberries.

When I stepped back and looked at the bed, I felt a flush of pride. I built a curving path running through it—cardboard to keep the weeds down, wood chips on top. I shored up the downslope with cement blocks and large stones to prevent erosion. The strawberries were scattered all around, a few lemony sorrel plants in their midst, and in the middle stood the persimmon tree we had planted. Persimmons put out leaves late in the spring. The tree would shade the bed after the berry season, helping to protect the plants from midsummer sun. I had planned it all.

The bed looked organized, tidy, nothing like the forest of quack grass I had found there. Over time the strawberry plants would spread and fill in; the sorrel would grow; the soil would all be covered in a mass of green. I could see what it looked like today, and I could envision what it would grow to become.

It was just how I had imagined.

Once it was done, I couldn't stop looking at the strawberry bed. I watched as the flowers bloomed. I obsessively trimmed any dead growth. By late May the fruit had formed. Come June it was ripening, each knobby berry blushing redder day by day. I was practically counting down to the first berry, the first Shuksan. After months of working toward this, hours of dirty, sweaty labor, I could hardly wait.

When the strawberries were finally ripe, I called my sister-in-law. Could the girls come over? I wanted them to taste what strawberries are meant to taste like. I wanted them to experience the delight of discovering scarlet treasure hidden among broad green leaves, to gobble them down still warm from the sun.

She called back and left a message: They were busy with swimming, playdates, afternoons at the beach. Some other time, she said. Maybe next week.

But the strawberries would not wait a week—not the Shuksans, these most perishable of all berries. I left another message. Was there really no time to spare? I could pick the kids up and bring them home. It wouldn't take long. The strawberries were ripe. They wouldn't last.

But she never called back, and after waiting a few days, I gathered the berries alone. I tasted a few, and it was all there: an explosive burst of the deepest flavor, sweet and slightly acidic, plush and velvety on the tongue. The berries were colored all the way through, a deep and tender red. I remembered the friend who, on tasting her first Shuksan, asked, "If this is a strawberry— *what have I been eating all my life?*"

It felt deflating—all that work, all those hours of digging, and what was the point if I couldn't share it with the girls?

I gathered the berries and put them in the freezer, for my mother when she returned from Canada. They were the best berries I had ever tasted, but I couldn't eat them. To me they tasted like failure.

9

. . .

CORN BY MOONLIGHT

ANOTHER FAMILY MIGHT HAVE collectively planned out an approach to this garden. Another family might have sat down and discussed how it was actually going to work. They might have decided, logically, whether they really had the time and energy to take on a neglected half acre overgrown with weeds.

That is what you do in permaculture—before you design an installation, you ask the most important question, the one that decides everything that will follow. It's not what vegetables you want to grow, or whether you prefer a woodland garden or want to raise cactus. The most important question in permaculture is simple: *How much effort do you want to put in?*

And then you round down, because everyone overestimates how much time and work they really want to take on. Everyone.

I liked to think about the family that would have done this. I imagined them as orderly Scandinavians—the sort with organized garages and wardrobes of white, all clean lines and minimalism. They would have sat down with graph-paper notebooks and spreadsheets and been honest about what they were willing to contribute, how many hours they could carve out of their week.

Maybe they would have said, *Yes,* we want to take on this huge, overgrown piece of land. Maybe they would have looked at their tidy calculations and said no and regretfully walked away. Regardless of the outcome, they would have been realistic about what they were getting into.

We were not that family. We did not have organized garages.

We talked about the garden—oh, yes! We talked about apricot trees and berry bushes, kiwi vines and kale. We assumed it would work. My mother would be in Seattle all winter, we'd both garden in the spring and fall, and I'd hold down the fort in the summer while she was in Canada. It sounded fine in theory.

Then she left, to be gone all summer. And it was not fine.

My mother had been out in the garden every day, weeding, amending soil, turning beds, planting kale and broccoli starts. Every time I came to the garden, it looked shaggy and rough, but I hadn't realized how much work she had been putting in just to hold the tide at bay. Once June came she left, just as Seattle summer kicked into gear. The rain stopped, temperatures rose, the garden took off running, and with it, the weeds.

Permaculture had given me a new perspective on weeds, one I appreciated. "Soil wants to be covered," explained my teacher Jenny. You could either do it yourself, she said, with plants or mulch, or the earth would do it for you—with weeds.

Now, when I saw bits of grass or dandelion popping up in my garden bed, I knew I was falling down on the job. I needed to cover the soil with some sort of mulch. I was okay with that.

What I hadn't experienced was opportunistic weeds, the sort that don't play by the rules. It didn't matter how well I mulched or tended, these bullies were hell-bent on taking over.

With the warm weather, bindweed—also known by the more romantic and entirely misleading name morning glory—twisted tendrils out of the ground, reddish stems and heart-shaped leaves, and began to climb everything in sight.

It climbed trees and fences and burrowed under the wooden shingles of the backyard cottage. It twisted around every small, tender chard and kale plant, threatening to choke them to death. It encircled the peonies and wound up the trunk of the apple tree and laced itself through the prickly raspberry canes. At one point I found a vine growing *inside the cottage,* having bored into cracks in the foundation and through the carpet. The castle in "Sleeping Beauty" that is suddenly overgrown with vines? The story says it was roses, but any gardener will tell you it was bindweed.

Then there was the blackberry, insistent, thick, barbed with thorns. If bindweed is a stealth invader of the garden, blackberry is the crusading army: It brings its own weapons.

I had grown up with blackberry vines, but I hadn't fully understood their persistence. I hadn't noticed that some stalks are thin and eventually form berries while others are thick and aggressive. I began to think of those as an advance guard sent out to tame new land before the women and children came to colonize and settle. They forced forward with disregard, pushing up against anything in their way. They never developed flower buds; they never produced fruit; they were all fight and conquer.

I cut the aggressive stalks back—using tree-pruning loppers and sometimes my own body weight to force the blades closed. I cut them to the quick wearing canvas gloves so thick it was hard to move my fingers, and still the thorns occasionally pierced through.

I had bought the gloves in the garden department of a large home repair store. I took them to the counter, along with another pair that fit better and were more comfortable but less thick and heavy.

"Which of these do you think would be better for pulling blackberries?" I asked the two women wearing shop aprons.

"Sandpaper would be better," one of them said, and for a moment I imagined my hands coarse, grainy, pebbled, and rough. Then I realized she was joking. I had not previously encountered gardener humor, which tends to the cynical and sarcastic. She nodded to the heavier gloves. I sighed.

"I was also wondering, is there anything you can do to get rid of morning glory?" I put the gloves on the counter and got ready to pay.

"You could try lasers," the woman replied. Again, I wasn't sure if I should believe her, but the idea of zapping the thousands of bindweed roots that laced through the garden sounded appealing.

She caught sight of my hopeful face the second before I realized she was again joking; then she responded more gently.

"Those roots might be coming from your neighbor's yard—or some house halfway down the block. There's nothing you can do but pull them up."

That lady is really lucky I didn't start to cry.

Suddenly it seemed ridiculous that I would be solely responsible for half an acre that threatened to go wild if you turned your back for more than two days. I had a job. I had a life. I did not want to be cooped up by myself in a garden, at war with a million weeds. I did not want to do battle against an endless and voracious invading army. What was I thinking when I decided this would be a good idea?

I say I had a job, but that summer it was debatable. After years of scut work in the publishing industry, eventually climbing up the ladder to become an editor, I had been given a contract to write a book—the contract that had allowed me to first come to Seattle. It was something I'd dreamed of doing since I was a little girl, my own literary version of Cinderella finally getting to go to the ball.

I'd had no idea how terrifying it would be. Nobody tells you Cinderella was scared senseless.

The writing was harder than expected. My whole first winter in Seattle I tried to write, and struggled, and cried, and went for long walks, and wondered what I was supposed to do with my life—because clearly this was not it. This dream I had chased after and sacrificed for: I never expected it to turn around and kick me in the teeth.

What is wrong with you? Do you know how lucky you are? Just pull it together.

I fell into a depression that winter, not realizing it was happening until it was over. I'd never experienced anything like a northwestern winter—it wasn't the cold or even the wet that was the problem. It was the dark, the low cap of dense clouds that hovered over the city so you never got to feel the uplift of a wide-open, expansive sky. It was the gray that felt like it was pressing down, making it seem hard to take a deep breath. No matter how I tried to pull it together, the threads kept unraveling in my hands.

The book came out the first spring my mother was in Seattle—this book I had struggled to write and never could make what I wanted. Everyone thought I should be excited, proud, but I wanted to run and hide. Instead of celebrating my book, I secretly hoped it would just go away.

It would be a long time before I learned how common these feelings are, how many artists are embarrassed by their own imperfect efforts.

When book promotion was over, I came back to Seattle shattered in a way that was hard to explain, hard even to understand. I felt like I had failed—like there must be something wrong with the person who is given their dearest wish and screws it up.

Who does that?

"Do you know how many people there are stuck in cubicles right now who would give anything to write a book?" my friend Sam said when we ran into each other in a bookstore. Sam knew how to call a spade a spade.

I imagined mindless work in an anonymous setting, gray walls that went on forever. Clocking in and out at a set time each day, a reliable paycheck every two weeks. Rather than stifling it sounded comforting; it sounded safe. I bit down hard on my inner lip, not wanting him to hear my voice quaver.

"The way I'm feeling right now, a cubicle sounds like a pretty good place to hide."

Sam looked at me with a measured gaze. "Then maybe it's not your dream."

I hadn't put such thoughts to words until he said it. I hadn't dared. What if the thing you think you want turns out to not make you happy? *What then?*

Going to the garden had started to feel like solace, like escape from a reality that had turned sour. I cried sometimes, deep in the weeds. I thought of Isak Dinesen, who once wrote, "The cure for anything is salt water—sweat, tears, or the sea."

That summer the garden was sweat and tears—and though the water that could be partially glimpsed through the trees was not the sea, it was wide and smooth and made me feel better, as though my problems were perhaps not so big.

That summer I started thinking seriously about alternate careers. Perhaps I should become a kindergarten teacher—I used to work with kids; I had gotten burned out but I loved it. Perhaps I should put my permaculture certificate to use and design gardens. In the short run, I needed to be working. The long run was newly open and terrifying.

"I'm thinking of doing some work with kids again," I told my friend Sarah as we walked the three-mile loop trail that encircles Green Lake in North Seattle, weaving in and out of inlets ringed with marsh grasses and willow trees. I hadn't told her how gutting the book experience had been—I hadn't told anyone. How can you when your friends are so pleased for you?

"Really? Why would you do that?" Sarah was a writer too. She couldn't imagine not wanting to write. Writing was what we did.

"I'm thinking about doing something different. Maybe just for the summer. The idea of not sitting at a computer sounds kind of nice."

A few weeks later my phone rang. It was Sarah.

"Were you serious about wanting to work with kids for the summer?" she asked.

"Maybe—why?"

"My friend Karen needs someone to look after her toddler two days a week—her mom usually does it, but she had a heart attack. Are you interested?"

I hadn't known how serious I was. When I went to meet Karen and Lucy, however, I liked them both. Lucy was a two-year-old, shy and inquisitive with a head of blond curls. Karen was a journalist, smart, funny, down to earth. When I emailed her a quickly-pulled-together résumé of my background working with kids—years of nannying, teaching, working as a summer camp counselor—she replied with a wry note that made me laugh.

"It appears that you're actually more qualified to watch Lucy than I am."

Slipping into that role again was easy; it was comfortable. It didn't challenge me the way writing did. It didn't scare me. It was my version of a cubicle: a good place to hide.

The clincher, however, the factor that tipped the scales and made me say yes, was this. Out of the entire city of Seattle, a civic area stretching 142 square miles, pockmarked with lakes, bays, and peninsulas, Karen, Lucy, and Lucy's dad lived in the same sleepy, unfashionable, off-the-beaten-path neighborhood as my mom. They lived three blocks from the garden.

In my imagination, Lucy and I would spend our afternoons in the garden. We would eat peas and cherry tomatoes; we would explore the woodsy areas, finding wild strawberries along the way. We would play with the balls and toys my mother had stocked. We would do all the lovely things I wanted to do with my nieces, whose schedule was often too busy to accommodate garden time.

The first visit started with strawberries. The Shuksans were done for the season, but my mother had bought everbearing varieties, which I had planted in the hollow centers of the cinder blocks that formed the retaining wall of the side garden. I had imagined my nieces picking berries as they walked by.

It worked exactly as I had planned: Lucy could reach out and grab them with her small fingers, her whole hand closing around the bright red fruit. When she brought it to her mouth, the flavor was a surprise. Her eyes widened and she looked at me, biting deeper into the tart, sweet fruit.

Once we had eaten our way through the strawberries, we came around the back of the house and into the garden proper. I showed Lucy the small watering cans my mother had bought for the niecelets—shaped like a rabbit and a turtle. Lucy liked to fill them up, stand on the edge of the patio, and dump water on the flower bed beside it.

Beyond the patio was the upper lawn—a portion of grass preserved as play area. Only we didn't have a lawn mower to keep it cut neatly, and my mother, in her dislike of lawns, refused to buy one. "Use the Weedwacker," she said. "It works fine."

But it didn't work fine. Or I didn't know how to work it. Or perhaps our weeds were not the sort to be easily whacked. I assumed a Weedwacker would have blades in it to cut the weeds, but ours functioned via two pieces of heavy plastic filament that were supposed to rotate fast enough to cut the grass. This seemed an improbable solution. The first time I tried to use the Weedwacker, I broke it. Or the weeds broke it. Our weeds laughed at plastic filament.

By the time Lucy and I came to the garden for our first visit, the weeds were growing tall. The grass was short—in the height of a Seattle summer, lawns actually stop growing for lack of water—but the dandelions were blooming proudly.

These were not the dandelions I was used to, which bloom in the spring and have abundant edible, jagged leaves. These dandelions had small, matted foliage and thin stems that reached upward, each capped with a bright yellow bloom. They were all over the lawn. The flowers reached my knees. On Lucy they came up to her waist; some were chest high. She got three steps into them and stopped walking.

"Go home?" she said hopefully.

"Not yet, Lucy. We're just going to walk across the grass."

"Noooooo."

"Come on—we're going to the cottage. There are games inside there."

"*No.*" Lucy retreated to the patio and sat down on a small bench my mom had bought for the girls. "*Go home.*"

That was our first and last visit to the garden.

I went to the garden, of course. After a day spent with Lucy, at the playground, on walks, playing with crayons, and reading books, I went to the garden. I filled up watering cans and did my duty, irrigating strawberries and moving hoses from tree to tree. The watering routine alone took about an hour. Then I would stand there, on the patio, and look down the long and sloping yard at everything that needed to be done.

And then I would flee.

On the evenings I stayed in the garden, it was bittersweet. The garden was huge, there was so much to do, and there was only me. I often heard voices as I weeded or dug, conversation floating over the hedge from the neighbors at the far end of the meadow—they ate outside in the summer; they often entertained. I heard laughter and the clink of wineglasses as I squatted in the dirt, in grasses that were now up to my waist, grubby and lonely and completely overwhelmed.

What was I doing here all by myself? This wasn't how I had imagined it at all.

It didn't seem strange to be spending my days with a toddler. That summer it felt like everyone I knew was pregnant—six friends all due within a month of each other. Most of these were second or third children. As we moved through our thirties, it was what people did.

What was strange to me, after years of nannying as a teenager and college student, was that now Lucy could have been my child. When we went to the playground people assumed she was—but people had been assuming the child I was caring for was mine since high school. "Go with your mama," a farmers' market vendor had told the first little boy I nannied for. At seventeen, I had been shocked.

Now, in my thirties, it was much odder that Lucy wasn't mine. Karen and I were about the same age. But Karen and her husband, Brian, had been together since they were sixteen. They had bought a house in their twenties, made a home. They had chosen to be a family.

I had chosen travel, adventure, writing. I'd spent more time alone than I had in relationships—and even though some had been passionate and thrilling, even though marriage and family had been discussed and considered, in the end none of them had felt right. My friends had long ago given up asking if I was dating anyone. They'd long ago given up trying to convince me I should.

One day I was looking through the website of a fellow writer. Amanda lived in Maine and was homeschooling her three children. Their days were filled with crafts and nature and books and the beach. In the winter they cozied up inside, she and her husband and their brood all in one small house.

I admired Amanda's life and felt drawn to it—but not because I wanted it for myself. I never imagined myself mother to a large family. And yet, there was something in Amanda's days of baking bread and walks in the woods and knitting sweaters and drawing and reading with her young ones that filled a hole in me that had long been empty.

Rather than wanting Amanda's life, I think I wanted to be her kid.

The photo that stopped me was of her children—a puppy pile in pajamas, arms and legs a flurry of wrestling and tickling; you could almost hear the laughter. Suddenly I was in tears.

Fun. They were having fun. Family could be *fun*.

It was a truth I had never known. And I wept because my family had not been fun. My family had been struggle and fear and frantic attempts to somehow hold it together. It seemed no small miracle that we all survived.

I remember one day on the deck of our old house in the country when my brother and I invented a game while folding laundry. We each took a corner of a long flat sheet and put a wooden block in the middle, so that it sagged in the center like a hammock. We swung the sheet back and forth like a swing until it picked up enough speed that we could spin it around and it would make a full revolution without the block falling out. We thought this was amazing. We could do this for hours.

I don't know how old we were. Perhaps I was nine and he was seven; maybe we were eight and six. What is striking about the memory is that there were no grown-ups around.

I know this can't be true—we had babysitters who took us to school and cooked and did the grocery shopping. But it is there in all my childhood memories: the feeling of being alone with no one in charge, the weight of responsibility, the fear of messing things up, of making life worse for our mother.

No matter how much fun we were having, no matter how much my little brother laughed, I was the one who had to stop the game. I was the one who had to say, "No. We need to finish folding the laundry."

When I was a child, people assumed I wanted to have a family. "You're going to make a good mother someday," grown-ups said when they saw me taking care of my brother or some other child in my charge. As I got older, it became a question: "Do you want to have kids?" As I entered my later thirties, the phrasing changed: "*Don't* you want to have kids?"

When this happened I told the truth. It wasn't the full story but it was enough. It kept people from asking further.

"I feel like I've raised a few already."

My friend Sarah was one of the pregnant people that year. All spring we walked around Green Lake, her belly growing bigger and bigger. Come June she had her baby, a little girl. I visited shortly after they had returned from the hospital, in the middle of a rare Seattle heat wave. We sat outside on the back patio and ate the cold noodles I had brought while the hot, steamy day drew to a close.

We passed the bundle of baby around the table, her delicate fingers and elfin ears protruding from a blanket as Sarah's older boys brought toys and books to show me and her husband worked the outdoor grill. Nobody wanted to be anywhere near a kitchen on a day like that.

"I need to get to the garden," I told them, finally breaking my lethargy and handing back the baby.

"Oh, stay a little longer," Sarah said, nestling her daughter onto her lap. "The boys will be going to bed soon and we can talk."

"Yes, stay," said her husband, Daniel. "It's far too hot to garden."

It *was* far too hot—and because their backyard had a breeze, because the water tinkling through the fountain that Daniel had installed was soothing, because new-baby time moves slow, I stayed. I stayed until it was ten o'clock.

By the time I got to the garden, the endless northern summer evening was finally at its close, a tiny bit of light still gathered at the horizon. I would have done a quick watering and come back the next day, but I was going out of town. Friends were getting married in California, and I would be gone for three days. The seedlings in the greenhouse, the ones I *kept meaning* to plant, wouldn't survive. I needed to get them in the ground.

I had run out of garden bed area but thought I might make one of my own. As an experiment, I took one of the large cardboard boxes left over from sheet mulching—ten feet by five when spread open—and laid it on the grass in a sunny patch of the meadow. Then I built layers on top of it—soil, compost, and a bag of straw and chicken droppings my friends had given me from their backyard coop. I piled it all up until the bed was more than a foot high, a loose version of sheet mulching. I wanted to plant corn and beans and squash in it.

This was a "three sisters" bed—a Native American tradition of companion planting. The beans fix nitrogen in the soil and provide nutrition for the corn, a heavy feeding plant. The corn gives the beans a trellis to climb, and they in turn help secure the tall stalks. The squash produces large, prickly leaves that mulch the soil and discourage raccoons, who might otherwise eat the corn. The plants work together to help each other.

I thought of this as I built up the layers, shovelful after shovelful, watering down the soil, nestling in the small corn, bean, and squash seedlings. How many people had done this before me, for how many centuries? I felt like part of a chain reaching back generations. Digging, sowing, watering: planting the harvest. Small, vital acts to ensure our survival.

This work required many trips back and forth, from the patio where we kept the watering cans, shovels, and bags of soil, to the new bed I was building in the back field. The exterior lights illuminated the house, but to walk down the hill was to walk into darkness, to depend on the dim glow of the moon and the stars and my own growing familiarity with the land. It was still warm, even toward midnight, and I strode back and forth wearing a tank top and skirt, the dark and humidity a physical thing, a weight I could feel on my skin.

I tossed off my shoes, something I had never before done in the garden, and walked with bare feet on dry grass, feeling the damp beginning to turn into dew. With my soles I could read the land—the curvature of the path where so many had trod. In the dark I felt strong, powerful, a primal feeling of belonging. I was one with the wild grasses and the stars and the gathering breeze.

In that moment, at the end of a hot day, in the dark garden under a dim quarter moon, planting as so many had before me, there was no other place on earth I wanted to be.

10

• • •

A HOPE FOR MAGIC

AFTER KNOX, MY NEXT friend to come to the garden was Kim. Though we had known each other only a few years, Kim and I had intertwining history. We had attended the same college— years apart—and had both worked in the book industry; we had helped run different literary festivals. It was as if we had been destined to meet all along. It just took me moving to Seattle to seal the deal.

I thought Kim, more than anyone else I knew in Seattle, might be able to understand the potential of the garden, how there was a chance for this to be a magical place. In many ways I was still the young girl who wanted to climb trees and read books and daydream. I had a sense that Kim shared that too. I hoped she could see past the weeds, the cracked patio, the moss growing between the shingles of the cottage roof. I hoped she could see the wonder.

Kim arrived wearing the linen tank top, long shorts, and

leather Top-Siders that made up her summer uniform. I met her in the driveway where I'd been weeding, keeping an eye out for her. I wanted to be there when she first saw the garden.

That spring had seen a variety of people come into the garden, mostly workmen. They walked in from the gate, and the scene spread out in front of them: covered patio to the left, high banks of camellias, azaleas, and rhododendrons, and a wide lawn that began to slope down toward the cottage and the patio that stood before it. They'd all had the same reaction, every last one of them.

"Wow, this is a really big yard," they said at first glance.

Then their eyes would travel further, and they'd realize the cottage was not the end of the yard. The garden was a figure eight, the upper lawn simply half the equation. When they saw there was a field down there with fruit trees and wild grasses, they stopped in their tracks.

"*Whoa.* This is a *really* big yard." There was always a note of awe in their voices. Or was it fear?

Kim was not like the workmen. She was not awed by the garden; she was not scared. Kim was the most competent person I knew. She stood on the edge of the patio at the top of the yard and looked down, past the greenhouse and the cottage to the field and fruit trees beyond.

"Well," she said briskly. "I can see what you've bitten off here."

We wandered across the lawn, which was turning dry and golden as the summer progressed. I showed her the vegetables, the spot where a semicircular bed of weeds had been cleared to reveal surprise raspberry bushes. As we walked past the cottage, I described the overgrown blackberries. We peered into the greenhouse, which was sprouting tall grasses from its earthen floor.

"This is a lot of work," Kim said in a businesslike tone. "And your mom is gone all summer?"

"Yep," I said, looking around. It was always a surprise to see the garden through someone else's eyes. Kim saw weeding, mowing, berry vines that needed to be cut back.

But as we walked up to the house, past the bank of rhododendrons that reached ten feet high, she peered into the shrubbery, quickly realizing the long, oval leaves concealed space behind them, tunnels and holes in which you could hide.

"You know," she said slowly, "if I were a kid, I would think this was magical. There are so many places to slip off and read a book or make a fort." She looked around again, her sharp eye sizing it all up. "Your nieces are going to love it here. What amazing memories you will make for them."

That was exactly what I was hoping for.

Most of the time the garden didn't make sense: this huge space, all this work, no one there in the summer to enjoy it. I went over to water and weed several times a week, often staying until dark. On weekends I tried to put in a full day. But then I went home. The garden grew and bloomed and flowered and fruited, all without anyone there to appreciate it.

"You're doing this all wrong—you realize that?" Knox had told me. "The best part of a garden is after the work is done, kicking back with a drink and enjoying it. You've got all the work and none of the enjoyment!"

He was right. I had never sat in the garden at the end of a day and enjoyed my accomplishments. At the end of the day, I was tired and dirty and went home.

I started cutting flowers, something my mother would not have approved of. She preferred them growing on the stem. But with her gone all summer I helped myself to dahlias and hydrangeas. It seemed only fair that I get to take something home with me to enjoy. Otherwise, what was all this work for?

There was food, of course. I carried home baskets of kale and

chard each weekend. There were peas in the spring, snappy and
sweet, and green beans as summer rolled on. There was lettuce
and arugula that needed to be used before it got too hot and the
plants bolted, putting out flowers and becoming bitter. My grocery bill shrank, but even that was a toss-up. Was it really worth
spending all my free time in the garden just to save twenty dollars a week?

"Why don't you just have a little P-Patch, shop at the farmers' market, and have your weekends free?" Sarah asked, when it
became clear that the garden was taking over my life. I sometimes wondered the same.

The garden was lovely, of course. In the summer evenings,
when the light slanted golden and the dahlias that had been
planted all those years ago glowed and the breeze rustled through
the feathery cilantro that had gone to seed, I again felt what I
had experienced at Picardo, a feeling that can only be described
as peace. But then I loaded up my baskets and went home, and
the garden continued on without anyone there to appreciate it.

The only time the garden made sense was Wednesdays. That
was the day the niecelets came to play.

I'd hear them even before they came running around the
side of the house, tearing through the gate into the garden.
"Tea-tea! Tea-tea!"

Usually one was trying to outrace the other, to be first to
launch herself at me—sometimes into my arms, sometimes just
at my knees. At five and six years old, they were still young
enough to want to be cuddled, picked up, tossed about.

As Cate came barreling toward me, I reached out and
launched her into the air, long, skinny limbs flying in all directions. I caught her and tickled her as she wriggled and shrieked
with laughter, the sound of it cascading down the sloping hill.

"My turn next! My turn next!" Abby jumped up and down
in anticipation.

Before I put Cate down, I kissed the top of her sun-bleached head and breathed deep the scent of her. She smelled like swimming pools, sunscreen, fresh towels, a childhood so free of cares it brought sudden tears to my eyes.

"You smell just like summer," I said. She giggled, and I turned to her sister. More shrieks, more laughter, another kiss on the head.

Their first question was always the same: "What are we going to do today?"

I answered with a question of my own: "What do you think is ripe?"

Early in the summer it was raspberries. We waded deep into the canes with plastic containers, picking the small ruby thimbles that crushed between our fingers with too much pressure.

"Your daddy and I picked raspberries like these when we were your age," I told them, as the sun beat down on our backs.

"Really?" they said, sounding surprised. "He never told us that."

"Does he tell you about how things were when we were little?"

"Not really."

The niecelets were full of stories of their mother's family—of great-grandfather John who played the violin, of the great-grandmother everyone called Hellcat, even to her face. Their great-great-grandmother Jocabed had been the youngest of twenty-one children.

Stories of our side of the family didn't seem to exist, unless I told them. I wondered whether this was because my brother was at work all day or whether he didn't want to talk about our early years, in the same way survivors sometimes do not want to revisit their past.

"We lived in a house in the country," I told the girls as soft red berries plunked in our containers or were poked into mouths.

"We had a small creek that dried up in the summer but became so big with the winter rains that sometimes it flooded. Grandma planted a garden for us, and there were apple trees you could climb and stay up there all afternoon reading a book. If you got hungry, you just picked an apple to eat."

"That's cool," said Cate.

"I liked the apple trees because your daddy was too little to climb, so I could go up there and be all by myself."

Abby giggled. As an oldest child, she knew what it was like to long for solitude.

"I have an idea," said Cate. "Let's go up in the loft of the cottage and *tell secrets*." The final words were drawn out as if they were something dramatic.

So we ran off, abandoning our berry containers awhile. We'd come back to them later in the day. We'd come back to them later in the season, when there would be blueberries and blackberries, each in turn. The summer stretched out in front of us, endless and sweet. Now was the time to tell secrets.

As we climbed the wooden ladder in the cottage and curled up under the sloping eaves, I smiled. I had imagined the girls doing this the day my mother and I came to steal berries in the garden, long before the house was hers. I imagined the cottage their clubhouse, a special members-only password and a KEEP OUT sign posted on the door. I liked to think of them trading secrets like currency, whispered confidences large and small, forgotten and remembered.

I just hadn't imagined I would be there with them, that I would be invited in. I never imagined we would have our own special club of three.

When Abby was born, I had wondered how I was going to be a good aunt to her, living so far away. My brother was busy with work, and my sister-in-law never got on the phone to talk. How was I going to know this child, this miraculous thing that had entered our lives?

"Don't worry about it," my friend Michelle said. "These days kids have email by the time they're eight." Her own niece and nephew lived on the other side of the country. They emailed regularly, she said.

But eight years was a long way off. What was I going to do until then?

We had all gathered in Seattle for Thanksgiving the first year of Abby's life. I brought her a picture book about the holiday and made sure to inscribe my name on the cover page, so when she was older she would know I had been there. She was only ten months old, not quite walking. My sister-in-law's parents had visited recently and taken pictures using a camera flash, which Abby did not like. Every time I pulled out my camera, she frowned at me. I went home with dozens of photos of this small blond child giving me the stink eye.

By the next Thanksgiving, Cate had been born—four months old with a mohawk that stuck straight up; we called her the cockatiel. Abby was almost two years old, walking and talking. We went to the park and scuffed in the leaves, and when my sister-in-law got sick the weekend after Thanksgiving, I extended my visit to help with the kids.

When opportunity came the following spring to spend some time in Seattle, I took it. I fully intended to return to San Francisco after the summer. By then the girls would have baseline knowledge of who I was. "I don't want to be the semi-stranger who shows up each year for Thanksgiving," I told my friends.

What I hadn't expected was that I would fall in love with my nieces. I'd spent time with children my whole life; I started babysitting at age eight. I loved all the children I had cared for, but not the way I loved my nieces.

That first summer in Seattle I took care of each of the girls one day a week—Cate on Wednesday, Abby on Friday—while their mother took the other child to a toddler gym class. I worked on the weekends to make up for the time. It was worth it.

Together we went to the park, to the wading pool. We picked berries, and each Wednesday Cate and I waited for the garbage truck, the highlight of her week. We read books and played puzzles, and Abby and I visited a farm, where she fell in love with a purple cabbage and insisted on holding it in her lap the entire drive home. I came home those days tired but filled up in a way I couldn't quite put words to. It was as if I had been thirsty a long time and not known it.

One day, that first summer I was in Seattle, Abby and I were driving back to the house where I was living. It was chilly that morning, and she was wearing a puffy white jacket with embroidery on it, sitting in her car seat. As we drove down Roosevelt, headed for the University Bridge and the ship canal, her little voice piped up from the backseat.

"Tea-tea."

"Yes?" I looked at her in the rearview mirror: tiny in her jacket, wispy blond hair held away from her face.

"Tea-tea," she said, looking out the window at the traffic alongside us, "I love you all the time."

At that moment my heart cracked open; it has never gone back to being the same again.

Late that first summer, my brother and sister-in-law took the girls to the East Coast to visit her family and asked if I would drive them to the airport. We all piled into their car, everyone in high spirits. When we arrived at the airport, the girls grabbed their tiny roller bags with their baby dolls strapped to the outside and nearly ran into the terminal, so excited were they for the trip. My sister-in-law raced after the girls; my brother was juggling luggage and travel seats for the kids. I waved to them all and got in the car to drive home.

It wasn't until I pulled away from the curb that it hit me: *What if something happens to them? What if the plane crashes?*

Suddenly I was wiping away tears, unable to see the road ahead of me, so overwhelmed I took the wrong lane and drove into the parking garage rather than onto the freeway. I sat there in the dark a few minutes, bent over the steering wheel of my sister-in-law's huge and unfamiliar SUV, weeping, terrified at the idea of losing those girls, shocked at the vulnerability of loving them so much.

So this is what it feels like to not be able to call your heart your own.

"Tea-tea, look what I found!" Abby came running from the back field, holding something in her hands, Cate hot at her heels.

"What is it?" I knelt down to see whatever small wonder she wanted to share with me. She stopped running and came close, until we were face-to-face; then she threw the contents of her hands high in the air. Dry grass seed showered down on me as she and Cate erupted in giggles.

"You *stinker*!" I said, shaking the grass seed out of my hair but smiling along with them.

I was surprised to hear this phrase come out of my mouth. My grandfather had called me *stinker* when I was young, but he had been dead twenty years. When I was a child, he used to visit us from his home in Florida, but when he died more than a decade later, I hadn't seen him in years.

Stinker was a reference to my nature, a spiritedness he neither understood nor could control. It was equal parts endearment and scolding. Now, thirty years later, I was delighted to find my nieces were stinkers as well. The family mischievousness was in good hands for another generation.

"You guys want to see the hammock I put up?" They looked at me curiously.

"What is a hammock?"

"Follow me and I'll show you."

I had strung the hammock under the rhododendrons,

stunned that a bush could grow big and sturdy enough. Ours towered over the garden, more than ten feet high. The hammock was hidden from view by those leaves Kim had realized served as a screen. The girls followed me to where the faded striped fabric made a long sling, and I showed them how to scramble in and swing back and forth.

"Push us, Tea-tea. Push us harder!" Their skinny legs went sprawling out of the hammock as I pushed them back and forth, and they laughed in delight; the sound washed over me like unexpected summer rain, the sort you hold your face up to drink in.

"You're really Weavers now," I told them. "We love our hammocks in this family."

We'd always had a hammock, ever since I could remember. I used to crawl in and wrap myself up as if I were in a cocoon, weaving my small fingers into the strings to keep it closed. My brother did the same, and I pushed him, making up a game where I twisted the cocoon so many times it would spin to unravel, and my brother would emerge dizzy and laughing, begging me to do it again.

There was never anyone to push me when I was young—my brother was unreliable in the quid pro quo department—but I figured out how to rig up one of the straight rakes from the garden to help me. I buried the tines in the dirt and leaned the handle up against the hammock at a perpendicular angle. Then, as I lay there reading, I could push against the handle, and, as a result, the hammock would rock back and forth. I remember feeling pleased at my invention, at having solved this small problem. There was no one to help, but I could help myself.

"Push us, Tea-tea," my nieces cried. "Push us *harder*."

And so I did, feeling glad to be there. To push them, to catch them; these children would need no rake. It felt like a joy I had not known before, a gift for all of us.

It felt like progress.

I began to plan our days in the garden, to think of things the girls would like, fun ways to share with them what I thought important: nature, adventurousness, imagination, wonder. There were days when we lay in the tall grass of the back meadow and looked for shapes in the lacy clouds that floated overhead: a boat, a rabbit, a snake. Studies say the average American child spends only minutes outside each day. I was glad to know that was not true of these two.

Sometimes I intentionally let them do nothing. They always gravitated to the meadow, running their hands through the tall grass collecting dried seed, as dreamy and self-occupied as I had been growing up in the country. In the rush of their own busy lives of soccer, swimming, tennis, choir, I was glad they had time to wander and daydream.

Other days we watered the garden, the girls each with her own small watering can. On hot days I set up the sprinkler, and they ran through, the droplets sparkling and catching light as I marveled at their pure joy from the simplest thing.

Years ago a high school teacher had quoted John Ciardi to our class—"Man is what he does with his attention"—and the idea had stayed with me ever since. What we spend our time and energy on is who we are, what is important to us. I chose to give my attention to these girls, to be there for them, to share my version of what was valuable in life.

One day I discovered a secret space underneath the large azalea bush perfect for hiding. We'll read here, I thought when I saw it. It will be our bower.

The Victorian novels I'd devoured as a child always had people reading books in garden bowers. That week, when the girls were coming to play, I spread a soft blanket under the bush and put one of my favorite books there: *The Secret Garden.*

"Look at this perfect hiding spot," I told them when we had

eaten our fill of berries and swung from the hammock and climbed the trees and the long afternoon shadows were beginning to slant across the grass of the garden. "Why don't we read a book? I have one you might like."

"It's a little den," said Abby, as charmed by the setting as I was.

"Can I sit in your lap?" Cate was always fast to claim that spot.

"Of course you can." We ducked our heads and cozied up on the blanket with Cate on my lap and Abby snuggled to my right, ready to turn the pages, and I began to read the familiar lines about Mary, who was born in India, a peculiar girl with a yellow complexion and sour nature.

"*Bugs,*" Abby shrieked. "There are *bugs* in here!" She leapt to her feet, crashing through the bushes and onto the lawn, trying to get away from the small gnat that had crawled onto our blanket.

Cate jumped from my lap and followed. *"I hate bugs. Get them away from me."*

I sighed and followed them. Nowhere in all of those lovely Victorian novels did anyone mention bower bugs.

Late in the summer, when the grass had dried to a crunchy yellow and the garden was festooned with blackberries, the girls and I had a campout. It was almost fall, one of the last weekends of warmth and sunshine we would have. Before the end of the summer, there was one more thing I wanted us to do.

We pitched a tent on the dry grass, lugged sleeping pads and bags, and I gave them each their own flashlight—one shaped like a ladybug, the other like a bumblebee. They were in high spirits with the excitement of sleeping outside, something they had never done. They had pitched the tent in their living room, but this was the real thing.

After dinner we roasted marshmallows, building a small fire in a galvanized metal tub for lack of a proper fire pit. The girls ran off to find sticks, threading their marshmallows and holding them over the fire. They had made s'mores before.

"Tea-tea, why does the fire turn into mosquitoes?" Cate asked.

"What do you mean?"

"See, the fire goes up and turns into bugs." She pointed to the flames, and I saw what she meant. Tiny bits of ash floated up from the fire and into the shadows. For a moment, as they circled lazily on the updraft, the small flakes did indeed look like roving mosquitoes. Then they disappeared into the darkness, to descend far outside our small circle of light.

In that moment I realized: *These kids did not know fire.*

They had roasted marshmallows before, but over a gas insert in the patio table my brother and sister-in-law had in their backyard. They watched movies in front of a gas fireplace turned on by a switch. When our small campfire blew smoke in their faces, they didn't know why their eyes were stinging. What had been an integral part of my life growing up in a country house heated by a wood-burning stove, was something entirely foreign to them.

How is it possible not to know fire? This is what has sustained our species—allowed us to cook enough calories to develop larger brains, helped us build the tools we needed to survive. And yet, children today were growing up with no knowledge of this elemental substance. Perhaps there were those who saw this as progress; to me it seemed dangerous.

"This is smoke," I told the girls. "This is ash. This is what happens when you burn wood. This is important."

Later that night we snuggled into sleeping bags. It was the peak of the Perseid meteor showers, and I left the rain cover off the tent so we could see the night sky. Every August the earth passes the orbital path of a far-off comet. When the debris of this

comet enters the atmosphere, the result is a burst of meteor activity: thousands upon thousands of shooting stars.

I had grown up watching the Perseids at summer camp in
the mountains of California. One night we had lain in our sleeping bags in a wide-open meadow and counted thirty-two shooting stars before we finally fell asleep. I wanted the girls to know
this wonder, the sight of stars streaking across a dark night sky.

Abby fell asleep immediately, curling up in a tight ball, but
Cate and I lay there, eyes open, looking for the trail of light that
might signify a meteor.

Suddenly there was flash and motion when before there had
been none. "Look, Cate! Do you see it?"

"I see it, Tea-tea. *I see it!*" She wriggled closer in delight, and
I wrapped my arms around her, smelling the campfire smoke in
her hair. Soon there was another, and another. We counted four
before we dozed off, the lateness of the evening finally over-
coming us both.

But before she fell asleep entirely, I heard Cate's voice from
deep inside her sleeping bag, lazy and slow, almost a whisper.

"Tea-tea. You're my best friend who is a grown-up."

There it was—just as I had hoped, just as Kim had said it
would be.

Magic.

PART THREE

. . .

TEND

11

. . .

A FOUNTAIN OF GREEN

It was a long winter of kale and potatoes and onions before we made our way back to the garden. Winter often felt endless in Seattle—day after day of dark gray, the ground soggy, the days short, the garden on hiatus. When local gardeners said, "We're so lucky to be able to grow year-round in the Northwest," I wanted to laugh. Lucky compared to where? Alaska?

The truth is, not much grows in the winter in Seattle, not even the grass. It's as if the persistent winter drizzle pushes it down. You can keep some kale plants going until spring, perhaps a bit of chard if the frosts aren't too hard and it doesn't snow much. If you've planted your winter vegetables early enough, you may have carrots or beets to tide you over. The collards will continue to produce, at a much slower speed, and you might be able to coax along a cabbage or two, but unless you have a greenhouse, there's not much going on.

I remember a farmers' market stand I once saw in Seattle in

March. The farm itself is large, well established, and respected. From late spring into winter, their stand bursts with gorgeous vegetables and bags of grain, but in March that year, all they had to sell were subscriptions to their summer produce box and a huge pile of parsley. That was it: nothing but parsley.

Don't believe what they say: Late winter in Seattle is slim pickings.

What was growing that winter was our family. The girls had a new baby brother, born in the early days of December. I went to the hospital at the end of his first day and met this tiny thing with clear eyes and a steady gaze.

Who will you be? I whispered as I took this small bundle into my arms, so tender and warm. *Who will you be in our family?* His name was Graham. With this new arrival, the circle was growing larger.

People complained about the Seattle winter—sometimes even me—but in truth I liked the downtime. I liked not having to go up to the garden, not having to weed or water. Summer is a frenetic period in Seattle. The days are long, the weather good, and residents feel an urge, a compulsion, a *responsibility,* to pack all the fun into two or three months. All the hiking, the camping, the swimming, the sunning, the picnics, the parties, the boating, the lazing. It all must be done in July and August. After that you're living on borrowed time. September could be nice, October even, but any day it could start raining again.

As much as I loved the northwestern summer, I had come to love that it did eventually rain. Finally I could slow down. Finally I could stay home and read books and plan cozy dinner parties. Finally I could hibernate. For all my travel and adventures, it seemed I was a homebody at heart.

When it came to home, however, I was soon to be out of mine. I had sublet a tiny apartment on the top floor of an old brick building with a view of Puget Sound and the sun setting fiery behind the snowcapped Olympic Mountains. It was impractical, out of my budget, and temporary, but the moment I saw a photo of it, with the sun slanting through large windows and the mullioned panes of the French doors onto hardwood floors, I knew it had to be mine. It was only for nine months. I would make it work.

"It's like a magic carpet ride," said a friend when she first saw the apartment. With large windows on three sides and the lights of Ballard twinkling below at night, that's exactly how it felt. In the daytime I sat at my desk in the corner between huge windows and watched the sun arc across the sky. Small floatplanes bound for remote islands drifted by my perch, snowcapped mountains carved a jagged horizon across calm waters, and sunset painted the wide expanse in shades of brilliant pink and orange. In those moments I felt as deeply happy as I had ever been.

Come spring the original tenant, who now lived in Europe, offered to let me take over the lease. It was tempting, but the rent was going up, I'd be locked into a yearlong commitment, and I'd begun to have fantasy dreams in which the closet somehow morphed into a bedroom. Though I knew I would miss the view for the rest of my life, I sadly said no. The small studio apartment was a magic carpet ride, not a long-term place to live.

"Why don't you stay here for the summer?" my mom asked one day when we were working in the garden. She was getting ready to leave for Canada and would be gone three months. When she returned, I planned to go to Japan for a long-overdue visit. "You don't *need* a place until November," she pointed out. "That's six months. Just think of all the money you'll save."

I sat back on my heels in the garden bed where I had been transplanting and thought about it. I knew immediately I didn't like the idea.

"I don't want to live in *your* house," I told her. "I want to live in *my* house."

My mother's house smelled of sandalwood and Japanese indigo dye, an unusual scent that often made westerners wrinkle their noses; it smelled of *her*. I wanted someplace that smelled like me. No matter how practical, there was something strange about living under my mother's roof at this stage of my life.

"Suit yourself," she said, "but the garden needs you."

That was true. The garden needed me. The garden needed a lot.

Almost every day that spring my mother had been out there, hoeing, weeding, planting, working on the three large beds along the south side of the yard. I had begun to think of this area as her private kale garden.

When she gardened she wore old sweatshirts, many of them castoffs from my teen years. The cotton fabric was so faded only I knew what color they had started out as. There were holes sprouting from cuffs, and the hems hung low, yet my mother wore them still.

As a child I had dressed up in her clothes, trying to be a grown-up. Now I was a grown-up—even if I didn't always feel that way—and my mother was wearing the faded remnants of what had been mine. Every time I saw her slight figure at work, a rush of emotion went through me. My tiny mother, so determined, so driven. Even now, at an age when others took up bridge, my mother was working hard. She was a hummingbird, constantly in motion.

"Can't you just sit down so we can have a conversation?" I sometimes asked. "You're *always* working." It was the same thing I had been saying since childhood.

"My work ethic has really paid off for you over the years," she'd respond tartly.

I knew what she meant: the private college I attended that she had paid for; the time spent in Europe and at summer camp; the theater tickets and museum visits and piano lessons; the bicycles, computers, and large checks written. She meant a million things, big and small, that she had given my brother and me. Things no one had given her. And here I was, ungrateful.

She took my words as criticism. She never understood their real meaning. She never understood that when I asked her to sit down, when I wanted her to stop working, just for a moment, to talk to me, to look me in the eye, I was saying one thing, over and over.

I want *you* more than I want those other things. *I just want you.*

But she never stopped. She never sat still. There was always something she needed to do. And I never found the words to explain what I really wanted from her, what I needed.

In the prior couple of years, my mother had tried to calm her hummingbird ways. More than once she had declared *this* was the year she was going to slow down. These announcements came as New Year's resolutions or after some injury. She had broken her foot twice now, once running for an airplane, once tripping down the stairs in a rush.

"I really got the message this time," she told me after a particularly bad injury. "Time to *slow down*."

But her version of slowing down never looked very different from what had come before. I couldn't tell if there had actually been a change.

"What do you think would happen if you did slow down?" I asked once, in a moment of tenderness between us after a fight, when I felt more like the mom than she did. "What would happen?"

"You know," she said slowly, all the bluster worn out. "I've been going so fast for so long . . ." Her voice was low and serious, no drama. "I think if I really did slow down, I might just die."

My mother's work in the kale garden had paid off that spring. The three broad beds had filled with sprouts of green as the seedlings took root and grew tall. The shiny green leaves of the pak choi were dark with white veins, the lettuces ruffled like petticoats in shades of rust and speckled lime. The chard unfurled on stems of lurid magenta and goldenrod, and the kale put forth grayish-green leaves so bumpy they reminded me of the topography of a globe. It was a fountain of green in my mother's garden that spring.

What were not plentiful that spring were apartments or houses I wanted to move into. I had fallen in love with my neighborhood and the view that looked toward the Olympic Mountains. After a few years in Seattle surrounded by trees, living in shadow, I knew my happiness over the long winter depended on as much light as I could get and a view of the setting sun. I might be leaving my hilltop perch, but I didn't want to leave the hill.

Permaculture had helped me settle on this neighborhood, a collection of streets lined with small homes and tidy front yards. I had taken the lessons I learned about mapping and flow and drawn routes to all the places in the city I went on a regular basis—farmers' markets, the library, my mother's house, my brother's. There were other things I wanted: a direct bus line downtown, a view toward the west, access to parks and green. When I marked them all on a map, it became clear. I picked the hilly neighborhood right in the middle and was surprised by how happy I felt there. There was no effort in my life any longer; everything I needed was close at hand. It was an ease I hadn't previously known. Always before life had felt like hard work.

There were other old buildings on the hill, full of the vintage details I loved, and I put my name on the waiting list for the next available space in one of them. The units were bigger there—a small dining room in addition to bedroom and living room. It wasn't the magic carpet ride, but it would do.

While I waited I looked. The neighborhood was filled with small Craftsman houses: long on charm but too large for one person and more than I wanted to pay. As my springtime departure grew closer, I looked harder. There were rental units in some of these houses, but usually they were converted basements. Winter in Seattle was dark and damp enough without living underground. I did not want to become a mole.

"You're *sure* you don't want to live here for the summer?" my mother offered again.

I was sure, but as months ticked by and I still didn't find anything, I began to reconsider. Maybe I could live in the garden cottage. I could put my desk there and write with a view of blooming flowers and fruit trees.

I imagined wandering out to pull weeds when faced with a particularly tricky passage that needed some pondering. When I had research to do, I could read in the hammock. I wouldn't be living in my mother's house—I would be living in the garden. Then I would be off to Japan. With the money I would save, I could stay longer, travel more.

It wasn't ideal—but it was practical. And from summers spent working as a wilderness instructor, I was used to throwing things in storage for the season; I'd spent months living in a tent. Surely the cottage would not be so bad. And as my mother said, the garden needed me.

A month before my lease was up, the woman from whom I rented the apartment returned to move her belongings out of the studio with the view. My mother was out of town, so I stayed at her house for the week, a trial run of sorts. I didn't bother to set up the cottage.

But staying at my mother's house meant sleeping in the upstairs guest bedroom, a poky space facing the street with high windows that were long and narrow. After the wide view and huge picture windows of my apartment, it felt closed in, like sleeping in a coffin. I hated it.

I spent most of my time in the downstairs room my mother had converted to her office. It had a view out large windows looking down the hill to the cottage and the field below. In late spring, it was a glorious sight.

The magnolia was festooned with blossoms—magenta on the outside, a pale shell-pink on the velvety interior. The irises and tulips were giving up their bright colors, deep purple shriveling up into a dried golden husk. The raspberries were covered with tiny white blossoms, and carrots that had been started from seed were pushing feathery green tops out of damp soil. To watch tiny seeds cleave soil took my breath away—all that life somehow emerging from a speck of brown. It seemed miraculous. It was.

I sat there, at my mother's desk, and took it all in.

I had never spent the night at Orchard House; I had never seen the garden at dawn. Within a day or two, I started sleeping downstairs, on a foldout futon in the office, so I could see morning break over the garden. From where I slept, I had a view down the lawn all the way to the orchard and the houses beyond. One of them had small white lights strung on its back deck. At night they twinkled and looked like the fairies I had imagined as a child. The whole scene felt like it was touched by magic.

In the mornings I opened my eyes to an entirely different landscape. There was fog some mornings. The tall cedars wrapped in mist looked ghostly and beautiful. Some days were clear and sunny, still cool in the morning when I took my cup of tea out on the patio and prepared to start my day. Some days I took a blanket with me, to wrap around bare feet as I sat there in silence. The only sounds were the chickens clucking and crowing in the neighbor's yard next door. Though the house lay within Seattle city limits, it felt miles away.

One morning I woke up to hazy white covering the garden, on the grass and the plants. I blinked, not believing what I was seeing. Was it frost? It couldn't be—not in late May. Was it *snow*?

I opened the door, preparing for cold, but felt only a mild breeze. As I walked across the patio barefoot, I saw it wasn't frost at all.

A heavy blanket of dew had condensed and now hung from every blade of grass and sprig of flower or vegetable. From a distance it looked like a frosty haze, but when I got close, each drop glittered in the early-morning sunshine. Each drop reflected the world back to me, as if they were a million tiny mirrors. Each drop revealed beauty.

How lucky I am to see this. If I hadn't stayed, I would never have known. The magic would have happened without me.

When my mother returned, I told her I would stay there for the summer. Two weeks later, when the apartment building where I had put my name on the waiting list called to say there was a unit available, I told them no thanks. I would be spending my summer in the garden. It needed me.

And maybe I needed it too.

I hadn't moved often. Not the way most Americans do—with rental trucks and packing blankets and furniture wheeled out on a dolly. I left for college with exactly two duffel bags and a box sent after me. I moved to Japan with three suitcases and several crates of books. And when I moved into San Francisco, from my mother's house across the bridge, I did it gradually, taking little bits here and there in my car. I felt an odd pride that nothing I owned was too big to fit in the back of my station wagon. Besides one very heavy black desk, nothing was too big for me to carry. I could do it all on my own.

I even tried to move the desk by myself once, too impatient to wait for help. That is how I hurt my back, an injury that continued to aggravate me years later with occasional flare-ups. Sometimes it incapacitated me. This usually happened when I picked up something heavy or unwieldy without waiting for help. Some of us are slow learners, or maybe just stubborn. Some of us think we can do everything on our own.

My first Seattle move, however, to the charming studio sublet, had been a different experience. In Seattle, it seemed, you didn't do things alone.

"Your homework is to let people help you move," my friend Mary told me, as I started to plan and pack.

"What do you mean?"

"You have such a hard time asking for help—this is the perfect opportunity."

"I don't think I can do that," I told her. I didn't mention a friend had once nicknamed me Lone Wolf.

Then Mary sat me down and told me a story.

When she and her girlfriend moved into the house they now share, they decided it was time to hire movers. They weren't in their twenties anymore—it was no longer okay to ask friends for help in exchange for pizza and beer. It was time to be grown-up. So they threw money at the problem and hired out the labor. The move went smoothly, and all was fine until Mary's best friend found out what they had done. Then he got mad.

"Why?" I asked. Wouldn't most people prefer *not* to hoist boxes and lift furniture on a sunny Saturday? No one wants to spend a weekend that way.

"He said I hadn't given him the chance to help—I had taken away the opportunity for us to become closer."

I thought about this. In San Francisco I had never been asked to help anyone move, but in Seattle I already had been. When friends moved out of the city to a nearby island, I had packed my car full of their artwork and breakables and driven it onto the ferry and to their new house at the other end. Then I helped unload the truck until my back got so inflamed I had to lie on the floor in their new yellow living room. My friend and her baby lay next to me, and we laughed at how crazy the whole moving process is. When someone walked in carrying a box of angst-filled journals from my friend's younger years, we joked that the warning label should not read "heavy"; it should be *weighty.*

Helping *had* made me feel closer to my friends. I liked feeling that I was a small part of this new adventure in their lives, as if I was part of their family of friends. Years from now we would still share those memories of dusty packing boxes and exhaustion, the small yet rich details of life as we live it.

"Oh, yes," my friend Sarah said when the subject came up on one of our walks. "Moving is how you know who your friends are." And then she volunteered to help me move.

I was still not convinced—the whole idea made me feel uncomfortable. What if I asked and no one came? What if they came and saw the contents of my messy drawers and ran away? What if they thought worse of me? It seemed easier to keep it all at arm's length, to do it myself, to pay people if needed. Asking for help made you vulnerable.

I probably would have tried to pack and move the contents of a three-story house by myself, but I wasn't given the choice. That old back injury returned to haunt me. An awkward twist with a packing box and suddenly I was in pain. I couldn't lift heavy things, and I certainly couldn't carry them up three flights of stairs. I needed my friends. I needed their help.

There was an uncomfortable email sent to those who had offered: *So, about that moving thing . . . I might need your help after all.* To my surprise, people actually showed up.

Jennifer and Carrie packed my kitchen, taking far more care wrapping dishes than I ever would have. Kairu brought boxes and packed up my children's-book collection. Marianne drove those boxes across town in her minivan, Anne mopped my living room floor, Sarah helped carry furniture, and in the midst of the frenzy, Viv volunteered to scrub out my refrigerator.

"You sure you want to do that? It's pretty gross."

"Oh, yes," she said far more enthusiastically than I expected.

It made me squirm to have someone scrub the congealed smears and spills from inside my now-empty refrigerator, but I let her. I simply could not afford to turn down help. I gave it a cursory wipe down, then tried to be okay with someone else seeing the grossest bits of my life. It felt like being naked in public.

Halfway through the process, intent on her work, Viv called out for me.

"Do you have any Q-tips? I want to get the cracks really clean."

By the time she was finished, the fridge was cleaner than when it had come off the manufacturing floor, and Viv was beaming. "Isn't that better?" she said. "You can call me any time you want your fridge cleaned."

I sent her home with handfuls of fresh herbs and grateful thank-yous, baffled that this dreaded chore seemed to be something my friend truly enjoyed. "It lets me practice my OCD," she said with a laugh. "I find it very satisfying."

Somehow, despite my injured back, my friends helped me out of the house and into the little apartment in the sky—and not a moment too soon. I carried up the last box at 9 A.M., after a night of no sleep, got into the car without showering, and drove to California to attend a summit that started that evening. I never would have made it on my own.

It would be three weeks before I returned to Seattle, but when I did it was to an apartment of carefully wrapped glasses and plates. Every box I opened, every lumpy bundle of crumpled newspaper and bubble wrap, felt like a present from my friends.

I do not know if I have ever felt so loved by so many people.

———

When it came time to move out of the sublet, however, I didn't feel I could ask friends. I had learned my lesson—*help is good*—but it seemed like anyone dumb enough to move more than once in a calendar year forfeited the right to assistance. This time I would be carrying things down the stairs, not up, and many of my things were already in storage; how hard could it be?

I somehow didn't calculate that I would have to *walk back up* three flights after each load. Multiply that by thirty or forty, and the stairs became their own circle of hell. I didn't anticipate that I would get sick, and that packing and hoisting and carrying are much harder with a fever and body-rattling cough. I never imagined I would cling to the banister, pulling myself up hand over hand. I never imagined it would be as bad as it was.

I cursed every box of books I owned. I cursed the twelve pasta bowls I hadn't put in storage the first time—*who needs twelve pasta bowls in a studio apartment?* I cursed the winter coats and snow boots and the box of damned Christmas tree ornaments. I considered throwing them all from the top of the stairs, just to see the angels take flight, the glass balls shatter, tinsel and glitter strewn everywhere.

Mary was right. We should not do these things alone, if only to preserve our own sanity. It is sometimes as thin and fragile as a glass Christmas tree ball.

My mother had offered to help, but I had turned her down. We were not a help-out family. All my life I had watched her do everything alone, and I had picked up the message hidden in her actions: to ask for help is somehow shameful; it means you can't do it on your own.

It's not that I never asked my mother for help. I just tried to do things myself first. It was only when it became clear that I couldn't, when I began to get panicky and desperate, that I called my mom. To ask her for help meant I had failed, that I wasn't as strong or as capable as she was.

I was never as strong or capable as she was.

I knew she would come, but she was the court of last appeals: I would be helped, but I would be judged. My mother was there for me, but she was never a soft place to land.

And anyway, she was packing herself, to go to Canada. I didn't want to ask when I knew she had work of her own to do.

It never even occurred to me to ask my brother. This seemed like another part of family he liked to keep at a distance. And anyway, he was busy helping his wife and children.

When I called my mother that day, coughing and exhausted and near desperate, she came. She interrupted her own packing to help with mine. When she saw my apartment filled with boxes in various states from full to empty, she sighed. "Why must you always be so disorganized?" she said, and then she got to work. We carried things down the stairs and filled up her car. I was weak on my legs, light-headed as I shoved things into the nooks and crannies of her trunk.

"I'm done," she said, standing by the side of her now full car. She meant she was done with helping; she was done with me.

"Can I just run up and get the plants?"

The woman I had sublet the apartment from had left her plants, even though, when she asked, I'd said I didn't want them. They were big, spiky things that took up room, but after nearly a year of keeping them alive, I had a hard time tossing them in a dumpster. My mom had agreed to take a few. Others I had put in the building lobby with a note, and they had eventually disappeared. Adopted, I hoped, by other residents.

My mom slammed the car door in irritation. "I'm getting too old for this shit." Then she looked at me and sighed. "Go get the plants."

I turned and quickly went back into the apartment building, stomping up the stairs. *Why* couldn't she be a supportive mother? *Why* hadn't she shown up a week ago with boxes and packing tape? *Why* didn't she want to sit on my floor and wrap candle holders and gossip and go out afterward for pizza? I had helped pack up her garage—*why didn't she come help me?* Why did I have to ask? *Why* did she have to judge? Why wasn't she just *there*? *Why couldn't she be the mom?*

I ran out of stairs before I ran out of complaints.

When I came back down, clutching a pot filled with a spiky thing for which I had no name, my mother had three words for me.

"Call your brother."

"Do you think he'd come?"

"Of course he would," she said. "He's your brother."

I didn't say anything. I turned away and waved her off and quickly went into the building. There I sat down on the steps and I cried. I wept at the idea my brother might show up. That he might be there for me.

And then he did. That night, after his children were in bed, my brother came and carried boxes with me—all the boxes that were going in storage. He carried boxes and he teased me. ("No one who has been out of college as long as you should still have a futon.") And he acted as if it were the most normal thing in the world, though to me it felt astounding.

"I *told* you he would come," my mother said when she called later that night to check on me. The apartment was nearly empty; I was washing windows and floors, scrubbing the bathtub, tossing the last few bits of trash into bags and boxes, running on fumes and adrenaline.

When I was desperate and at the end of my rope, my family had shown up for me. I had asked, and they had come. It was the most mundane thing in the world, but for a family with little glue to bind them, it felt like a small miracle.

That first week in the garden, I barely got out of bed. I felt beat-up, so sore from the move and the endless stairs. I was still wracked by coughs, the deep, body-shaking ones that bring up phlegm and mucus, the ones that make you feel like it might actually be possible to cough up a lung or your own spleen.

My mother was gone to Canada for the summer, and I slept most of that week. Not a fitful sleep; I slept like the dead. I stayed upstairs in the coffin room, because it was next to the bathroom, and who cares about a view when you're not awake?

When I finally staggered out of bed, I was hungry.

It was more than hunger. I wanted something warm, something soothing that would make me feel better—something I could wrap my hands around to feel comfort. It is hard to comfort yourself when you feel miserable. Comfort requires something from the outside.

There was nothing in the fridge. My mother had cleared out her perishables before she left, and the only things I had brought from my apartment were condiments. I stood at the open fridge door, looking in despondently. Then I noticed the container of green Thai curry paste.

I took the plastic tub to the stove and filled a saucepan with water, spooning in as much curry as I could stand. I added bouillon as well and rummaged in the cupboard for a packet of rice noodles. I set another pot of water to boil.

As the saucepan simmered on the stove, I left the kitchen and went outside, slowly making my way into the garden. In my free hand, I carried a pair of scissors.

Across the grass lay the kale beds—an assortment of greens my mother had planted and tended. I clipped floppy leaves of chard, long green chives, and ferny bits of cilantro already beginning to bolt. I cut pak choi and tender sprigs of broccoli. I gathered them together and carried them back into the kitchen: the yield of my mother's efforts, a bouquet of green in my hands.

In the kitchen, I washed the greens quickly, cut them roughly, and stirred them into the simmering broth. As the leaves wilted into the steamy soup, I removed the pot from the heat. I drained the noodles and added them, with a tiny bit of fish sauce for saltiness, some lime for sour.

I poured the whole thing into a bowl and wrapped my hands around the warmth of it. I leaned forward into the sour-tanged steam and tried to breathe deep. When I sipped the broth, the heat and fiery chilies began to open my long-clogged nose and chest. Though my taste buds were muffled, I sensed lemongrass, the sharpness of lime. Soft noodles slipped down a throat that ached from coughing, and the greens were chewy and tender. I knew they were good for me.

My mother wasn't there to comfort me—she had rarely been able to give me what I needed. But here was a garden of vegetables she had worked hard to grow. Now, when I needed it most, she was nourishing me. She couldn't give me herself. Instead she had given me the tools to be strong on my own. Perhaps that was her greatest gift to me: resilience and strength, the ability to survive.

Maybe this is how my mother loves me. Maybe this is the best she can do.

I drank down the entire bowl of soup, chewing the soft noodles and toothy greens. I ate another bowlful and went back to bed. The next day I made more, picking more greens from the garden. The supply there seemed endless.

I made that green noodle curry over and over, for weeks on end, until I was fully well again. I never grew tired of it.

12

THE YIELD OF A BERRY PATCH

I HADN'T INVITED FRIENDS to the garden. Not really. Knox and Kim had taken tours, given feedback, and been on their way. I hadn't invited anyone over just to hang out. This was not surprising. I'd spent a lifetime not inviting people over.

I had learned early, from neighborhood children, that my house was weird. We had no television, no candy, no cool toys. None of the neighborhood kids wanted to come to our house to play. They told me so.

Our house was filled with Asian carpets and calligraphy done by Buddhist masters. There were no comfortable chairs, no places to lounge. I longed for a house with wall-to-wall carpeting and a boring beige sofa set. Boring was safe.

There was usually no mom at our house—and when she was there, she was a liability. My mother was more likely to dole out carob-studded trail mix and unsweetened apple juice than cookies or lemonade. She might try to give you tofu or seaweed. Her eccentricities made us stick out. Her refusal to fit in became a burden for which I did not have her strength.

As I got older things shifted, never for the better. The occasional high school friend who came to visit widened their eyes at tatami-mat floors and the Asian art that decorated the home my mother had created. *"What is that smell?"* they whispered, picking up the ancient, unfamiliar scent of indigo dye. The truly unlucky asked about the bamboo whisks lined up on the kitchen windowsill.

"They're used to make ceremonial green tea," my mother explained, seeming delighted to have been asked. "Would you like some?"

I kicked my friend under the table, gestured behind my mother's back—I shook my head. "It's *really bitter*," I warned.

My mother brushed away my concerns. "It's not so bitter."

Too often the friend said yes, and my mother selected a handmade bowl and carefully measured out powdered green tea using a tiny bamboo scoop. Tea ceremony is an agonizingly slow process, and I cringed through every deliberate moment. My mother whisked the powder into warm water until it was a frothy mixture of brilliant green that tasted deeply of grass. Each friend who fell into this trap took a single sip before coughing and sputtering, taken aback by a concoction so strongly flavored it's meant to be served with tooth-aching sweets for balance. My mother never bothered with that part.

Couldn't she see she was only making things worse?

I wanted a mother who asked about school or drama club or the cross-country team—who showed genuine interest in her daughter's life and this new friend. Why couldn't she put me first?

Some friends seemed taken by the exoticism of a visit to my house—so very different from their own homes. They were curious about a mother who did not serve on the PTA or work as a real estate agent or dental hygienist. My mother had been far

more adventurous with her life than most women of her generation.

But I didn't want to be a curio. I wanted friends to be able to
open the fridge and get a snack without fear of what they might
find there, collapse on a sofa, put their feet up on a coffee table.

There were no coffee tables in our house. What little furniture we had was arranged around the edges of a large Chinese
carpet. The center of the room was vacant. In the place where
there should have been comfort, there was only emptiness.

My solution was to hide my family from the outside world—
dividing life into separate categories of school and home. I defended the boundaries like my survival might depend on it.
Sometimes it felt like it did.

I stole the notification postcards for back-to-school nights
out of the mailbox. I lied when necessary—*my mom's out of town;
I'm not allowed to have friends over.* If my mother ever wondered
why she wasn't being called to school to meet my teachers, why
I didn't have friends over to play, she never mentioned it.

As I grew up and had homes of my own, I overcompensated.
I read etiquette books and cocktail guides and lists of suggestions
for how to be a relaxed hostess (*put out your serving platters the
night before the party; make sure to relax with a drink and preselected
music twenty minutes before your guests arrive*). I bought tablecloths
with matching napkins, sets of glasses for different types of wine.
But none of the books held the answers I really needed: how to
feel okay with letting people see who I was.

This sometimes called for heroic measures. Other people
clean before company comes over—I've been known to purchase entirely new furniture. The words of the neighborhood
kids still rang in my ears.

The things I bought never covered up the fear that I was
doing domesticity wrong. My mother hadn't been taught—her
own mother had died too early. And my grandmother's mother

had died early as well. I was the third generation to be raised feral, making it up as we went along.

But in fundamental ways, we were different. My mother saw she would never fit in—*and decided not to.* She had blazed her own path, to Asia and an unconventional life. I was the opposite. Not fitting in made me want it more. I craved the safety and the validation of the group.

In some ways I marveled at her—how strong to walk away, to not care what other people thought. In other ways it seemed inhuman. Even animals are dependent on the group for survival; no one makes it on his own; the lone wolf is actually a myth.

Sometimes I wondered if my mother's unconventional choices were her billboard to a cruel world: I DON'T CARE WHAT YOU THINK OF ME. Had she chosen to walk away, or did she withdraw early to avoid failure? Were my mother's eccentricities a strength, or just the way she covered up her own vulnerabilities? I knew from my own life that it's easier to pretend you don't want the thing you cannot have.

I feared rejection as well. The isolation and lack of community I had been raised with made me feel—not that I was doing things wrong, but that I *was* wrong. I feared opening up my home would reveal all my messy, broken bits, all the ways I continually failed. If anyone got close enough to see, I was sure they wouldn't want to know me.

After years of shutting people out, how could I possibly let them in?

I hadn't planned on the raspberries.

The new garden had a berry patch, a large and neglected plot. We hadn't noticed them at first because they were overgrown with weeds. The first year the plants seemed stunted, shorter than I was used to and anemic looking, without much in the way of fruit. At the end of the summer, I cut back the old canes, thinned them out, and piled up dried leaves around the roots as mulch, to protect them and enrich the soil. The next summer they grew taller, bushier. By April they were covered with tiny white blossoms.

Things felt good in the garden that spring, even if I still felt awkward in my mother's house. I had survived the onslaught of greens, the baskets of kale and chard, the lettuce and arugula that thrived in the unusually rainy spring we'd had that year. As June turned into July, the weather finally warmed up; peas began to flower and form; the raspberries came ripe.

That first June morning was a revelation: walking out to the garden in pajamas and bare feet *to pick breakfast.* The grass was damp with dew, the cilantro in delicate white flower, lettuces all shades of snappy green and speckled rusty reds. There, standing behind them at chest level, was the thicket of raspberries.

I approached the jungle of green leaves, loaded with clusters so heavy the stalks had begun to droop. I remembered the wonder I'd had as a child in my mother's berry patch: these tiny thimbles, like hats for fairy children. Each one was a collection of even smaller spheres held together as if by magic. When I put the first berry in my mouth, it collapsed at the slightest pressure into a burst of tart sweetness. Ah, *raspberries.*

Each morning I waded into the berry patch, trying to avoid damaging the thin canes. Each morning I picked and picked, filling two quart-sized plastic containers to the brim. I ate berries for breakfast with yogurt, berries for snacks midday, berries for dessert after dinner.

I'd always thought berry picking a treat. I'd never thought of it as a chore, an obligation. But that summer I discovered when berries are ready to be picked—*they must be picked.* Especially the delicate raspberries. When it rained they began to mold on the stalk and were wasted.

By the second week of picking, I was sick of raspberries. Really and truly sick of them, something I had not thought was possible. I didn't want to see another raspberry for a long time. But what to do with them? They kept coming.

I stashed quarts in the freezer for my mother when she came home at the end of the summer, but freezer space was limited. I made jam, but still the berries kept coming. I made raspberry curd and raspberry cordial, for an *Anne of Green Gables* picnic with friends, but still the berries kept coming. It was time to branch out into baked goods. Even though I was not much of a baker, I decided it was time to bake a pie.

I entered the kitchen that afternoon with trepidation. Pies scare me. There's technique involved in getting a flaky crust. Torn piecrust seemed irreparable, the ice water never cold enough. What if the dough didn't come together? What if it looked lopsided and sad? Cakes can be disguised with frosting; pies are naked in their homely beauty.

I shouldn't have been as worried as I was. I might not be much of a baker, but I knew people who were—people like my friend Kate.

Kate McDermott taught pie making around the world; I had taken her class several years before. It hadn't made me a baker, but it had given me some perspective on the art of pies. Mostly I had been taken by her attitude.

"I make ugly pies," she told me. "They don't have to look perfect."

That day Kate had ably patched ripped piecrust, shoring up weak spots where the dough had been rolled too thin. She didn't think it needed to be perfect. "Just fix any mistakes you make," she said without concern. "It doesn't matter."

Kate's approach was breezy and relaxed. She barely followed a recipe. "See how it feels," she told me. "Trust yourself." As I ran my hands through the butter cut into flour, I felt emboldened. Things didn't have to be perfect. Kate seemed at peace with imperfections, her pies beautiful in their rustic uniqueness, no two ever the same.

Perhaps the secret was finding comfort in the way things were: a process of accepting rather than hiding.

The irony was that I liked it when other people let me see them as they truly were: less-than-perfect houses, disordered garages, overdue library books. The imperfections in my friends' lives didn't make me like them any less—*they made me like them more.* I felt more comfortable with the flaws in my own life, more intimately connected to them; it made me feel like family.

I knew this intellectually, but it was harder to apply. I might be able to appreciate rustic charm in a pie, to enjoy the comfortable clutter of a friend's house, but I held myself to a higher standard—one I never managed to achieve. My friends didn't have to be perfect. I just couldn't give myself that same compassion.

But rolling out and patching the rips in my pie dough that afternoon, as Kate had shown me, I began to wonder if there might not be another way. And when I pulled the pie out of the oven, bumpy, irregular, burnished and glossy and smelling like raspberry heaven, for a moment I thought it was beautiful. My beautifully imperfect pie.

I hadn't counted on the fact that you cannot eat a pie on your own. You can try, but by the time you finish it, you won't like pie any longer. If you draw it out over days—a slice here and there—it will go soggy and unappealing. Pie begs to be shared. It is the most sociable of desserts.

Sharing pie would involve inviting friends over to the garden, something I had not planned on. I couldn't entertain them elsewhere—I no longer had a place of my own. It would have to be the garden. The messy, weedy, out-of-control garden.

I might have survived the onslaught of spring greens, but I had not survived the onslaught of weeds. The bindweed had woken up and was twining and twisting up everything that stood: fence slats, trees, azalea bushes, sturdy kale plants.

"Is there anything you can do about bindweed?" I asked a friend of mine who had a farm in California. I was getting desperate.

"Nope," she said. "Bindweed is like herpes—you just gotta live with it."

I was coming to think that bindweed was something that ought to be disclosed on real estate contracts—along with foundation damage and a history of flooding. Potential buyers should be warned.

I tried to keep on top of the bindweed, but it was impossible. And then there was the lawn.

We'd had an argument about that lawn, my mother and I. She was all for letting the grass grow. This lawn that had been carefully tended for decades, that had once been like velvet nap with mower lines—she wanted it all wild.

I was in favor of keeping the lawn. "The kids need someplace to play."

"You can have this part." She gestured to the far upper section, near the patio, a tiny strip.

"That's not enough; they need more space."

"They're not *that big*."

"But they're growing—and that's not enough space to run through the sprinklers or play croquet. We need room to be able to string a badminton net."

"Fine. You can have the upper section for lawn, but I'm letting the field go."

Thus the yard was partitioned: my upper play area, my mother's meadow in the distance, a riot of wild grasses that now grew waist-high.

But I hadn't counted on the upkeep a lawn required. I had

neither time nor equipment to mow or edge the grass, and the dandelions that grew in my mother's meadow blew their seed over to colonize. By midsummer they were stretching up sunshiny faces. I occasionally weedwacked them down, but they grew back, shorter the second time. I felt sure they were mocking me.

Above the weedy lawn, next to the house, chaos had broken out. Lacking a shed or storage space, my mother had leaned all the garden tools up against the house, under the broad overhang. Flowerpots and bags of fertilizer and soil fought for limited space with pitchforks, wheelbarrows, piles of cardboard for future mulching projects, watering cans, hoses, rolls of chicken wire, and garden stakes in a variety of sizes. There was no system of organization, no sense to the mess. Between the rusty shovels and pickaxes, the towering stacks of unused flowerpots, and the dandelion-strewn lawn, the yard had a dilapidated air to it. In well-tended North Seattle, it looked like hillbillies had moved in.

I was annoyed my mother had gone off for the summer and left such a mess. I couldn't invite anyone over with things looking like this. What would they think?

But then there was the pie . . .

I sprang into action, hauling abandoned flowerpots—*wheelbarrows* full of abandoned flowerpots—back to a storage area behind the cottage. I wrestled bags of compost and fertilizer and wood chips around to the north side of the house where no one would see them. I stacked cardboard neatly, tried to organize shovels and rakes, and sorted through piles of twine, gardening gloves, various soil testing kits, bits of copper wire to ward off slugs, and stakes to prop up drooping plants. I threw out plastic plant tags, broken pottery, and a packet of lima bean seeds from 1986 that had come up from California with my mother. I was covered in dirt and sweaty, but eventually some semblance of organization had been imposed on the clutter my mother left behind.

Why does she keep all this crap?

I hadn't cleaned everything—it would take an entire summer to do that. Instead I dragged things I didn't know what to do with around to the north side of the house, where a narrow passageway ran along the fence that marked the property line. Here I piled up pots, cardboard, pieces of a large composter, and the ladder that had no other home. It blocked the path but would be out of sight for the friends I had invited, who would be arriving soon.

I had sent Marianne and Viv the address, with careful instructions that they should follow the path around the south side of the house. I would be in the back, I explained. I could have met them at the front door, but all these years later I was still uncomfortable with friends entering my mother's home.

Looking at the garden, I wondered what they might see. They'd notice the weeds, the cracked patio, the kale plants nearly as tall as I was. It was a riotous mess. Even with all my cleaning, it was ramshackle and cluttered, overgrown and untidy.

I hoped they'd also see the light glinting through the wild grasses in the field, how plump the pea pods were on their vines. I hoped they'd notice the clematis flecked with magenta, the blooming honeysuckle, the small tree covered in tiny little apples. I hoped they'd see the wonder as well as the weeds.

"Hello! Hello!" I could hear my friends' voices. I looked up the path to the driveway; it was empty. Where were they?

"Hello?" The disembodied voices floated into the yard, and I rushed back to the patio. *"Where are you?"* I could hear them even if I couldn't see them. Suddenly I knew what had happened.

There, coming around the north end of the house, picking their way through the garden junk I'd carefully hauled away, were my friends. All that crap I'd hidden to make sure no one could see. Blood rushed suddenly to my face.

"Wow," Viv said. "Look at this place." I couldn't tell if the note in her voice was awe or horror.

"Yeah, it's a little out of control."

"It's so *big!*" said Marianne. "I can see why you've been so busy."

Viv had pulled out her camera and was taking pictures of flowers, lettuces, the blackberry vines blooming along the fence. It made me nervous. Viv was always taking pictures, but I hadn't calculated on our mess being captured for posterity. Or worse, for the internet.

"Here, let's sit in the shade." I had set up the table on the patio, next to the raspberry bushes, where we would be sheltered from the afternoon sunlight. Marianne and I began to arrange food.

I turned to find Viv taking pictures of the rusty garden tools leaned up against the house: rakes, shovels, pitchforks, a scythe. *"What are you doing?"*

She laughed, a tinkling sound, light and pure. "It's just all so . . ." She paused, searching for the right word while I cringed, the harsh language of the neighborhood children rushing back to my ears.

" . . . *novel,*" she said happily. There was no judgment in her voice, only pleasant curiosity about a life unlike her own. Viv and her husband lived in a downtown high-rise, far away from pitchforks or scythes.

I laughed. We all laughed. And I realized something I should have figured out long before. I had been too wounded, too guarded, to see it.

When you find your real friends, they will not judge or mock you. *They are your friends.*

I brought the pie down from the kitchen and set it on the table. There was a honey-rosemary soda I'd made with herbs from the garden, and my friends had brought a bottle of Lillet and vanilla ice cream to go with the pie. The raspberry filling pooled around the crust and melted the ice cream so a single bite was both creamy and tart, warm and cold. On a summer day, to sit in the shade with friends and eat pie and drink wine felt like the best thing ever.

"Are *those* the raspberries?" Viv had caught sight of the stalks next to the patio. She knew the fruit was from the garden but seemed surprised to see it growing inches away from where she sat.

"Yep."

"Really?" she said, a note of wonder in her voice. *"They're right there?"*

I laughed. To me this was no longer novel. "You can pick some if you want."

"Really?"

"Sure. I'll get you a container."

I hadn't realized how accustomed I'd become to eating what I had grown. About 70 percent of what I consumed came from the garden: morning berries, lunchtime salads, the vegetables in evening noodles or frittatas. I still bought beans and pasta and eggs, but that was about it.

If Viv was the romantic, Marianne was more practical.

"This place is a lot of work," she said, looking around.

"I know. I can't keep up with it all."

"You need help. This is not a one-person job."

"If you want, I could come help you weed one day." Viv was back from the berry bushes, her hands cupping a small mound of red.

"Really?"

"Sure—and Carl would love to weedwack those dandelions."

I smiled to think of my high-rise-dwelling friend and her husband mucking around the garden with me.

"You would do that?"

"Of course." She smiled. "It would be fun."

We sat in the shade of the patio as the sun sank slowly toward the western edge of the sky. The magnolia swayed in the breeze, the chilled wine slid down my throat, and I laughed and talked with my friends, the sounds of our conversation weaving together and floating out over the grass and flower beds to the meadow beyond.

Later, when we were packing up the trappings of our pie party, I handed back the bottle of Lillet. It was still half-full.

"No," Viv said. "Keep it. For the next time we come up here."

I looked at my friends, at the berry bushes, at the fruit I had grown and the pie that had brought us together, and suddenly the neighborhood kids and their harsh words felt a far distant memory. Ancient history.

I took the wine bottle, I smiled at them, and in that moment my imperfect garden felt very perfect indeed. As sweet as raspberries, not a thorn in sight.

13

. . .

TO PRUNE A TOMATO

IN THE GARDEN OF my childhood my mother grew corn and asparagus, beans, zucchini, and more, but the thing I remember most is the cherry tomatoes, bushy in their cages, the leaves slightly sticky, funny smelling. My mother wore long-sleeve shirts to weed the tomatoes.

I remember her plucking them off the bush, my brother and me opening our mouths like baby birds for her to pop them in. I closed my eyes to experience the exact moment my teeth pierced the smooth skin and the tomato exploded in a burst of acid sweet, the seeds slightly bitter in their jelly pouches. The sensation was so unexpected each time it happened that my eyes flew open. And there was my mother, smiling at me. That is what I remember.

My mother did not smile often. We have pictures where she is smiling, me or my brother nestled on her lap. You can tell she loves us. Her body language shows it. But mostly we knew she loved us because of how hard she worked for us. Usually else-where.

But the garden—the garden was her project. In the little time she had not devoted to work and cleaning and trying to hold her small world together, my mother grew food.

My brother and I didn't help in the garden, but we were usually playing nearby. We always wanted to be nearby when she was home. I remember her letting us crawl through the dried cornstalks after the ears had been harvested. I remember running my hands through the asparagus that had been allowed to go to seed. I remember eating plums from the old tree that lived in the corner of the yard. I remember her feeding us tomatoes fresh off the vine and still warm from the sun.

When I think of those tomatoes, it is not the flavor that moves me. They were shockingly sweet and tangy, but that is not what I remember the most. It is not what I yearned for.

Eating cherry tomatoes meant my mother was home; it meant she was smiling at me.

The Good Shepherd Center in North Seattle was formerly a home for wayward girls. The ornate stone building and surrounding parkland now housed an elementary school, senior center, artist studios, and nonprofit organization offices. One of these nonprofits was devoted to gardener education and support—with classes, children's camps, a demonstration garden, and a P-Patch. Among the many programs and events that the gardening organization Seattle Tilth sponsored was a big spring plant sale that they held one weekend in April or May.

As I approached the building the Saturday of my first plant sale, I was surprised to see a line snaking around the wide lawn and under gnarled old apple trees in full bloom. I wondered if there was a music concert nearby—surely there must be some trendy event to pull this sort of crowd. But all these people were

waiting for the plant sale. I felt a slow swell of pride at the real-
ization that I lived in a city where people lined up for parsley and
lettuce, tomato seedlings and chard.

Heading for the back of the line, I noticed people carrying
plastic or cardboard flats, some pulling small red wagons. I hadn't
brought anything to carry my plants home; I hadn't known that
I should.

This was my first clue that I was entirely unprepared for the
experience.

Once the line had slowly, politely moved forward and entered the main enclosure, the feelings of overwhelm began.
There was an ocean of basil, fragrant, broad leaves that seemed
too big for their stems—Genoa basil, Thai basil, purple basil,
lettuce leaf basil. The delicate, feathery leaves of chervil stretched
up from pots, as did cilantro and summer savory. There were
names I had never heard before: anise hyssop, Vietnamese cori-
ander, pineapple sage.

To walk down the rows of herbs was to feel transported,
carried away, almost high from the scent. I hadn't known mint
came in such wide variety: licorice mint, orange mint, apple
mint, chocolate mint, lemon balm. There were so many kinds of
thyme: lemon, silver, variegated, English, French, and Proven-
çal. The fragrance must have gone to my head because suddenly
I wanted to grow them all.

This might be the reason for what happened next. Or perhaps gardening is a sort of socially condoned addiction. I'm not
entirely sure. But somehow I found myself on the far side of the
plant sale an hour and a half later with three flats of seedlings and
a receipt for more than a hundred dollars. It took me two trips
to get them all in the car.

It was the tomatoes that really did it. Those too came in unimaginable variety. I had known about beefsteak, Roma, Early
Girl—and the knobby multicolored fruits sold under the catchall
name "heirloom," but there my knowledge stopped. I had never

heard of Cherokee Purple, Stupice, Juliet, or Siberian. I didn't know about Lemon Boy, Jubilee, Garden Peach. I hadn't realized you could raise a Celebrity! A Champion! An Early Swedish! I wanted to try them all. I had the space now—why not?

This is how I ended up with eighteen different tomato varieties. I was like those people who cannot stop taking in strays and suddenly are living in a house with thirty cats. I kept picking more and more plants: I just wanted to give them a good home.

I would have told you I had a strategy. I wanted to try as many as I could so next year I'd know which ones did best. I was being *scientific*.

I felt rather proud of myself. Just think how much money I'd save come August when the red-filled crates at the market no longer called to me. I would have my own tomato farm at home.

If my mother seemed taken aback by my large investment in tomatoes, she didn't voice her feelings. She let me take up two shelves in the greenhouse and never questioned my haul. She made a good partner for pie-in-the-sky schemes.

That spring was a poor one to be planting tomatoes. For that you needed soil temperatures of fifty-five degrees. You also, ideally, needed it to stop raining. Neither of which was happening in Seattle that year.

We were luckier than most. The tomatoes stayed warm in the greenhouse, sheltered from the cold and the wet. They continued to grow, becoming leggy and unhappy. As the chilly, gray spring dragged on, their leaves began to yellow, and the stems turned purplish.

"You need to do something about those tomatoes," my mother told me, on a day that was still not warm enough to plant outside. "They need to be in the ground."

"I know, but it's too cold. I can't plant them yet."

"Then you should put them in bigger pots. They need more room."

She was right, but repotting eighteen tomatoes would be a pain. We didn't even *have* eighteen pots the right size. The greenhouse was full that spring. Instead I delayed, thinking next week would be better. Then the next week, and the next. But Seattle that year was a city spring forgot. It was one of the years natives are talking about when they say you can't expect reliably good weather until the Fourth of July. It might be sunny before then, but it might not.

"Don't worry about it," the man at the nursery told me when I confessed my unplanted tomatoes. "You just want to plant them under."

"What does that mean?"

"Dig a deep hole, and plant them up to here." He pointed to a spot halfway up the stem of a nearby plant. "Take off all the leaves below that point. You can put up to two-thirds of the stem underground."

"What if I can't dig that deep?" The side garden was formed by a retaining wall. I didn't know how far down I could go.

"Don't worry about it," he repeated. "You can even plant them on their side—they'll turn and stretch toward the sun."

It sounded far-fetched, but I figured he knew more than I did.

When the weather stabilized, I did as he'd said. I removed the leaves from the lower halves of the tomato plants, loosened their tightly bound roots, and planted them on their sides. Then I hoped for the best.

The problem with my first serious attempt at growing tomatoes was not that I kept them in the greenhouse too long— though I probably did. It wasn't even that I planted them on their sides and trusted the nurseryman that they would find their way upright (they did). The problem with my first serious attempt at growing tomatoes was that, once the weather finally warmed up, the tomatoes took off. They started growing like crazy. They are tropical vines, after all.

I hadn't planned for the sprawl; I hadn't planned for out of control foliage; I didn't know what I was doing. I tried to put them in tomato cages to support the growth, but who has eighteen of those?

A month later the side garden was an acrid forest of sticky green leaves. It was hard to see into the jungle, hard to harvest, and with such a short summer, most of the tomatoes were still green or orange when it started getting cold and rainy again. I wasn't sure what I had done wrong, but my plans for crates of juicy red fruit had failed.

I felt like a character in a cautionary tale of how not to grow tomatoes. *Did you hear about the girl who tried eighteen different varieties?* I promised myself next year I would do better. That is the mantra of the gardener: *next year.*

I had no excuse for not growing a good tomato crop. I had an ideal tomato-growing climate in the side garden: all-day sun on a southern exposure with a cement foundation behind to absorb and retain heat. The area was sheltered from strong winds and cold. Sure, Seattle was a challenging climate for them. But if I couldn't grow tomatoes in Seattle, nobody should be able to.

The following year wasn't a particularly good summer for tomatoes either (I was beginning to wonder if any Seattle summer was). Another long, rainy, and cool spring kept temperatures low until the end of June. But by then, I was prepared.

I had researched tomato varieties. When I went to the plant sale, I wasn't swayed by Garden Peaches and Celebrities. I went straight for varieties known for ripening well in the Northwest: Cherokee Purple, Paul Robeson, Siberian. This time I was not messing around.

I didn't keep the tomatoes in the greenhouse long. That spring I had driven into the northern mountains of central Washington, to a small town a few miles away from the Canadian border, to interview a farmer for an article. Billy Allstot grows strawberries, peaches, cherries, arugula, and eggplant, but he is known for his tomatoes. I stood with him in a greenhouse that held thousands of plants, all being trained upright on cords strung from the ceiling. The plastic siding magnified the heat, the soil smelled warm, it was like summer in there—even though it was still cold and raining in Seattle.

That morning Billy had told me he talked to his plants, something my mother did as well; I have always been skeptical.

"I walk the farm twice a day," he said, "always along the same route. By the end of the season, the plants on that route are twice as big as the other plants." He laughed. "I kind of feel sorry for the other guys, like I'm playing favorites or something."

He told me this as we were standing on the top of a hillside, looking out over strawberries, cherry and peach trees, all planted in the glacial till soil of the Okanogan River. Later, when we returned to the greenhouse, Billy knelt and ran his hand through the sticky leaves of the tomato plants, an expression of deep satisfaction on his face.

"Are you going to talk to them?" I asked.

He cocked his head to the side, a slight challenge in his eyes as he kept his hands buried in the lacy foliage. "How do you know that I'm not?"

"What do you mean?"

Billy grinned mischievously. "Haven't you ever been touched in a way that said more than a thousand words?"

I swallowed. I might have shivered. I knew exactly what he meant. I laughed or smiled awkwardly, but I didn't give him the real answer, the one that leapt immediately to mind.

Not enough, Billy. Not nearly enough.

When I left the farm that day, Billy gave me a tomato plant. It was a Sun Gold, a prodigious producer of tangy orange fruit. "Do I need to keep this in the greenhouse?" I asked him.

"Nah, plant it outside. The stress of the weather will make it strong."

"Should I plant it under?"

"You can take off some leaves and plant it deep, but don't make it go twisting and turning. I don't like that. Those people who plant their tomatoes upside down—I won't even sell my plants to them. How would *you* like to be hung from your heels?"

I drove back to Seattle with the tomato in the rear seat, delighted to be taking a small piece of Billy's farm home with me. I knew I would not be able to equal the affection he lavished on his plants, but I was determined to try.

I might even try talking to them.

If Billy taught me about tomato love, the other thing I learned that year was tough love. I learned about pruning.

I knew what pruning was, of course. I had grown up around trees and vines. Pruning meant taking off deadwood, or controlling growth, or shaping the plant into what you wanted it to be. Cherry trees get pruned, grapevines get pruned, but I had never heard of anyone pruning a tomato. With their sticky leaves and soft stems, tomatoes seemed an odd candidate.

Tomato pruning, it turns out, is something else entirely.

Tomatoes come in two types—determinate and indeterminate. It was right there on the tag, though I had never noticed before. Determinate tomatoes set all their fruit around the same time; they tend to sprawl. Indeterminate tomatoes will continue to grow and set fruit until frost. Indeterminate tomatoes like to be staked. They like to be pruned.

Left to their own devices, tomato plants will make more branches. For almost every leaf an indeterminate tomato puts out, it starts a new branch, nestled in the crook between leaf and stem. That branch will grow and make more branches, so a tomato plant ends up looking like a family tree—with dozens of new lines branching off here and there. This makes for a lot of foliage. It does not make for a lot of fruit.

My tomato jungle the summer before was a prime example of a family tree gone wild. No wonder nothing had ripened. The sun could barely penetrate the thicket.

I resolved to do better. I staked my tomatoes to wooden poles and old branches we had lying around the garden. I followed the example of my mother's ragbag and ripped up a pair of beloved pajamas that had finally sprouted holes, and I used the strips of fabric to tie the tomato stems to the poles. Every time I saw the blue checked fabric fluttering in the breeze, I thought of the friend who had given the pajamas to me and smiled. It was much better than throwing them in the trash.

Then, I kept watch. When I saw the leaves of a new branch forming in the crook of a stem, I pinched it off and threw the acrid, sticky leaves away. I was vigilant. I took this pruning thing seriously.

The problem with pruning is that it requires hardening the heart. It's difficult to cut back an otherwise healthy plant. It was easy to pinch off the new tomato leaves, but what if I missed the new branch for a week or two? What if it was fully formed? *What if it had flower buds on it?* Left alone, those buds would become tomatoes. For a gardener who spends her time trying to make things grow, it's hard to also be the executioner.

I was no stranger to this dilemma. I had been dealing with it for years.

When my mother lived in California and I still lived in San Francisco, she called me every January or February. "The wisteria needs to be pruned. Can you come do it?" She had planted the climbing vine when we first moved into the house. Over the years it had wrapped itself around a support column for the upstairs deck and woven in and out of the railing. On its own it would have taken over the place. Every spring, it needed to be cut back.

I don't know why my mother thought I was more capable of doing this than she. Perhaps, after years of doling out tough love to her children—having to be mother and father, good cop and bad—she was sick of it. She didn't want to be a hard-ass. Not even to her plants.

Most every year I spent an afternoon tangled up in wisteria. I took out deadwood; I clipped thin or unhealthy shoots. I pulled out the wayward vines growing between slats of the deck and inching under the shingles of the house. Over time they could do serious damage.

Every year, as I did this, I thought about my own life. If pruning allowed a plant to focus its energy by getting rid of its excess, what in my life needed to be pruned? Was I spreading myself too thin, going off in all directions, trying to do too much? The answer was usually some version of yes.

Maybe there were friendships that no longer fit, clubs or activities that didn't hold my heart the way they once had. I was coming to realize that trying to do everything meant not doing anything terribly well. It was time to make choices. What in my life had become deadwood? As painful as it sometimes might be, perhaps a quick snip was better. Sometimes you have to cut things back in order to grow.

Standing in the side garden that summer, I had the same thoughts: Where did I need to focus; what was I ready to let go of? So much had changed with the move to Seattle. I no longer rushed about. I took walks now, long baths, and I woke with the sun. I hadn't been unhappy in San Francisco—busy had been fun, it had made me feel important—but I was developing a life now that suited me better.

And yet, there were gaps. I had a growing community in Seattle. I was finding my people, making the sort of friends who understood who I was without explanation, the sort of friends who showed up when you needed them.

The outer ring of my life was becoming well populated, but the innermost circle was a question mark. Leaving San Francisco had let me step back and look at my life. I had been too busy to really pay attention. It had been all go-go-go all the time, and I hadn't bothered to check where the boat was heading. When you are reasonably happy and well occupied, you don't look at the big picture. You don't ask if this is the shape of the life you really want.

When it came to that, I didn't have a vision. I had grown up trying to be there for other people, trying to be what I thought they wanted from me. I knew what I wanted from my career, but I hadn't thought about what I wanted for myself. I was too busy trying to keep my world afloat.

What freedom I had found had come from leaving—from moving away from everything I knew. Living on the other side of the world, I'd no longer had to try to hold my family together; I hadn't been trying to make anyone else happy. It had felt like such a relief.

I hadn't been trying to build anything either. What life I constructed on the other side of the world would eventually be torn down. It was never meant to last. I couldn't imagine anything lasting.

I was used to pieces that didn't fit together—the constant hustle to shore up the cracks before everything washed away. I had no confidence I could build a successful family of my own. My mother hadn't been able to, and she was stronger than me. I knew I could fall in love and be loved in return—I had proof of that. But I never believed those I loved would stay.

The one man I should have been able to trust had left. My father had attached wooden blocks to the pedals of my tricycle so my small feet could reach, then he walked away and never came back. There had been no one to teach me to ride.

A relationship, a home, a family of my own—did I want these things? I'd spent so many years saying I didn't, I no longer knew if it was true. And here I was, spending my time and energy tending my mother's garden. I was not growing my own.

Life had taught me it's easier to pretend you don't want what you think you cannot have. It's safer that way.

With dutiful pruning the tomato plants grew tall and were laden with ripe fruit: red, yellow, and orange. When the arborist my mom hired came by one September day to look at our fruit trees, she told me there were more ripe tomatoes in my garden than in any garden she had seen in Seattle that summer. I felt like I had won a prize.

When my mother came back from Canada at the end of the summer, the staked plants were heavy with fruit, and the cherry tomatoes—Billy's included—had grown up the side of the house, reaching nearly six feet tall. Every day we harvested baskets of them, tangy and sweet, bursting with seeds.

It was hard to know what to do with so many cherry tomatoes. I started roasting them. The baking sheets went into the oven filled with cut fruit that emerged soft and oozing, flesh and skins collapsed, flavor made bolder by the low heat of the oven. We couldn't stop eating them.

The tomatoes rarely made it into anything I cooked. Mostly we ate them with our hands, standing in the kitchen, exclaiming how good they were. And when the tomatoes were gone, we ran our fingers along the battered baking sheet to sop up the oily residue, rich with tomato flavor, not wanting to waste a single drop. That sucking fingers thing my mother sometimes does— this time I was standing alongside her, doing it myself.

And in those moments, my mother and I were together. We were eating cherry tomatoes from the garden. We were smiling at each other, trying to outmaneuver the other for a particularly luscious bit of syrupy juice, grinning like crazy conspirators.

14

. . .

FALLING

WHEN I FIRST MOVED to San Francisco, I lived in the upper flat of a large rambling house with three roommates, one of whom was moody. Whatever the cause of her discontent, I always knew the exact shade of her bleakness as soon she opened the door.

"It's pretty amazing," she'd say. "You know when I'm in a bad mood before I even get in the house."

I smiled; I shrugged. The truth is she didn't take pains to hide it. She was a social worker. After a long day of listening to other people, I think she just wanted to vent.

The other part of the truth is that I am the oldest child of a single mother. We are a special breed.

I have only vague memories of the yelling that happened when my mom came home at night, exhausted and worn out, and had to face everything that had gone wrong over the course of our day. Mostly I know she yelled because she's told me that she did. And because I remember when I got old enough to yell back. But I remember her coming home angry and at her wit's end. I remember trying to make it better.

Oldest children of single mothers develop a special sort of sensitivity to what is happening around them, a skill honed by trying to make things work when they so clearly do not. It's a version of the same skills women have developed throughout history. When you are not in a position of power over your own destiny, when the quality and shape of your days are dependent on the favor of others, you become sensitive; you become savvy. You learn to soothe and coddle, influence and meddle, all under the radar. Call it female intuition, call it outright manipulation, call it womanly wiles if you like. I call it survival.

My childhood gave me the skills to read emotions, to suss out power dynamics and unspoken dangers. It has allowed me to live in countries where I do not speak the language—it's not the words that are important; listen for what isn't being said. As with a sixth sense, sometimes I just knew.

I always knew when my mother wanted to talk to me. Not the quick conversations about where I left the pruning shears or when I was going to move the table in the garage (the one with *my* stuff on it). I knew when her panic began to kick in. My mother functioned on the basis of fear. There was no middle ground. If too much time went by and she hadn't heard from me, I was probably dead.

I didn't always call her when I got that feeling. Sometimes I was busy; sometimes I didn't want to cater to her fear or be ruled by it. Sometimes I didn't want to talk, or I just plain forgot. And sometimes I thought that—if she really so desperately needed to check that I was still breathing—she could damn well call me herself.

But I always got that feeling, a prickle on the back of my neck. I knew when my mother needed me.

I got it the summer I was staying in her house, in late July, when the corn was up to my waist in the side garden and wispy threads of golden-green corn silk had emerged. The whole thing amazed me and made me want to stop people on the street to tell them, "Did you know *I grew corn*? It's true!"

That July I ignored the feeling about my mother. I had a friend in town for a few days, and we were busy exploring the city. By the time we got home at night, it was too late to call. In the mornings we headed out early, trying to make the most of our time. And if my mother really wanted to talk to me, she could call me herself. At least that's what I told myself.

I called a few days later, once my friend had gone home, and got the answering machine. I left a rambling message and hung up. It often took a few tries for us to connect in the summer. I called a day or two later, and my mother answered the phone.

"How are you doing?" I asked.

"I'll tell you in a sec," she said. "Let's talk about you first." My mother rarely wanted to talk about herself. She always, however, wanted to talk about me.

I told her my news—my friend's visit, the fifteen-mile hike we had gone on, the state of the garden, the state of my corn: all the mundane details no one else would be interested in. I thought nothing of the conversation. My radar was silent.

Finally I turned the tables: "So, how are you doing? What have you been up to?"

"I've injured myself," my mother said slowly, carefully. "I've broken my back."

Suddenly the world got very quiet. *"You've what?* Tell me what happened!"

She had walked out of the cabin first thing in the morning, dew still on the deck. While going down the four small steps that led to the ground, she slipped, feet flying out from underneath her, and landed on her tailbone. She bounced down the wooden stairs, *clunk, clunk, clunk*. Somewhere between step one and step four and somewhere between vertebrae T5 and T8, my mother had broken her back.

The pain had knocked the wind out of her, and she'd lain gasping on the ground. "I still don't really know what happened," she told me.

Because the cabin sits on its own few acres, because no one would hear if she shouted, and it could be a week or more before anyone came by, my mother did the only thing she could do. Once she caught her breath, she crawled up the stairs on her hands and knees and into the cabin. She somehow made it to the telephone.

She was taken off the island and to the nearest hospital that afternoon in an ambulance, a journey that involved two ferry-boats. She spent the night there, but there was little they could do for a series of fractured vertebrae. Eventually they sent her home. Each detail she shared felt like a knife.

"Why didn't you call me?"

My fear gave me an edge like anger, though mostly I was angry with myself. How could I have ignored that feeling? How could I have known my mother needed me and not responded?

"I thought about it," she said, her voice unusually small and calm. "But it's not like there was anything you could do."

"If *I* were hospitalized in a foreign country, *wouldn't you want to know*?"

"Of course," she said. "But that's different. I'm the mom."

In that moment, it didn't feel different to me. It didn't feel different at all.

Though I lobbied for her to return to Seattle, my mother decided to stay in Canada. "In Seattle I'd only have you—and maybe your brother, but he's really too busy. I have more community here," she told me.

My mother had never been good at making friends. In Seattle she had barely tried. But on the island there were people she'd known for years and a stronger community ethic. People

were looking in on her, she promised me. They had been bringing her food.

It felt like a million small pains to be so far away when all I
wanted to do was feed her soup and watch over her, but I knew
I wouldn't change my mother's mind. I've almost never been
successful at that. And in another few weeks I would be there,
with the niecelets, a visit that had already been planned.

"Really, I'm just lying down until then anyway," she promised.

It took all I had not to jump in the car and start driving
north. If I left immediately, I could make the cabin by nighttime
or first thing in the morning.

"I promise, all I'm doing is resting and reading books," she
said. "I'll be *fine*."

She didn't tell me until later about the weeklong therapy
workshop she conducted, despite her broken back, for students
who had come from all over the world to study with her.

"I didn't want to disappoint them," she said meekly when I
got angry. "I spent most of the time lying down. But, yeah, that
was a really dumb idea."

Because of that, what had been predicted to be a ten-week
recovery would take longer; it would be more painful.

It didn't matter that she was the mom. I should have jumped
in the car. I should have known she needed me. I should have
listened when she called out.

The island where my family used to live lies between the long
and narrow landmass of Vancouver Island and the Canadian
mainland, one of dozens of islands scattered in the Strait of
Georgia. They rise wooded and rocky out of calm, clear waters,
the coastal range towering above to the east. I did not know it as
a child, but after years of travel, I can now say it is one of the
most beautiful places on earth.

What I knew as a child was that it was fun. It was fun to run barefoot down to the beach and build entire villages out of driftwood and pinecones. It was fun to jump in the lake for afternoon swims and to straddle the logs that sometimes floated on the water. It was fun to pick berries and to see the horses, sheep, and goats that dotted the island. It was fun to collect bottles of milk delivered to a small wooden box nailed to a tree just off the road.

My memories don't go all the way back to when my mother and father put me, only five weeks old, into the car and drove from California to Canada to live on this small island. We didn't know then that it wouldn't work out. But while they were there, they made friends—friends who had two boys a little older than me and would go on to have another two. Years later, my brother and I spent summers with them, all six of us kids running wild. These are among my favorite memories from childhood.

But memory is fickle. Memory twists and changes and grows larger than the thing it started out as. In my memory we spent every summer on the island, though I know that not to be true. Somehow those golden days when all six of us ran barefoot and blond-headed became magnified and pushed out more mundane recollections. In my mind the summers stretched endlessly, and we jumped off rocks into the lake as if we were immortal, as if we could fly.

Those summers were the only extended time my brother and I spent in a family with two parents. There were routines and boundaries and meals served at the same time every day and enough grown-ups to worry about the grown-up things. I still had to look after my brother—and he didn't always make it easy—but I could be more of a kid than I usually was. It felt like freedom. It felt like flying.

I hadn't understood the pull this place had on me until I had been away from the island for several years in my twenties.

When I returned, after a five-year absence, I rode my bike to our friends' house to spend the day with them. As I cycled out of evergreen woods and saw their fields unfold in front of me, the orchards and gardens of their small farm with the house lying low and views across calm waters to the mountains beyond, I was surprised by the feeling that welled up in me, unexpectedly strong and vehement.

This is home.

Miles away from my own house and mother, this was the one place in all of my childhood where I felt secure. Sometimes home has nothing to do with family or even with love; sometimes home is simply the place where you feel safe.

I wanted my nieces to know the island the way I had, to jump into the lake and build things on the beach and run through the woods as if they were wild. They were growing up with security and safety I could not have dreamed of as a child—two parents, generous financial means, and a whole cast of characters in their extended family. But I wanted to give them the island. Maybe it would be to them what it had been to me: a wondrous and golden place.

My mother wanted the girls to know the island as well. The year before, she had flown the three of us up on the floatplane that lands on the island once a day, a trip more expensive than flying from Seattle to New York. We had stayed only a few days, but we walked the rocky beach and collected shells, and the girls swam in the lake and picked berries. It had been just a taste, a preview. This year the plan was a full week.

"Are you sure you still want the girls to come, with your back?" I was feeling protective of my mother, not at all sure she was up to the energy of small children.

"I couldn't do it alone," she answered, "but if you're there, it will be fine."

I might have been worried about my mother, but my friends were worried about me planning to take small children on a car trip that can run ten to twelve hours. There were three ferries and one international border crossing involved. In the summer, there were often long lines.

"I don't even think I'd volunteer to do that with my *own* kids," Sarah said when I explained the journey to her.

"You're taking two kids on a ten-hour road trip without an iPad?" another friend asked. "Go buy one immediately!"

But I remembered long drives with my brother when we were young. Our own childhood visits to the island had started in California and took three days. I didn't want to plug the girls into a device; I didn't want to lose the time with them. I told my friends we'd be fine.

I was more concerned about leaving the garden. I had asked my brother to water while I was gone. I felt bad for burdening him, but if I was looking after his children, he could at least check on my tomatoes.

I used to take care of my mother's leafy yard in California, when I was still living in San Francisco and she was gone all summer. Every year she wanted to go over what needed to be watered, and when, and how. "While you water in the front, put a drip hose on the ferns by the side of the house," she used to tell me. "Not a full stream, just a dribble."

"I know, Mom. It was the same last year and the year be-fore." It was the same every year, but each June she insisted on telling me again, as if she didn't trust me to remember.

I now knew that trust was not the largest factor when you're leaving your garden. You might trust the person who will be filling in for you, but they don't know the plants the way you do; they don't have a relationship with them.

Would my brother notice if the pumpkin vine I had nursed back to health started to wilt again? Would he think to pluck the budding heads off the basil plants so they'd continue to produce leaves? And what about blossom-end rot on the tomatoes? Would he know what to do about that? A garden is a complicated and nuanced thing. It's not just watering—I had a relationship with the garden that my brother would never be able to approximate.

You might think looking after his children would be far more complex, and in some ways it was, but the girls generally told me when something was wrong. My tomato plants would suffer in silence. Making sure they were thriving required a close eye and consistent concern. In some ways, children were more straightforward.

I made one concession to entertainment on our road trip. I asked the girls what music they liked. At five and six years old, Cate and Abby already had pop favorites. But when I went to download their requests, I couldn't find the connection cord and searched and searched without luck. With an early departure the next morning, I finally gave up. We would be on our own, accompanied by the radio and our own imaginations.

It was an hour into our drive when I told the girls about the music. The early excitement had worn off—the anticipation that had them hopping into the car almost before I had come to a full stop in front of their house. They each had little roller bags and books to read and were more wired than I had ever seen them. We were going to the island! We were going to see Grandma! Their parents stood in the driveway and waved as we pulled away, but the girls barely looked back.

An hour into the journey, things had calmed down. We were driving through the green farmland of Washington's Skagit Valley. The sky had grown light, and I braced for the first meltdown of the trip when I told them I'd failed to bring the music I promised.

"That's okay, Tea-tea," Cate said amiably. "You can do it some other time."

"Actually," said Abby, "our favorite game is called Song Turns."

"How do you play that?" I asked, cautiously optimistic at their good nature.

"We take turns singing to each other," said Cate. "Here, I'll show you," and she launched into a tune I had not heard before. Then Abby took a turn; then I sang a song.

We sang our way up the Skagit Valley, across the Canadian border, and onto the large ferryboat that would take us to Vancouver Island. The windows were down, the air was soft and salty, and suddenly it felt like vacation.

We explored the huge boat and, as we approached the city of Nanaimo, we ate Nanaimo bars from the cafeteria, sweet with layers of custard and chocolate. I hoped the girls would remember this special treat. I hoped it tasted like adventure to them.

As we drove up Vancouver Island, on the highway that had been built in the years since I was a child, we played the alphabet license plate game, and when we reached our next ferry terminal just minutes after the boat had pulled away from the dock, the girls didn't complain. Not one cross word. I was impressed with them; I was proud. My friends' fears had been for naught. I'd had faith in us all along.

When we missed the ferry, I pulled out two small kites that I keep in the back of the car, and we walked down to the docks. This was a spot I knew well. My brother and I had spent hours of our childhood here, waiting for the ferryboat. The girls unfurled their strings, and the kites sailed up into the sky, dancing on the breeze, reflecting in the calm waters of the harbor. They laughed in delight, and I felt a throb in my throat.

Here we were, years later—not me and my brother, but me and his children. Somehow we had survived the years of struggle; we had made it through, messily, with our wounds. But here was another generation, these golden girls in their sundresses, to redeem all that had been difficult and dark. It felt like uncommon grace and I wanted to cry from the sheer wonder of it. Instead I watched as their small kites swooped gracefully upward into the widening sky, lazy arcs soaring over still-shimmering waters, as our laughter filled the harbor and echoed out all around.

The most arduous part of the long day—the only arduous part—was the final twenty minutes. We were off our third ferryboat, on the island at last, but still had quite a drive to the cabin. I remembered this from my own childhood, the mounting anticipation as each familiar landmark came in sight. But the girls didn't know the island the way I did; they didn't know what to look out for. I tried to help them.

"If you look to the left," I said, "soon you'll see the funniest library ever." And they looked and around a corner it came: the open-air hut that served as unofficial lending library for the island, where you could exchange a book you already had for one that was new to you or purchase it outright for fifty cents a paperback and a dollar a hardcover. The girls laughed.

"If you look to the right, soon you'll see the harbor." And there it was—a flash of golden light on water, oyster floats, rocky outcroppings.

"Soon we're going to see the lake. Do you remember swimming in the lake?"

The girls did remember, and they were excited, but twenty minutes can stretch into infinity. Soon Cate was squirming in the back of the car. "Are we *there* yet? We've been driving *foorrreeevvveeeerrrr!*"

"We're almost there," I promised. *"Almost there."*

Finally we turned off of the pavement and bounced down the dirt and gravel road to the cabin, driving under evergreens whose boughs swept the top of the car. My mother heard the engine and hobbled out on the deck, and the girls tumbled out of the car and ran toward her. When they met on the stairs, two small children embraced their grandmother, and she bent her frizzy gray head toward them, and I sat in the car and felt a throb again in my throat.

It all felt so fragile suddenly. This tenuous bond we had, this life. One wrong step on the stairs and it could tumble down around us. The only binding agent, the only glue we had, was love, and sometimes it felt like we didn't have enough of that.

Our visit unfolded as expected—only a week but it felt longer in all the best ways. We picked blueberries at our friend's farm, coming home with flats of juicy purple fruit. We made fruit crisps, staining the inside of my mother's enameled pot a deep purple, and ate them with milk on the deck for breakfast. We swam in the lake and visited our friends at their farm. But often Grandma needed to lie down, to rest, and when she did the girls played board games with her.

Sometimes I needed to get them out of the cabin to burn off energy. In the afternoons, while Grandma rested, the three of us took long walks down the dirt road, past the horses that lived in a large paddock, and into the woods. One day I brought a paper envelope with us, and we collected seeds from the purple fox-glove that dots the forest so we could plant them in the garden when we got home. And another day we drove to the other side of the island so my mother could have an appointment with our friend John.

John was a Chinese medicine doctor and had been treating my mother since long before the back injury. He and his family had moved to the island in the years I was away, and when I returned I was surprised to find them friends with my mother. John and his wife, June, often flew through Seattle when they traveled, and when they did they stayed with me. It was on one of those nights that John tried to help me understand my mother.

"You're never going to get out of her what you want," he told me. "You can try and try—but it's never going to work. You need someone warm and comforting, but that's not her. So go find yourself a granny and appreciate your mother for what she is."

No one had ever spoken to me about my mother like that before—as if they knew her better than I did. And how did he know what I wanted? He barely knew me.

I had always assumed my mother wasn't warm because she had never experienced warmth; that she couldn't delight in me because no one had delighted in her. To John, however, this was better explained through Chinese medicine. Each person has an elemental type, he told me. My mother's type was metal, he said, which is rigid and unbending and demands perfection. Metal is sharp. Those who were metal were often steeped in sadness and overly critical.

My type was earth. We are known to be compassionate nurturers. Earth people like community. They like to cook and dance and be joyful. None of these were things a metal person would find valuable.

I needed cozy, John told me, but metal was the wrong place to find cozy. Metal was more cutting than cozy.

Was that why I was always bitten by my mother's comments, by her judgments? An earth type could be motherly to a metal type, but not the other way around. I could give my mother what she needed, but she could never do the same for me.

"You can try," he said again, "but it's like getting water out of a stone. You have, what—ten more years together? Why waste that time trying to get something she can never give you? Why not appreciate her for what she is good for?"

"What is that?"

"Metal is good for inspiration. She could help you set up a business."

This felt like cold consolation. When one wants comfort—wants a *mother*—getting a business partner seems like a lame trade.

Later, however, I thought about my mother and her willing-

ness to jump in on large projects—like sheet mulching, or growing eighteen varieties of tomatoes. Her enthusiasm extended to
other things in my life as well. When the publishing company I
had worked for many years earlier turned down an idea I had for
a book, my mother suggested I do it anyway. "I'll pay for the
first printing," she told me.

These offers of hers scared me. I wasn't the type to plow
forward the way she did. If I shared plans with my mother, she
often grew frustrated with my slow progress. She didn't understand I had to battle my own fears before I could move forward,
that I was made of less stern stuff. Rather than encouraging, her
support felt like pressure.

My mother believed in my ideas more than I did. Her faith
in me was terrifying.

The girls liked going to John and June's house because it was
home to a large rabbit named Pushkin who roamed loose on the
deck. Occasionally June had to scare off hungry bald eagles
when they tried to carry Pushkin off in their claws for a juicy
meal.

While my mother had her appointment with John, June told
us of a new animal who had taken up residence that summer.

Walking in the woods one day, she had found a baby deer
lying next to the body of its dead mother, who had been at-
tacked by wolves. Knowing the baby would die without protection, she brought it home and bottle-fed it milk. Now the deer
wandered the property, his hindquarters still marked with the
white spots of youth.

"If you are gentle," June told the girls, "you might be able to
pet him."

The four-year-old who lived next door had named the baby
deer, so when June walked to the kitchen door and called for the
animal she did it by name.

"Squeak-fish," she called out gently. *"Squeak-fish!"*

Soon Squeak-fish the deer came, and the girls were given carrots and warned not to make sudden movements. Then, as if in a fairy tale, they walked out the kitchen door and stood calmly as the baby deer ate out of their hands and nuzzled them with a soft black nose. Abby and Cate slowly ran their small hands over his white-speckled rump.

They looked up at me, and I could see it in their eyes: *wonder.*

When my mother was done with her session, the girls ran to tell her about Squeak-fish (*"We pet a deer, we pet a deer, Grandma, we pet a deer!"*), and John quietly took me aside. "I need to talk to you," he said. In the midst of the children's excitement, it was easy to slip away and we stood awkwardly in the hallway next to the bathroom door.

"This injury," he said, "it's a big deal. The severity of it, and your mother's age. If she doesn't recover—and I mean really recover—it could start a downward spiral."

"What can I do?"

"You need to make sure she takes it easy—really easy."

"She's not good at that."

"I know. That's why you need to make sure that she does."

I nodded silently, soberly.

John looked at me hard. "She really needs to be nurtured—that's all she wants."

I dropped my eyes to hide tears that had suddenly formed. I didn't really care if John saw me cry. He would think I was sad or scared for my mother, and I was. But that's not why the tears came.

John would never know what rose unbidden in my throat; I would never tell him. I would take care of my mother, I would do my best, but I would never ask the question that came to me that day.

But who is going to nurture me?

15

· · ·

BITTER HARVEST

THE FIRST FEW WEEKS after she returned from Canada, my mother slipped on the stairs twice. Her feet just slid out from underneath her. "My slippers don't have any traction; they're too slick on the carpet," she said.

That's when I yelled at her not to wear those slippers—the same way a parent yells at a child who has just barely avoided an accident, an anger that comes from fear. *Do you know how close you came? Do you know what could have happened? Do you know how much I love you? Do you know how scared that makes me?*

"Okay, okay," she said. But still she wore those slippers.

I knew then I wouldn't be going anywhere that September, not to San Francisco as I usually did each September, not to Japan as I had hoped. I needed to stay in Seattle. I needed to keep an eye on my mother.

She was supposed to be lying down, resting, but often I

found her in the garden, loppers in hand, trying to cut back the blackberries, the rhododendrons, the azaleas.

"You're not supposed to be doing that," I said, feeling like a teacher assigned to yard duty.

"I know. I just need to clip a few—"

"Give me the loppers. I'll do it. You go lie down."

"Okay, okay," she reluctantly agreed. It wasn't as if she could argue—*she had a broken back*. But before I knew it, she would be up doing something else. It felt like a giant game of Whac-a-Mole. Every time she popped up, I told her the same thing: *I'll do that; you go lie down*.

The doctors wanted her horizontal, resting, for ten weeks, but my hummingbird mother had no sit-back-and-relax setting. She functioned on one of two speeds: *overdrive* and *off*. Once she was done sleeping, she wanted to get up and be productive. She did not want to lie down. She didn't want to rest. She didn't know how.

Resting now meant spending time on a platform bed in the living room. Her own bed was too soft, not supportive enough of her back, so we set up a futon next to the large picture window in the upstairs living room. From there she had a view down the long yard to the fruit trees in the distance. She could see the whole garden.

This meant she could see every weed that needed to be pulled, every branch that needed to be trimmed. Before I knew it, she would wander out to take care of them. That's when I would find her with loppers or pruning shears. That's when I would tell her to go inside and lie down again.

The bed in the living room made me uncomfortable. It reminded me of the elderly gentleman my mother had bought the house from. We'd heard he had spent ten years in a bed set up in the living room. "This is where I am going to live when I can't get out of bed anymore," my mom said when we first saw the house. "You can all come to pay your respects."

My mother was getting older. She was becoming more frail. I was prepared for that—as prepared as one can be. I could imagine taking care of her once she was bedridden.

What I was struggling with was the timing. She had only been in Seattle two years. She wasn't that old. She was still my bossy, stubborn, know-it-all mother. How could she be bedridden?

I hadn't thought we'd be here so soon.

It had been odd living in my mother's house that summer; it was even odder to be there with her. Always before when I visited, it had been in a house where I had once lived—a house that was also my home. This new house was very much my mother's territory.

Little things set us off. When I woke up in her house that first morning after moving, I noticed my mother had put the toilet paper on the wrong way—with the paper dangling out the bottom rather than hanging over the top. I changed it back, thinking she was off her game. Then I noticed the downstairs bathroom was the same.

"Did you *change* the way you put on the toilet paper?" I asked when she returned from Canada.

"*I did,*" she said, a note of glee in her voice. "It took me a long time after you kids left for college to decide how *I* wanted the toilet paper. I like it better this way."

Parents shouldn't be *allowed* to change what they've taught their children, I fumed silently. All my life I had been trained to hang the paper over the top. Now she was changing the rules?

Of course the real worry lay deeper: *If we could no longer agree on toilet paper, what hope was there for our relationship?*

My mother was growing older and changing in ways I could not anticipate or control. Ground I had thought solid was shifting beneath my feet. It felt like a small betrayal, as if I didn't know her anymore. Maybe I never had.

One morning, as I came up from the downstairs office where I was still camped out, I heard a voice talking on the phone. There was no one else in the house, so it had to be my mother, but it sounded nothing like her. She sounded younger, softer. I hesitated on the stairs. If I walked into the kitchen, she would see me, and I knew her manner would change.

That summer on the island my mother had made a friend. I had met her myself when I took the niecelets up there. My mother's new friend Priya had brought her granddaughter to the cabin. The three young girls piled into the hammock with their sun-bronzed legs and their long braids, and I had a moment of wonder remembering how I had made island friends in the summer when I was a child, so glad they were getting this experience too.

I didn't speak with Priya much. I was exhausted by the logistics of our visit—keeping an eye on the girls and my mother all on my own, making sure she rested and they got the activity young kids need and everyone got fed and somehow the dishes got washed. When Priya and her granddaughter arrived, I sat back and watched the girls swing in the hammock and their grandmothers sit in the sun and talk, but I noticed right away that something was different.

My mother does not have relationships of parity: She is mother to her children, teacher to her students, therapist to her clients. She has few friends. This means there is rarely anyone to call her out—to tell her she's being irrational or suggest she rethink a decision. She is the law. This also means there is no one for her to lean on.

Perhaps it was the broken back, perhaps it was just a good match of personalities, but my mother was leaning on her new friend. There was a softness between them I had rarely seen, a level of comfort unusual for my mother. And when Priya left, she gave my mother a jar of homemade yellow plum compote.

"On some miserably gray day in Seattle, you can open it up

and remember summer," Priya said. My mother looked at her and smiled.

I knew then that my mother had told Priya things—how she hated Seattle in the winter, how she struggled. Priya knew more about my mother's life than I did.

It was Priya on the phone that morning. I heard laughter, giggles. My mother sounded like a young girl. I wasn't trying to eavesdrop, but I sat down on the stairs and listened—not to the words, which were muffled, but to this noise I had never heard before: the sound of my mother's girlish laughter.

That fall my mother was scheduled to have a laser treatment on her skin. Afterward she would have to stay out of all sunlight for three days. There was a dark downstairs room where she could camp out during the day, but she would need someone to bring her food and water until the sun went down and she could move about the house freely.

"Is this a chemical peel?" I asked, surprised that my mother would be doing anything so image focused.

"No—I don't care about things like that," she said. "You know that."

She wouldn't tell me much more. Only that the doctors were going to treat some spots on her face that were cancerous and had suggested she do the whole thing. She would have to be dropped off and then picked up at the end of the day. That was it. When it came to her medical condition, I was on a need-to-know basis.

She had always been like this. Once her doctors had accidentally called me with the results of a medical test. I was her emergency contact, and when they couldn't reach her, the office called me to say her neurological exam had come back fine. My mother was furious.

"What neurological test?" I asked. "Why did you need one? Are you having problems?"

My mother wouldn't talk about it. No matter how I tried, the conversation was closed.

"*I'm* going to be the one who has to make medical decisions on your behalf if you are incapacitated," I told her. "Don't you think I should know what's going on?"

But still, she refused to talk. She had no problem discussing her concerns about my health—she aired them frequently—but her own was off-limits.

I drove her to the hospital the morning of her procedure. It was in an area called Pill Hill by Seattle locals, in reference to the many medical facilities there.

"I always get lost here," my mother said, staring out the window at the view of Lake Union as we drove down the highway.

"It's the James Street exit, right?" I knew the neighborhood, though I did not know which of the many hospitals we were going to.

"Yes," my mother said. "James Street, and then turn left."

"What do I do next?" The left turn had taken us up the hill to a large intersection. "Right or left?"

My mother looked around blankly. "This is where I always get lost."

"Come on, Mom. Right or left!" I sat poised on the edge of the intersection, the cars behind me starting to honk.

"I don't know."

"What do your directions say?" She had pieces of paper in her hands, printouts from the hospital with notes written on them.

"I didn't write the directions down."

"Jeez, Mom—*come on.* You've been here before. When you get to this point, what do you do? Right or left?"

My mother looked around the neighborhood as if she had never seen it before. "When I get to this point, I call the hospital, and the nurses tell me what to do."

"*Mom.*" I swerved across oncoming traffic just before the

light turned red again and we were stuck there. I held my tongue and began to drive down the street. "Does *this* look familiar?"

"None of it looks familiar."

"What about this?" I pulled up in front of the entrance to one of the hospitals. "Is this where you've been?" But it was Harborview, not Virginia Mason—wrong hospital. I finally exploded in frustration and fear.

"This is no way to live!" I shouted at her. How could the mother I had known—always in charge, always in control—be reduced to this? For a second I took my eyes off the road and glanced in her direction.

My mother—so small she sat on cushions in the car, using them like a booster seat—was staring at the road, tears beginning to slip down her stony face. She made no move to wipe them away.

"I know," she said quietly, still staring straight ahead. "Don't be angry with me. Getting old is no fun."

Winter in Seattle is a challenging prospect. The cliché is that it rains all the time—and sometimes it feels like it does—but rain is not the hard part. What is hard is the dark, the bleak. On the worst days, there is no dawn, just a subtle lightening of the pervasive gray. On the worst days, you keep the indoor lights on all day.

At the height of winter, the sky doesn't begin to lighten until after 8 A.M., and sunset starts at 2 P.M.; it is fully dark by 4 P.M. Office workers commute in pitch black. People hibernate. Unless you are proactive, you may not see your friends until spring.

The garden called it quits in the winter as well. In some ways this was a relief—incessant rain means the grass barely grows; most weeds go dormant. If you do a good job of cleaning things up in the fall, the garden sleeps throughout the winter without much need for tending or maintenance. Even things that continue to grow slow down. The rate at which kale produces leaves in the winter requires great patience.

Being with my mother that winter required great patience as well, which I didn't always have. I buried myself in work, hiding out in the downstairs office, though work was not going well either. The economic downturn was making itself felt in all corners. Where before work had been, if not plentiful, at least available, budgets had now been slashed. And I had spent the summer working less than I should have. When it came to my career and finances, I was bailing water on a sinking ship. That winter felt hard all around. Inescapably hard.

The only bright spots were the afternoons the kids came to play. I was usually working when they arrived, but soon I heard them gallop to the stairs and they burst into the downstairs office, hurtling their small bodies at me. "Tea-tea!" they cried in excitement. "Tea-tea!" On days when my work felt stalled, when it felt like I was failing, having small people simply delighted to see me was like unexpected sunshine, cheerful and warm.

My mother threw herself into these visits. She spent the day before shopping, buying foods she knew the kids liked, making sure she had organic milk in the house. The day after their visits she spent cleaning up the games or crafts scattered around, rehanging dress-up clothing in the closet, sweeping up crumbs and bits of food from under the dining room table. I knew she loved them coming, but I wondered how long she could keep it up.

The days Graham—the girls' new brother—came to play were easier on her. His needs were simpler, the pace of a baby slower. She was perfectly happy to sit on the floor and roll a ball back and forth with her grandson, for hours if he wanted. It reminded me again of how much seniors can offer, what a good match they can be for small children.

The baby looked exactly like my brother—blond hair with stickup cowlicks and big wide eyes. It was as if my brother had managed to clone himself. As Graham started crawling and toddling on uneven legs, it felt like we had gone back in time. To see him playing on the same Chinese carpet my brother and I had played on was to feel as if thirty years had somehow vanished, as if I were seeing my brother again as a child. As if no time had passed at all.

To see my mother with the baby was even more affecting. When my brother was born, she had been overwhelmed, newly abandoned by her husband, suddenly responsible for the care and support of a family of three. There had been no time to enjoy her baby. She was focused on survival.

Now, thirty-odd years later, my mother no longer had to work so hard. And here was a child who looked exactly like the child she had missed out on. She poured herself into the baby, marveling at his development, his intelligence.

"Do you know what Graham did today?" Her conversation opener on the days he had come to play was always the same.

"Why don't you tell me?"

"I was making lunch, and he wanted his quesadilla, but they weren't done, so I told him we needed to be *patient*. Then, later in the afternoon, when we hung the birdseed balls in the yard, I looked for birds and finally said I guessed they weren't coming. Do you know what he said then?"

"I don't know."

"He looked at me and said, 'Grandma, *patient*.' Can you believe that? That's pretty abstract thinking. I tell you, that kid is just *so smart*!"

My mother was smitten. Like I had never seen her before.

When I went upstairs to get a cup of tea, or saw the two of them together in the garden, a wave of emotion washed over me. My mother with her gray hair, a little boy who looked exactly like my brother. They walked hand in hand, looked at each other with such adoration; they spent hours playing with blocks or studying some small rock or pinecone in the garden. She had all the time in the world for him, and he loved her for it.

Sometimes, if you're really lucky, life gives you a second chance.

Once the children had gone home, however, it felt as if all sunshine had gone out of a bleak sky. The house was big and cold, and my mother and I were left there, just the two of us with our sharp edges, puzzle pieces that never seemed to fit together.

We fought that winter—and not just about toilet paper. On the worst days, we fought about deeper things: how judgmental she was, how I feared I disappointed her, how we each failed to meet the other's needs. John may have used Chinese medicine to explain our dynamic, but that didn't make it any easier to live with.

"Loving you is like trying to hug a porcupine!" I shouted at her in the midst of a particularly bad fight. "Do you realize that?"

My mother stopped and laughed, a short, angry bark. Then she paused.

"Yes," she said slowly. "I imagine it is."

The next day I could barely remember what had set us off. It almost didn't matter. The subtext to our arguments was always the same.

Why don't you see me for who I am? Why can't you accept and love me the way I need to be loved? Why are you making this so hard?

It was late at night that October when I got the email from my friend Sarah: *Are you still awake? Can we talk on the phone? I have something to tell you.*

Sarah and I had seen each other a week or two before, on a walk through the wooded trails of Carkeek Park. She had told me how busy her schedule was, how she didn't have time for the medical appointment she had made. "Why don't you postpone it until after your deadline?" I asked. She had a book project taking up too much of her time.

I had plenty of friends in Seattle by then, but none with

whom I shared as many commonalities. Sarah understood my fierce Northern California politics; she had lived there herself in high school. We were both trained journalists, with the cynical second-guessing that brings along with it. She also shared the gallows humor and worst-case-scenario thinking I had been raised with. I had assumed this a feature of my mother's personality but was coming to realize it was cultural. Sarah's ancestors had seen the same hard times mine had.

It was this worst-case thinking that made her ignore my suggestion to reschedule a medical screening for which she was ten years too young on a week she was on deadline and had no free time. It's good she didn't listen to me—for there she was on the phone, telling me she had been diagnosed with cancer.

There would be surgery, she said, and then they would see. They had caught it early. Had she waited ten years for the screening, as medical guidelines recommended, she would have died. If she survived, it would be entirely due to modern medicine and her own fiercely suspicious nature.

I sat there on the phone that night wondering if my mother was right—perhaps we *should* expect the worst, perhaps we should plan on it. Life increasingly felt a fragile and dangerous proposition. We were all dangling by the thinnest of threads. How easy to start spinning out of control, how easy to plummet into the chaos. Really, it could happen anytime.

I spent the night after Halloween at Sarah's house, having dinner with her husband, Daniel, and the kids. She was in the hospital and had asked if I would help out. Her little girl—the baby we had all passed around that hot summer night—was a toddler now, and the evening routine was hard to do alone.

That night one of the boys refused to eat vegetables but still wanted candy afterward. When I said no, he started crying—big tears that turned his face red. Daniel was putting the baby to bed, and I pulled the crying child onto my lap. He resisted at first, then went limp, snuggling his head under my chin and sobbing as if his world had broken in two. When he wrapped his arms around my waist, it took all I had not to cry along with him. I knew exactly how he felt.

His mother's in the hospital; give him the damn candy already.

When chemo started I began going over for dinner on Wednesdays, when Daniel worked late, bringing with me a big pot of soup. When you cannot make things better, when there is nothing you can do to make a problem go away, it's therapeutic to chop vegetables. It makes you feel like you are accomplishing something.

Each week as I chopped the vegetables—kale from the garden, mustard greens, chard—I thought about all I hoped for my friend. I hoped the soup might make her strong. I hoped it might bring her some comfort. I wanted her to have something easy to heat up on days when she was busy or not feeling well. It was only soup, but it was all I had.

When the soup was ready I took the still-warm pot off the stove. I doled some out for my mother, then carried the rest to my car. I put the pot on a kitchen towel on the floor of the passenger seat and drove to Sarah's. She and Daniel lived only ten minutes away from my mother's house, the soup still warm when I carried it into her kitchen, dodging small, excited children. "Tea's here!" they shouted. *"Tea's here!"*

When we sat down to dinner—the two boys, the toddler, Sarah, and I—the family went around the table, everyone sharing two good things about their day and one bad thing. The bad things were predictable—a broken toy, a lost book, perceived unkindness on the part of a sibling, all the small but significant heartbreaks of childhood. The good things ranged from a favorite dessert to a new game, or a visit from a friend. But on the nights I was there, each of the boys said that one of their best things was that I had come for dinner.

After the toddler was asleep, after I had read the latest chapter of *How to Train Your Dragon* with the boys, after we had cleaned up the leftovers and had a cup of tea and a chat at the table, the alarm for Sarah to take her medication would ring, and it was time for me to go. She always thanked me, over and over again. Over and over again, I said it was nothing, it was my pleasure, and really it was.

What I don't think she knew, what I don't think she ever understood, was that she was helping me through my long, hard winter as well. Those evenings with her and the kids felt warm; they felt joyful, even in the midst of fear and uncertainty.

To walk through the door and have small people cheer just because I had shown up (*Yay!* It's *you!*) was an antidote to my mother's grimness, her frustration with me, and my own feelings of failure at work and at life. At Sarah's I felt appreciated in a way I rarely did at home. I could make her daughter laugh just by hiding behind a doll blanket. I marveled at the boys' latest Popsicle-stick creations, and they glowed bright with pride. With my own family, I felt guarded, always fearful of judgment or rejection. Being at Sarah's felt validating. It felt redeeming.

Sometimes a kitchen-table chat with a friend is exactly what you need to soothe the barbs of the day. We all have our small but significant heartbreaks. We all need help in hard times. But sometimes help works in mysterious ways. I might have been helping my friend, but she was helping me just as much.

That is the mark of a good friendship, I thought, driving home late at night on quiet, dark streets. When you each give all you have and you both think you are getting the better deal; when walking through the door of a house that is not your own feels like coming home.

And week by week, soup by soup, we got through the long, hard winter together.

PART FOUR

. . .

GATHER

16

. . .

PLANTING THE SEEDS

FOR AVID GARDENERS THE season starts early, in January or so, even in the Northwest. It may be cold and wet outside; it may be muddy and dark before 4 P.M., but January is the month the seed catalogs start arriving in the mail. January is the month gardeners begin to dream.

It might sound outrageous to compare the pages of garden catalogs to pornography, but really, it's just a different kind of lust. Hidden in those shiny centerfolds is a perfection that also calls with a siren song. To a gardener, pictures of juicy tomatoes, beguiling flowers, frilly lettuces, and fruit trees hung thick with cherries tempt and tantalize. This perfection may be equally unattainable—but don't mention that in January or February. That time of year anything is still possible.

That winter my mother suggested we take a seed-starting class. I said yes because I knew she wanted to go. After an evening spent learning about vermiculite planting mixes and grow lights, she came home and set up a sprouting station next to a south-facing window. There she hung lights that would give the seeds more hours of illumination than our short winter days could provide. She spread out a heating pad from the nursery to keep the soil warm and filled containers with the special mix used for starting seeds.

Some gardeners, I was beginning to realize, do not go to the plant sale in May and buy their entire garden, pre-sprouted and already three inches tall. Some gardeners grow their own.

There were many reasons for this, as I was learning from the gardening books I read those long winter nights. Cost is the most obvious, but seed diversity was also important. A hundred years ago there were 497 varieties of lettuce available from commercial seed companies in America; now there were only thirty-six. We'd gone from 285 cucumber varieties to a mere sixteen.

Each lost variety led us down an increasingly precarious path, reducing the resilience of our food supply. The greater selection of plants that were grown, the better chance there was of surviving a crop failure. Had the Irish not been so dependent on a single potato variety in the 1800s, the blight that caused the Great Potato Famine would not have been so devastating, and the course of human history would have been different.

The U.S. government had, at one time, understood this. Starting in 1839, seeds were collected, propagated, and distributed by the U.S. Patent and Trademark Office—they were considered essential for the growth and security of the nation. By the end of the 1800s, the government was distributing more than a billion seed packets each year.

Commercial seed companies didn't like this. It was hard to make a profit on a product that could be obtained easily, traded, and saved from year to year. It took forty years of lobbying, but in 1924 an association of commercial seed companies convinced Congress to shut down the government distribution program.

The seed breeding being done by commercial seed compa-

nies wasn't a new pursuit—its roots go back to the dawn of agriculture. For generations, this is how our species survived. At
the end of each growing season, the biggest beans, the sweetest
tomatoes, were set aside. They were not for the dinner table but
to start next year's garden or crop. But it wasn't until the 1900s
that seeds became big business.

The first step toward profit was hybrids: crosses of plants
developed for certain beneficial characteristics. Hybrids do not
grow true—if you saved the seed and planted it again, you
wouldn't get the same product. At the end of the season, farmers
who grew hybrids had to buy more, improving the bottom line
for agricultural companies but making farmers dependent on an
outside source of seed. If you wanted to grow Early Girl tomatoes, you had to pony up each spring for seed.

The next step took place in 1980. Until that point, a single
plant could be privately owned, but the genetic code that made
up the plant belonged to all. The Supreme Court's ruling in
Diamond v. Chakrabarty changed that—a scientist who developed a new plant or life-form could now apply for a patent and
own the rights to it. The same government that once distributed
seeds for free was now issuing patents on nature. The staff of
life—once considered so vital to our survival—had been priva-
tized.

Seed companies were quickly bought up by chemical and
pharmaceutical corporations. A single corporation, Monsanto,
between 1996 and 2013, acquired seventy-nine different seed
companies. Bayer bought up thirty-two, Dow Chemical twenty-
four. While some independents remained, there are farmers who
would tell you it's hard to keep the big agricultural businesses
out of your fields or garden. The small, seemingly homespun
company you may be buying your seeds from could be owned
by one of the giants.

It wasn't just seed profits these companies were interested in.
Chemical companies developed seed strains that were resistant

to their pesticide products. A farmer could now plant a field of corn and spray the whole thing with weed killer. Because the corn had been bred to resist that particular chemical combination, the weeds would die, and the corn would continue to grow. Seeds were a way to get farmers to purchase more chemicals, which led to problems with pesticide runoff into rivers and streams and tainted land.

For this reason and for others, there were those who said seed saving was a political act. Hybrid seeds could not be saved from one year to the next, but others could—and had been for centuries. They were called open-pollinated seeds. Some open-pollinated seeds were heirloom varieties, stretching back generations; others were more modern, but in each case you could save and share the seed. I started looking carefully at the seed packets I bought, choosing companies I knew to be independent and committed to preserving seed diversity. To grow them, it seemed, was to save them.

That winter my mother started her seeds, laying the sprouting mix out in a long tray of small, square compartments, tucking away in each of them a tiny seed capable of turning into a plant, a flower, a zucchini vine. A week or two later, when the seed had sent out a shoot that broke the soil and grew upward, reaching for the light, it felt miraculous. This is how we have survived as a species; this is how we have reproduced and grown strong: this simple but deeply wondrous ability to produce our own food.

As my mother was tending her seeds, spring was slowly coming to Seattle and to the garden. I was used to it now—the gradual way that spring comes in the Northwest. I had missed the subtlety at first. I had been expecting spring the way it comes in California: early and insistent. I hadn't noticed the music had already begun to play.

It started with snowdrops blooming tiny and white. I had noticed little clumps of these scattered around the garden the year before and brought them all together in a border at the base of the kitchen stairs. Now snowdrops were one of the earliest signs of a change in season. Their small white flowers felt like hope.

Next came the crocuses, sticking their thin necks up from the earth, and daffodils, which grew tall before revealing hidden gold. There was forsythia as well, delicate sprays of small, cheerful yellow flowers. I had planted a forsythia that Knox had given me in a spot where my mother would be able to see it from her desk. It hadn't bloomed yet, but there was always hope that this year it would. Gardening is the kingdom of second chances.

Once my mother's seeds were on their way, she turned her attention to the next thing on her list. My mother wanted to get chickens.

We were not new to the world of chicken raising. We'd had them in the country, when my brother and I were young. We had chickens again in my teen years, when the man my mother bought our house from had a flock and didn't want to take them with him. Did my mother want chickens along with her four-bedroom, two-bathroom home set on a leafy quarter acre at the base of Mount Tamalpais? Of course she did: fresh eggs for her children.

Her children, who thought sleeping in on weekends a universal right of all teenagers, were not impressed when we had to wake up early to let the chickens out. When it came time to clean their coop, we were less impressed still.

Now, in Seattle, my mother wanted to do it again, but I was dubious about what I had dubbed Project Chicken. For all the same and different reasons.

"Who is going to open and close the chicken coop when you're gone all summer?" I asked. "You know it gets light at 5 A.M. in the summer. You can't expect me to drive up here every day just to let chickens out."

I had finally moved out of Orchard House that spring and

back to my hilly neighborhood, into the building where I had kept my name on the waiting list. The view wasn't as stunning as in my magic carpet ride, but there was more room—a full bedroom, French doors, hardwood floors, and five closets that were all mine. After the long winter at my mother's house, after living out of boxes, I was happy to be there. Happy to feel like I was returning to my own life. Chickens had no part in that.

"Well," she said, "I'll just have to figure something out."

A few weeks later my mother told me the neighbor girl would be opening up and closing the chicken coop. The neighbors had their own flock, and once she took care of them, she would come next door and do my mother's chickens. My mother would pay her five dollars a week. She was eleven years old, and this would be her first job.

When my mom wants to get something done, she gets it done. This time she wanted chickens.

On an early spring afternoon, I met my family at Seattle's Portage Bay Grange so the kids could pick out their chickens. I was a few minutes late, and as I parked my car, the girls came running. They had both gotten haircuts—my sister-in-law finally giving in to pleas for shorter hair and bangs. For a moment I didn't recognize them. Who were these tall girls with bobbed hair swinging as they bounded toward me? Surely they could not be *our* kids. How were they growing up so fast?

When Graham toddled after them, I picked him up and held him close for a moment. This one still smelled like a baby, but even that would soon pass. It was all going by so quickly.

The kids got their chickens that day—tiny little fluff balls. My mother wanted Ameraucanas, an American-bred version of the Araucana known for their blue-green eggs. This meant our fluff balls were not the charming yellow chicks of Easter. Our fluff balls were a somewhat unappealing shade of brown.

"Can we hold them? Can we hold them?" The kids jostled

to be able to see the chicks in the small, folded brown box they had been placed in.

"No, sweetie. Not yet," my mother explained. "They're too upset from all the commotion. I'm going to take them home. You can come over tomorrow and hold them. We don't want to put them in shock."

At this point the toddler started crying. He just wanted to hold his fluff ball.

That weekend we gathered at Orchard House, on a rare sunny spring day. The chicks were living in a large cardboard box filled with wood shavings in the kitchen. There was a lamp set up next to them with a red lightbulb that was kept on day and night. It looked like they were getting light therapy for jaundice, as newborns sometimes do. The chicks were fine—they just had no mother to keep them warm. The light would do that job for them.

The kids pushed toward the box, each wanting to be the first to hold his or her chick.

"No," my mother said firmly. "We must all be calm and gentle. We don't want to upset them. They don't know you yet—and you're really big and scary compared to a little chick."

She had the kids sit cross-legged and, one by one, slowly picked up the tiny balls of fluff and placed each one in a child's small outstretched hands.

The looks on their faces when they got their chicks said it all—wonder, pride, excitement, the mystery of holding new life, tender and warm. That look was my first hint that I might have been wrong about Project Chicken.

The kids selected names for their chickens—they had picked them out before they got to the house that day. They had decided on their own, without any adult input.

That is how we ended up with chickens named Pancake, Cookie, and Raisin.

The chicks were keeping my mother busy with ministering to their needs in the kitchen. One of the chicks developed a blockage of the cloacal vent—where the eggs (and everything else) come out. This is known colloquially in poultry circles as pasty butt.

It is easy to remedy with a Q-tip and warm water, but I steered clear. It was another piece of Project Chicken I wanted no part of.

The chicks were clueless about manners, my mother said. Water dishes and feed dishes were things to be walked through. "They really are a mess," she reported, aflutter and distracted in a way that made it seem as if she was actually enjoying it all. It reminded me of the day, a few years prior, when she told me she was thinking about getting a dog.

"But you don't like dogs."

"I don't *dislike* them," she said, "and studies show people with pets live longer."

I'd read those studies too. I wondered if the longevity was a result of added companionship, or if having a pet gave you something outside of yourself to take care of—an occupation and feeling of usefulness that might otherwise decline with advancing age. When my mother suddenly had to hang up the phone, to get back to the chickens, I thought about this some more.

The chickens, it seemed, were going to be my mother's dog.

While my mother was busy tending chickens, I was busy in the yard. I had decided to plant an asparagus patch, like the one my mother had when we were kids.

The asparagus in my mother's garden emerged from the ground in spring, thin stalks pointed upward. Once they got tall enough, you could pluck them at the bottoms of their stems, these odd-looking vegetables. We've all seen bunches of asparagus in the store, bound together by rubber bands, but to see them emerging singly from damp soil is to be reminded of something primeval. They look spooky, ancient.

The taste of asparagus just plucked from the ground is unlike anything else. It is tender and sweet, a mild flavor—clean and fresh and almost nutty—so full of water it practically melts in your mouth. There are notes of mineral in the background, something you can't quite put your finger on. Asparagus reminds me of clear skies, freshly cut grass, and daisy chains. It is the flavor of spring.

You weren't supposed to pick them all; I remember that. In the first few years, you're barely supposed to pick asparagus at all. It needs to establish its root system. Then you begin to harvest, always leaving some stalks to go to seed. From the scaly, needle-like tip of the stalk, branches emerge, impossibly thin. Eventually they grow into feathery fronds that sway in the breeze. From a distance, a forest of asparagus going to seed looks like a delicate green cloud hung with tiny red berries, an ethereal version of holiday decorations.

If you were the sort of child who grew up reading books about fairies, as I did, an asparagus patch was fertile ground for the imagination.

When it comes to asparagus, ground is important. You have to have a patch of earth you are willing to devote on a permanent basis—asparagus are perennial and, once established, will come back year after year. That patch also has to be cleared of weeds and other plants that might compete with the asparagus.

Despite having half an acre of space, we had no such spot in the garden. The vegetable beds were all taken; the side garden was strawberries and summer produce. The raspberry and herb patch took up room; we had planted kiwi vines. The rest of the garden was ten-foot-tall rhododendrons, lawn for the kids, and a big wild field of nothing but weeds. The asparagus would never make it there.

There was one spot I thought might work—a ten-foot square

behind the greenhouse. It was out of the way and could accommodate two beds of asparagus with a path down the middle. It
was, however, as weedy as anything else in the meadow—quack
grass, bindweed, dandelion, horsetails. All things nearly impossible to get rid of. Even if I removed every bit of root and sifted
the soil, as I had for the strawberry patch, it would all come
back. There was no way to separate this small patch from the
wilderness it lived in.

Unless you separated it physically, unless you put up a barrier. I wasn't sure it would work, but I started looking at bamboo
barrier—rolls of thick black plastic about four feet high often
dug in to prevent the spread of bamboo roots, which can turn
weedlike and take over.

If I could dig a trench around the asparagus patch and line it
with bamboo barrier, would that keep my little kingdom rela-
tively root-free? I could weed anything that grew on the surface;
it was the underground roots and rhizomes that scared me. Nature is not to be trifled with. Nature does not mess around.
When you are trying to plant an asparagus patch in an otherwise
wild and weedy meadow, nature can be a witch.

We had a little help in the garden that spring. My mother, on
occasion, hired men to do heavy lifting and digging projects.
Her back was still recovering, and I wasn't always around to
help—and never at the exact moment she wanted to get started
on a project.

That spring there was a rotating cast of characters. There was
one man who had a tendency to stop midway across the lawn
with a wheelbarrow of wood chips, put the handles down, wipe
his brow dramatically, and sigh. We called him The Poet, and I
wondered what his story was. It seemed clear he had not come
from a life of hard work.

My mother worked alongside these men, often growing irritated with them. "Some of them don't work very hard, you

know," she told me one day. "Some just want to take breaks. I'm nearly seventy-five, and they can't keep up with me."

"Perhaps you should be taking breaks as well."

"I don't have time to take breaks," she retorted. "I'm almost seventy-five—*I don't have much longer!*"

Our favorite of the men was Leonardo. He was older, perhaps in his fifties. He kept up with my mother, and he liked to talk to me as he worked, and he was the one to whom I explained my idea for creating a bamboo barrier moat to protect a future asparagus patch. He got it immediately.

"Oh, yeah," he said. "That will work. That's a good idea."

I wasn't sure if it was or not, but it felt nice to have a vote of confidence.

We worked together—Leonardo digging the deep trench for the barrier, me clearing the worst of the weeds. As we labored, he began to talk.

"I used to work in the asparagus fields," he told me. "Down in California."

"Really?"

"Yeah. Asparagus grow good in Washington. When you're ready, plant them in rows like this." He stopped and showed me the correct spacing. When he stood up, he looked at the patch we were working on. "With this much space, you can grow enough for a family of ten."

I smiled and nodded. What he said made me want to laugh and also made me sad. How many people in Seattle these days had families of ten?

In all the world, I didn't have ten people in my family. With the addition of the three kids, I was directly blood related to five people. That wasn't nearly enough.

Leonardo left at the end of spring, bound for Alaska to work the fishing season. I hoped he would come back, but we never heard from him again. I wanted to show him how the asparagus crowns were doing. I wanted to thank him for his help and advice. I wanted to share our asparagus with him. He had felt like part of the garden family.

The chickens grew quickly, but they were still small. They moved into temporary quarters on the deck, where they had more room but could still be brought in at night for warmth. Chicks don't lay eggs for four to five months. Because my mom wanted eggs sooner, she bought two pullets—teenage chickens— who would start laying earlier. She named these chickens herself: Domino and Snowy.

Domino was speckled black and white all over. She was a Dominique, America's oldest chicken breed, dating to the Colonial period. In my head, however, I called her The Dominatrix. She was mama hen of the chicken coop.

Domino arrived along with a smaller chicken, also a pullet, named Snowy. Though they were different breeds, Domino and Snowy looked like mother and daughter. Domino was bolder; Snowy hung back, moved slow. One day, my mother told me, she saw Snowy nestle up to Domino and Domino put a wing around her.

"I think she's going to be a really good mother," she said.

Snowy seemed to be struggling those first days, and my mother was often on the phone to the grange where she had purchased the chickens, getting advice on how to help. She followed all instructions, but Snowy did not seem to be recovering.

Five days into her time with us, Snowy was dead.

"Dead?" I repeated when my mother telephoned me with the news. "How can that be?" Had we done something wrong? Was it our fault?

My next thought: *How are we going to tell the kids?*

"The store wants me to bring Snowy in, so they can do an autopsy on her," my mother said.

"Are you kidding—an autopsy on a chicken?"

"Yes. They only had her for a day before I bought her. They want to find out what happened, so they know if it's a problem with the farm she came from."

When the autopsy results came back, we had our answer. Snowy the chicken had died of leukemia. "That's why she was moving so slow," my mother explained. "Her lungs weren't fully developed; she never would have been able to lay eggs."

My mother seemed to take the news hard, and so did Domino. Eventually the little chicks were put in the coop with her, but she never bonded with them the same way. Every time someone came walking up to the chicken yard, she trotted over and started to chatter and cluck. I always imagined her saying: *Thank goodness, a grown-up I can talk to! You have got to get me out of here. These hyper babies are driving me up the wall.*

As for the girls, they learned about Snowy on their own. Little Graham brought the news home with him from one of his visits to Grandma's house and told his sisters.

"What did he say?" I asked, curious to know how a toddler explains death. I had a hard time explaining it myself.

Abby looked at me with clear eyes, not at all upset by the topic.

"He said: 'Snowy dead. Grandma needs new friend.'"

We had a family brunch in the garden that spring, with the addition of my sister-in-law's family. Her parents had recently relocated to Seattle from the East Coast, and her sister came as well, bringing her two children, just a little bit younger than Abby and Cate. My mother doesn't entertain much, so to have everyone there was a rather big deal.

I had spent the prior year looking for a good outdoor table for the patio. The ones I liked were expensive—a new teak dining set can run more than a thousand dollars, sometimes two.

Instead I kept an eye on garage sale listings. Months and months went by without my finding one I both liked and could afford.

Then, just before my mother's birthday, just before our brunch, I saw what I was looking for: an extendable wooden table with six chairs. It was late at night, and I quickly emailed the seller, hoping to be the first to respond. When I spoke with her on the phone the next morning, I asked where she was moving.

"California," she said. "We have kids, and my husband's family lives there."

"I understand completely," I told her.

My obsession with dining tables was not new. My first big purchase in Seattle, before I ever thought I would live there, had been a dining table with long benches. It seemed like a symbol of the life I was yearning for—one that was slower, where we were all less busy and I could gather friends and family around for meals that lingered. The truth is I barely had any friends in Seattle at the time, and my family was held together by the most tenuous threads, but if I had the table, maybe they would come.

The table reminded me of a Dutch film, *Antonia's Line,* about a woman who returns to her village in the aftermath of World War II and builds a life for herself, befriending many of the town's quirkier characters. On Sundays they gather for a luncheon in the courtyard of her farmhouse, and over the years, the table they eat at grows longer and longer as more people join and more babies are born and life continues forward in all its sweetness and sorrow.

When I woke up early on my mother's birthday and drove across the bridge over Lake Washington to pick up this picnic table, that is what I was after. I wanted to gather the people I loved; I wanted to feed them. I wanted us together as life continued forward, in sweetness and sorrow.

We didn't all fit around the table that day—perhaps it already needed to be made longer. There were seven grown-ups and five kids, who quickly ran off and came back with the croquet set and pounded in the wire wickets. Croquet on our lawn was an interesting proposition. So many dandelions had blown over from the field and taken root that, even when the grass had been mowed, the ball did not roll straight—a mat of dandelion leaves or a patch of moss might shoot it off unexpectedly in a new direction. A friend of mine called it the "off-road" version of croquet: a more unexpected and exciting game, dependent on luck as much as skill.

The kids weren't old enough to really play. Mostly they hacked at the ball with mallets almost as tall as they were and were pleased when it moved at all. My brother and sister-in-law brought champagne and orange juice, and I brought glasses from my apartment, and the grown-ups sat among blooming tulips and irises and sipped drinks, and I had one of those moments I sometimes have where I wonder: *Is this really us? We look so WASPy and prosperous. How did we get from that old house in the country—from a single mother just trying to keep it together—to here?*

In truth, if you looked beyond the flowers, the garden was weedy. The patio of the cottage was cracked—whole pieces being pushed upward by the roots of the huge maple that had once towered over the yard. Even though the tree had been cut down years ago, and then ground down farther by an arborist my mother hired who swore he had killed it, the tree was still putting up shoots each spring, still trying to come back from what should have been irreparable damage, still trying to grow.

Perhaps that's how we got here: We never stopped trying to grow.

That day the girls showed their cousins around the garden, this place they thought of as their own. Abby had memories of a time before the garden, but Cate did not, and for Graham there had never been a time without it. As a baby he had spent afternoons napping in a woven Moses basket on this lawn where we now stood. The lawn he now ran across on short legs, sometimes tripping and tumbling, trying to keep up with his older sisters and cousins.

"Follow me," Cate told them, taking the lead. "Stay on the path—we're going down to the meadow. Here, I'll show you the good places to hide." She toured her cousins around the garden.

After we had eaten the scones studded with last summer's blackberries, the frittata of new broccoli sprigs, and the salad made with fresh cilantro from the herb garden, the party broke up. As everyone got ready to leave, people wandered out to the driveway on the path that ran along the side garden with the strawberry patch at its top. The same strawberry patch I had spent so many hours laboring over, cutting out the matted quack grass block by block, sifting through the soil for any remaining bit of root.

"This is where the strawberries grow," Cate told her cousins, gesturing to the green plants festooned with white-petaled flowers. "They're not ready yet, but just you wait, because they are the *best strawberries ever.*"

Even my sister-in-law, the one I had not been able to convince to come pick berries that first spring with the girls, had been won over by the sweet fruit.

"When are the strawberries going to be ready?" she asked. "They are my favorite."

17

. . .

HOW TO GROW A COMMUNITY

IN THE YEARS WHEN I was trying to decide between Seattle and San Francisco, I heard a speech given by a chef—Dan Barber of the Blue Hill restaurants in New York. He told of visiting an award-winning foie gras producer in Spain who didn't cage or force-feed his geese. They roamed and gorged themselves on crops he grew. What fencing he had was electrified on the outside only—to keep predators away. He did nothing to keep his animals in.

One day Barber and the farmer were in the fields when a flock of wild geese flew overhead. The farmer's geese began to honk, and the wild geese honked back, and suddenly the wild geese made a wide, sweeping turn and landed in the field with the farmer's geese.

Barber was amused. "They come for a visit?"

"No," the farmer said. "They come to stay."

Barber knew the DNA of a goose is programmed to make

them fly south in the winter and north in the summer. How could they suddenly change generations of evolution and stay at the farm?

When he asked this, the farmer shook his head. "Their DNA is to find the conditions that are conducive to life, to happiness," he said. "They find it here."

For me that story rang like the clear, high note of a bell. It was the best summation I'd heard of that thing we all look for—in a relationship, a job, a home. We are seeking *the conditions of our greatest happiness.* It is what we are programmed to do.

In trying to decide if I should stay in San Francisco or gamble on what I might be able to build in Seattle, I had made endless pro and con lists. But Barber's story made me realize it was time to make a new list. What were the conditions of my greatest happiness? Where was I more likely to find what I needed most?

When I did this, the results were surprising. Hidden in the list, the same concept came up over and over; it was something I hadn't truly considered before.

Community.

For all its woes and heartbreak, for every flea-beetle-eaten leaf of arugula and withered seedling, gardening is a fairly straight-forward thing. Nature will always throw curve balls—the unexpected late frost, the summer of drought—but in other ways the process is not mysterious. If you want to grow a sunflower, you plant a sunflower seed and make sure to water it adequately. A strawberry plant will, in most cases, give you strawberries. The instructions are there. How well you execute them is up to you.

Community, however, is a harder thing to grow. What seeds do you plant? How do you water? Books have been written about the micronutrients you need in your soil, the recommended balance of ingredients for a compost pile, but human life is a more complicated and variable thing. How do you find your people? How do you weave the sort of net you need—one you can cling to in hard times, one that will catch you if you fall?

My first summer in Seattle I wasn't looking for community. I had come to get away, to work on a book, to play with my nieces. I had exactly three friends in the city—enough to provide some social interaction but not enough to take me away from my work. I went for long walks and even longer bike rides and was happy with this smaller existence. It felt like a vacation from real life. I knew it was temporary.

Then I met a neighbor—a single mom with twin daughters just entering their teens. It was she who showed me how to mound up the raked leaves around my new raspberry bushes to mulch them. When I needed to get the large dining table I had bought home, she volunteered her minivan and wouldn't accept money for it. She invited me on berry-picking excursions in the country, and once or twice, when she knew I was racing a big deadline and consumed with work, she showed up on my doorstep in the early evening with a covered plate of whatever she had made her own family that night. "I know you're busy," she said. "Now you don't have to worry about making dinner."

I had never experienced anything like that. I had taken my neighbor to the emergency room when he was sick and needed to go, but it never would have occurred to me to make dinner for him. Seattle was a city, but sometimes it felt more like a village.

Not everyone experiences the warmth I found in Seattle. The city is known for a polite but sometimes frosty demeanor—people are friendly, but it can be hard to break through to actual friendship. They call it the Seattle Freeze, and there are many theories about the cause. Some speculate it goes back to the reserved personalities of Nordic settlers in the region; others point to the weather and annual hibernation that keeps people within their own social groups; still others cite studies that show Washingtonians to be some of the most introverted people in the nation. The rise of modern-day tech culture in the city probably doesn't help.

This was not my experience. The first winter I spent in Seattle, a man I had written a brief article about heard I was arriving in November and planning to stay the winter. "We must have you over," he emailed. "Otherwise you won't meet anyone until spring." That man became my friend Knox.

That first winter Knox invited me to a soup-swap party—an idea born when he grew tired of making big pots of soup and eating leftovers for a week. He figured his friends must be in the same situation and invited people over to swap their soup. When he put up a website, word spread; the event is now celebrated around the world.

That evening his house was crowded with friends, the windows steamy, rain jackets discarded on the porch. Everyone brought containers of frozen soup they'd made, and horse trading of sorts occurred, with people bragging about secret family recipes or tempting ingredients, the competition good-natured and humorous. Afterward we ate tacos in the kitchen, and I went home that night with six containers of soup made by people I did not know.

I doled the soup out over the next few months, each time marveling at how comforting it was to have food I had not made myself. It felt different than takeout. Someone had stirred this soup in their own kitchen. They had labored over it with all good intentions. And somewhere else in the city, someone was eating soup I had made.

Perhaps food was the key that unlocked the city for me. My first friends in Seattle were food writers, and through them I met more: writers and restaurateurs and enthusiastic home cooks. Food people are some of the most generous you can find— mostly they just want to feed you. There were picnics and potlucks and excursions to sample a new restaurant or café. Eventually I found myself invited into a club where we cooked from the same cookbook and gathered to share the results.

The first meeting I attended was a blur. We met at the home of one of the members. There were a dozen women, a few babies or toddlers. I knew only the woman who had invited me, but we had all cooked Diana Kennedy's Mexican food and sat together chatting and laughing for a few hours, a break from life and weekend responsibilities. Within the group were various connections and deeper friendships, but everyone was kind and friendly, and I went home having enjoyed my afternoon.

I was beginning to realize that friendship and community are not the same thing. Friendships are threads between people, either strong or tenuous, but community is a web. In San Francisco I'd had plenty of friends, but over time they slowly moved out of the city to far-flung suburbs for jobs or houses or better schools. They were still my friends, but I was losing my sense of community. I no longer had Paul living up the street, Michelle down by the park, Matt and Mireya a bike ride away. When I dreamed of gathering people around a table, it was community that I longed for.

It seemed to me that, these days, money often took the place of community. I could hire movers rather than asking friends, or order in soup or have tissues and prescriptions delivered when I was sick, rather than bothering someone I knew. The making of money also interfered with community—sometimes it felt like I was working so hard that I didn't have time for the kindness I might want to give. I sometimes wondered if, with money, we were chasing a false god, one that could not give us what we truly needed.

As our lives have changed, community sometimes now lived online. I could tell social media that I was sick and get responses of sympathy—from former work colleagues or people I went to high school with but haven't seen for years. It was nice, but it wasn't the same. I was connected electronically to people all over the world, but I didn't know the names of the people who lived across the street from me. If I needed to go to the hospital, my friends in London would not be able to help.

I'm not sure what it was about Seattle that made it feel different—the long winters, the rugged pioneer spirit passed down through history, the geography that puts it far away from almost everything else in the country. Or perhaps it was the economic boom-and-bust cycle. Seattle had known rough times, the sort that make people stick together.

Whatever it was, I liked it. Washington wasn't the rolling golden hills and dark oak trees of Northern California. The snowcapped mountains surprised me when I caught a glimpse of them; they stunned me silent. I was still unaccustomed to having to wait so long for spring. But in other ways—in ways that really mattered—it felt like home. It wasn't the home I had grown up in, but Seattle fit me. I felt grounded here.

Then there was the funny thing, the thing that felt almost mystical. My father had come from Washington, he had been born here. Though I knew almost nothing of his early life, I had researched his family enough to know that they had come to Washington in the 1800s. In the state capitol in Olympia, there was a portrait of my great-grandfather, a member of the Washington state legislature in 1925.

When I helped my mother pack up her garage that day in California, we had found books that belonged to my father, from classes he had taken at the University of Washington. His Seattle address was neatly written on the inside cover: *Brooklyn Avenue*. It was a name I knew well. It was the cross street to where my brother lived.

In a vast world of places my brother could have ended up, he had made his way to Seattle and bought a house just a few blocks away from where his own father had lived. A father he had never known. It was like those monarch butterflies whose descendants

migrate back to the same breeding grounds, though the grandchildren themselves have never been there. Somehow they just
know.

Perhaps, in ways that far exceeded my understanding, we
were all just making our way home.

The cookbook club met every other month, each time in someone's home. In late November we made Indian food, gathering
together on an afternoon when most people were battling holiday lines in shopping malls. There was a Persian food fest one
rainy spring, where the colors of the dried fruit hinted at blossoms yet to come. Our Julia Child feast included more butter
than anyone cared to admit, and for a January cocktail party, we
all dressed up and clinked glasses in a member's condo overlooking the twinkling lights of the city. By the end of that evening,
we were sitting around the edge of the indoor swimming pool,
fancy shoes long discarded, feet dangling in the water, talking
and laughing. It felt like an evening that would sparkle in memory for years to come.

There were offshoot events as well: apple picking in the fall,
weekend coffee-shop gatherings to craft and chat, an occasional
dinner party or camping trip. Postcards flew back and forth between members with surprising regularity. If I mentioned I was
sick, there were offers to bring soup, tissues, orange juice.

I was coming to realize that regularity was one of the keys
to community—gathering together, telling our stories, keeping
in touch. For some people, attending religious service works in
the same way, or team sports, or regular visits to the community
center or the coffee shop or the pub—people find comfort where
they may. Warmth and connection grow with repetition; the
reason for the gathering is almost immaterial.

One September evening we sat at a long backyard table lit by
candles, and I looked around at these women. In the period we

had known each other, there had been babies born, jobs lost and won, hard times with parents, breakups, minor breakdowns: life, in all its sweetness and sorrow. Through it all, every other month, we had shown up with our covered dishes, ready to share. Sometimes the cookbook felt like just an excuse to gather.

Now, when I rode my bike back from the garden, I passed the homes of people I knew—Martine, Lucia, Megan and Sam, Naomi and Brett, Kate, Renee, Jess and Jim. It felt cozy, as if the city was honeycombed with people I cared about.

I hadn't grown up with this, and perhaps that is why it mattered so much to me. My mother didn't have community when my brother and I were young—I'm not sure she realized it was an option. There's a give-and-take that happens in community that she didn't seem to have figured out. Perhaps she never had the time.

The garden was teaching me about giving—and about surplus. I had planted two artichokes the first spring. One made it; the other withered due to my own lack of attention. Knox gave me a third artichoke when he was dividing the plants in his yard. The first year or two they didn't do much, beside produce outrageously large silver-gray foliage that smelled a little piney, a little like a tomato plant. The leaves grew so large they blocked the path. They looked primeval. Every so often I had to hack them back just to get through.

Over time, however, they began to produce. The first flush yielded thirty-four artichokes, and there was more to come. I harvested them small and cooked them with potatoes and white wine and parsley, an Italian recipe from my friend Luisa's family, but there were too many to keep up with. When I mentioned this, the artichoke lovers in cookbook club raised their hands. A few weeks later I tucked some into Martine's mailbox and left a few more in a package with Kairu's doorman.

"I never knew artichokes had a scent," Martine wrote me in a note afterward.

It's true. Artichokes sold in grocery stores don't smell like anything. They are trucked in from California, days or weeks old. Even artichokes bought in supermarkets in California don't smell like anything. I felt pride in introducing someone to the real deal.

"That was the best artichoke I've ever had," Kairu wrote. "It cooked so quickly!"

I liked sharing things from the garden. With all this land, so much was possible. If I had extra, I wanted to pass it along. This was something my mother had never understood.

My mother was generous to strangers, to causes. She donated to many charities, served on the board of nonprofit organizations, sponsored students in developing countries. Once, when I was ten, we took in a Cambodian refugee to live with us. His family had fled the violence and genocide in that country. At the time we didn't have much to spare, but we had more than he did.

My mother might have thought her money could do more good elsewhere—and she may not have been wrong—but I think it went deeper. My mother never learned the give-and-take of community. She was okay donating where nothing was expected in return. To develop an exchange, to connect, was harder. You had to give, but also to receive.

I had problems with this as well. I was okay with the giving part, but the accepting made me feel awkward and indebted. I often tried to calculate the amount of money a friend spent on me, so I could adequately repay them. If I was given a forty-dollar present, I would pick up the tab for a forty-dollar dinner. I hadn't yet learned that true friendship transcends numbers.

If someone was *outrageously* kind—above and beyond the call of duty—it made me feel uncomfortable, unbearably so. I didn't know how to sit with that feeling; I didn't know how to submit to that kind of love. Instead of being gracious, I tried to pretend it wasn't happening. I tried to avoid the person who made me feel this way. Being outrageously nice was the easiest way to drive me away.

I knew it was ridiculous, but I couldn't stop myself. I had no model for this type of connection. Generosity on that level left me frozen and exposed, like a deer in the headlights. I had no-where to hide.

I lost friends this way, kind people who didn't understand why their gestures of affection were not being acknowledged.

Sometimes it seemed that I was too much like my mother: Trying to love me was like trying to hug a porcupine as well.

I knew this wasn't the way it should work. It made me feel good to be there for people I cared about. It would have broken my heart if any of my friends had been in need and not let me help. And yet, in turning down help, I was keeping people at a distance. By not letting them be there for me, I was preventing those bonds from growing. I knew it even as I was doing it.

The life I wanted—the community I wanted to be part of—was founded on the back-and-forth. That was how the web was built. I had to be okay with the discomfort. It was easier to stay on my own, but that wasn't going to get me what I wanted.

If the net was there to hold me, I had to learn how to be held.

The chickens had grown all summer, sprouting their adult plum-age and changing color. The baby chicks turned from scrubby brown fluff balls into beautiful hens. Their feathers were smooth shades of golden and russet red that glinted in the sunlight. All day long they darted around their yard with the energy of teeny-boppers. Domino, the older, white-and-black-speckled hen, looked positively bored with their juvenile antics.

As the summer progressed, they began to lay eggs. The first were small—the size of a large walnut—but they eventually grew larger and larger. By August we were getting four full-sized eggs almost every day. Domino's eggs were a pinkish brown, but the younger chicks laid eggs in shades of pale blue-green, like sea glass found on the beach.

With all the chickens laying, there were about two dozen eggs a week. I sent some home with my sister-in-law for the kids to eat and took some back to my kitchen, but I couldn't keep up with the production. I was reminded of a friend who grew up on a farm in the Midwest. When she was young, she said, eggs had not been a year-round thing. Chickens stop laying in the winter; eggs were summer food.

All summer I made frittatas and poached eggs. I put fried eggs on salads, on tortillas, on toast. But still the eggs kept coming. When I went out of town for nearly a week and came home to forty eggs, I laughed. We had an excess—an *egg-cess*. It was almost problematic.

I washed them up and put them in egg cartons and delivered some to my brother and sister-in-law. The rest I dropped off at friends' houses on my way home. I knew my mother would not approve—the eggs were *for family*. But we had plenty, and every day the chickens laid more.

When I ran up the stairs that day to leave eggs for my friend Kate, she opened the door.

"Hey, do you want some fish?" she asked.

I must have given her a funny expression because she laughed.

"My father-in-law went fishing in Alaska. Our freezer is full of fish. Do you want some?"

Usually I would have said no; I would have said I was fine. But I was trying to accept. I was trying to be gracious.

"Sure. I'll take some fish."

Kate returned with a package of salmon and a package of halibut.

"That seems like a lot," I said. "Are you sure? It's only a half-dozen eggs." I was still thinking generosity should be equal, that things should be even.

Kate waved off my concern. "We have a ton. Thanks for the eggs!"

This was what my mother didn't understand: When you pick the right people to be in your web, they give back. If you do it right, you let them. You say please and thank you, and everyone walks away gratified—having been of service *and* been served. This is how the web grows strong.

When I got home and put the fish in the freezer, I smiled. My mother would not have approved, but maybe her life had never felt abundant enough to include this sort of giving— generosity not to those who were starving or fleeing genocide but simply to be kind. Because you wanted to. Because you could.

But here is the thing that made me smile. Here is the thing I thought was funny.

The fish was worth more than the eggs I had given Kate; I'm pretty sure the fish was worth more than *all* the eggs I had given away.

Not that I was keeping track or anything.

That summer in the garden felt like a steamroller. I had gotten used to the overwhelmingness, the feeling like I was never going to keep on top of everything—not even of the weeds. But this year was different. It was drier than it ever had been. Spring had been unusually lacking in rain, something Seattle rarely lacks.

"Is this global warming?" I heard people say when it hit seventy degrees in May.

I liked it when we were playing croquet on the lawn in April and spreading out picnic blankets. By June, however, I could see the damage to the garden. The raspberries had not received their proper dose of moisture in the flower or fruiting stage, and the resulting berries were tasteless. In an average year, they were overwhelming—so many it was hard to keep up with them.

When it rained in June, as it usually did, you had to get picking, or the berries would soon be molding on their canes.

That year it didn't rain in June—it hadn't rained much at all—and the berries were so disappointing I barely picked any. They weren't good enough to eat. Instead of molding on their canes, they withered in the unexpectedly warm sunshine.

Water was something I'd thought about when trying to decide between San Francisco and Seattle. There are plenty of people who consider Seattle's rainfall a drawback, but I put it on the positive side of my pro-con lists.

In permaculture class we had seen maps created by the Department of the Interior that outlined areas of potential conflict over water—the whole Southwest, including California. When I thought about how the climate was changing, it had me worried. California had a year-round growing season, but not much grows without water. Seattle seemed a safer choice.

I felt a little crazy factoring precipitation rates into future life planning, worrying about drought or famine. I felt like my mother, expecting the worst, expecting the sky to fall. But perhaps I was also being like my ancestors, suspicious enough to ensure my own survival. A friend of mine who wrote about natural sciences had told me that animal migration patterns were already changing; they were heading to higher, cooler ground.

In all my consideration of climate, however, I didn't really think it would affect me. If water became an issue, it would be in the future, it would be in California. I hadn't thought I'd be dealing with drought just a few years later. I hadn't expected it in Seattle. But here we were.

A drought is survivable for a garden if you have enough water, but it means you must work harder. The watering routine that usually took an hour and a half now took twice that long; plants I had never watered before now needed it—perennials and fruit trees. Between general garden maintenance and watering, I was run ragged.

Early that spring my mother had arranged to have a catchment system installed to funnel rainwater off the roof of her house into covered holding tanks that could be used to water the garden.

Water catchment was not unusual in Seattle. For years the city had been offering rain barrels at a subsidized rate to residents. They were recycled food-grade plastic fitted with a spigot and connected to a downspout on your house. In times of intense rain, storm water runoff overwhelmed the city drainage system, becoming the largest single source of pollution in local rivers and the Puget Sound. It was better for the city to have water diverted and stored for future use. When I rode my bike to and from the garden, I passed many of these rusty-red barrels installed in people's yards and gardens.

I had suggested we get rain barrels, but my mother had done the city-issued fifty- or sixty-gallon barrels one better. The tanks she was considering had a minimum holding capacity of 250 gallons. Some were as large as 650 gallons.

"Are you sure we're going to need that much?" I asked, as we looked at the spot on the side of the house where the tank was to be installed.

"I figure if I'm going to do this—let's *really* do this," my mother said.

What she didn't say, what neither of us said, were the *what ifs*. But they hung in the air between us that damp spring day.

What if there was an earthquake? What if Mount Rainier erupted, as some said it was poised to do? What if climate change intensified and sped up? What if the worst came to pass? It would be good, then, to have as much water as possible. This was not drinkable water, but it could be boiled for cooking.

If the worst came to pass, we wouldn't be that picky.

We had all watched in frozen terror as a tsunami wiped out the coastal regions of northern Japan two years prior. Before that had been the earthquake in Haiti. That fall it was Hurricane

Sandy, a year later, Typhoon Haiyan. The worst *was* coming to pass for so many people. We needed to be prepared.

I couldn't tell if devastation was happening more frequently, or if modern connectivity just allowed us to watch it in horrifying real-time detail. Devastation had happened throughout history—war, pillage, fire, flood, famine. Those were the times that brought people together. Perhaps that was the truest definition of family: *the people you cared for in times of trouble, those you would shelter from the storm.*

I didn't want to think our times of trouble were here already, but I was glad to have gallons and gallons of water for the garden that summer—the fruit trees, the vegetables, the flowers. We needed it far more than I had expected.

None of my friends saw me much that summer; I was in the garden. My apartment quickly became the place I went to drop things, sleep, work, and leave. I showered there too, staining the bathtub with a dark ring made of garden dirt. My fingernails were never entirely clean. The needs of a garden in drought had taken over.

The physicality of it all surprised me. I remembered a young couple I once interviewed about the farm they had started. "This place beats us up," they told me, and I now knew what they meant. After nine hours in the garden, I woke the next day feeling like I had been battered, bruised in unexpected spots, sore in ways I never had been before. What was I doing this for again?

But sometimes, at the end of a long day in the garden, I looked up and noticed how the sunlight slanted through the tops of the blackberry bushes; how it was captured in the dahlias I had massed together, which now bloomed in fiery orange and pink, their pom-pom petals waving on long stems in the gentle breeze; how the alpine strawberry border I had planted was now studded with tiny white blooms and small garnet fruit, shock-

ingly sweet. In those moments it took my breath away. Instead
of seeing the weeds, as I usually did, I saw the beauty, and I
knew I'd had a hand in creating it.

In those moments the long days and unexpected bruises felt
worth it. In those moments it all made sense. None of us knew
how long we would be here, what the future held. How better
to spend your days than by creating beauty in the small corner
of the world that was yours? If that was all I did, it would be
enough.

I tried to be brave and invite people to the garden. My
mother had redone her kitchen that winter; now it opened up
onto the deck, and it was more pleasant to spend time there. We
had put the picnic table on the deck, and it was a nice spot to
have dinner. From the deck you could almost squint and not see
the weeds of the garden, not see how the vegetable beds were
wilting and gasping for moisture.

The kids came over. Sometimes it was just the girls; sometimes it was just the toddler; sometimes it was all three of them.
They each had their own garden plot. Graham grew carrots,
Cate grew carrots and flowers, and Abby wasn't particularly interested in growing anything at all. When some errant Shasta
daisies landed in her plot, she was happy to let them take over.

Graham had spent more time in the garden, with his
grandma, than either of the girls. He seemed more interested in
watering and planting than either of them had. That year my
mother bought him his own small red wheelbarrow. "I finally
got a master gardener!" she joked, as he watered and dug alongside her.

One day, when it was just the two of us in the garden, I led
him over to where I had set up the hammocks.

"Do you want to swing in the hammock?" I asked. He
looked up at me dubiously.

"Here, I'll show you"—and I spread the fabric to demonstrate how it could rock back and forth. He smiled shyly as he began to understand.

I lifted this little boy into the hammock—blond and sturdy and looking so much like my brother had when we were kids and I used to swing him in our hammock out in the country. When I placed Graham in the sling of fabric, he twisted around until he was lying on his stomach, his small face peeking out the side. "Okay," I said, and began to rock him gently.

The grin that appeared on his tiny face started slow and grew until it nearly split him open, so impish and wide I laughed aloud. "Welcome to the family, little guy. You're a Weaver now"—as if this were the induction ceremony to the run-wild garden tribe that we were. As I had with his sisters, as I had with his father, I pushed the hammock to make it swing. He wouldn't let me stop.

Eventually he reached out his arms so they stretched beyond the confines of the hammock. "Flying," he said. *"Flying!"*

I breathed deep and tried to hold on to that moment, that sunny afternoon in the garden when a little boy took flight for the very first time.

Then I stepped backward, onto a hidden underground wasps' nest. When I felt the hot stings on my ankle and realized what was happening, I snatched the toddler from the hammock and ran for the house as fast as we could go.

Despite the wasps' nests, I had offered to host the cookbook club's annual picnic. The year before we had gathered in a park, but when rain drove us under the shared picnic shelter, we'd had to squeeze between a Peruvian birthday party and a collection of drunken frat boys. In the garden, if it rained, we could shelter in peace.

This meant everyone would see the garden, in all its messy

and drought-strained glory. It wasn't just club members either. The summer picnic was the one gathering where partners and kids were invited too.

When I realized this, I was tempted to cancel, to think up some sort of excuse. But this was about community, about letting people in. Running away was not the answer.

In the past I had gone to great lengths to prepare for company. Once, when I was hosting a dinner for a nonprofit board I served on in San Francisco, I had painted two rooms of my house in advance of their arrival. I told myself it was good motivation for a task I had been meaning to do for ages, but in truth it was a cover-up. Not for the cracks on the ceiling of a charming old building—the cover-up was for me.

There was no way I could fix all that needed to be done in the garden. I didn't even try. I mowed the lawn. I swept up the patio and set out chairs. I bought new lavender plants—something I *had* been meaning to do for ages—but I didn't even manage to plant them.

When the first members of the cookbook club arrived, the lavender plants were sitting in their pots along the side border. They stayed there the whole party, a statement on my lack of perfection, perhaps, but what the heck? A garden is a work in progress—as a life is. It always will be.

I set up drinks on the patio. It wasn't fancy. There was a stack of mismatched vintage plates found at thrift stores—nothing too good to break. There were cloth napkins and Mason jars and homemade lemonade and a huge pitcher of Pimm's with mint and strawberries I had grown myself.

I was still carrying down the last of the beverages as people began filtering in. When one member asked if she could use the kitchen, I took her upstairs to show her around. When I came back onto the deck and looked out at the grass, it was covered in picnic blankets—stripes and checks and flowers. They made up a huge checkerboard quilt pattern on the lawn. They looked beautiful.

They also neatly covered up the matted dandelions on the lawn. *Bonus.*

That afternoon we ate and drank and lounged on the grass. A toddler staggered around on unsteady legs; a kindergartner made piles of wood chips and told us they were butterfly nests. People wandered down the hill to visit the chickens and went back for more food. It struck me that this is what I had been looking for when I came to Seattle. I had wanted this feeling.

And the sun arched overhead, and the breeze blew through the tall grasses of the meadow, and our laughter cascaded down the hill and filled up the space between the fruit trees. Maybe the neighbors even heard it over their fence.

The next day, when I walked across the grass to gather eggs from the chicken coop, I felt differently about the lawn. It was no longer that awful bit of grass pockmarked with dandelions that I still hadn't gotten around to digging out. It had been transformed by laughter. Now it was where my friends had spread their picnic blankets. It was the lawn on which we had spent the afternoon. It was the place my community had gathered.

. . .

18

PRETTY WONDERFUL

I PLANTED MY TOMATOES late again that summer, but this time it was on purpose. I had bought twenty-five varieties at the plant sales that spring—by staking and pruning I could fit that many in the side garden. I bought them as small seedlings and kept them in the greenhouse at first, potting them up once or twice as they grew. After a few years in the garden we had plenty of extra pots and, rather than a dreaded chore, I found it was pleasant to spend a rainy afternoon in the relative warmth of the greenhouse, my hands deep in potting soil.

"When are you going to plant those tomatoes?" my mother asked me in mid-May. She was tired of them taking up so much greenhouse space.

"Soon," I promised.

Spring seemed to come earlier in the Northwest every year; already I could see the effects of the changing climate. Plants were going to seed at unexpected times, flowering out of season.

I wasn't waiting for warm weather, however. I was waiting for the kids.

Finally, on a day when the girls and little Graham were all over at Orchard House, we planted the tomatoes—first ripping out the broccoli that had overwintered in the side garden and gone to seed. The kids liked pulling down the forest of yellow flowers and small leaves. My mother took the stalks to pinch off the flowers to eat. Waste not, want not.

"I've been thinking—when I grow up, I want to live on a farm in the country," Cate said as we nestled the small tomato plants into the earth. I was surprised. I hadn't heard of her future farming plans.

"Me too," said Abby.

"Aren't we lucky that Grandma has this big garden for us? It's almost like a farm."

"Yes," said Cate, "but it's not a *real* farm." She was dreaming of cows and horses.

"It's an *urban farm*," my mother said, using a currently popular term.

"Eww, Abby—you have a bug on you!" Cate pointed to her sister, who had a small black bug making its way up her arm.

With an expert flick of her fingers, Abby sent the small bug flying. "Who cares?" She shrugged. "It's just nature."

My mother and I looked at each other but said not a word. Were these the same girls who had run screaming at the sight of a gnat? The garden was changing us all.

The whole neighborhood was changing. The girl who lived next door—eleven years old—had fallen in love with my mother's wild back field and begged her mom to let their lawn go as well. Now there were two patches of wild grasses waving in the afternoon breeze.

"You're starting a trend," I told my mother.

"Good," she said.

Another day a neighbor from down the street stopped by as

I was bracing the lower limbs of the quince tree out front. "We were wondering if we could ask some questions about your water catchment system," he asked.

"You'll have to talk to my mother," I told him. "It's all her doing."

My mother left for Canada shortly after we planted the tomatoes. She would be gone again for three months, but I was used to the routine by now. Once she left I would clear off the patio, I would organize all the garden gear she left scattered around. When she came back she would complain that she could no longer find anything.

"That's because you're no longer *tripping* over it," I told her. We were still trying to figure it out, still trying to make things work. I promised myself that in the fall we would come up with a system that made sense to both of us.

The night before she left for Canada, I made my mother a care package for the road. I baked a loaf of the sour-tasting Russian bread I knew she liked, dark with coffee and molasses and caraway seeds. It was a recipe that called for eighteen different ingredients. I made it rarely, only for special occasions. That night I was up late waiting for dough to rise, but I wanted to do it for my mother.

I packaged up the bread, along with a spicy red-bean salad for her to eat for lunch. The trip to the cabin takes most of a day. I was sure she would have been too busy packing to plan a meal for herself.

When I showed up at her house the next morning, my mother was flitting around, squeezing last-minute items into the car, wanting to tell me all the things in the garden that I should water. As if I didn't know.

I gave her the bag of bread and salad and looked at her seriously.

"I know neither of us is very good at loving each other the way we need," I said, "but I stayed up last night making this for you because this is how I love you."

My mother didn't skip a beat. "That's nice, but I would rather you had gotten some sleep. You shouldn't stay up late just for me."

I looked at her again. *"This is how I love you."*

She paused, about to say something, then stopped. "Thank you," she said. "I will enjoy it."

That June it was Graham picking raspberries with me in the garden, the same raspberries I had brought up from San Francisco. The cuttings I had planted the first spring at Orchard House had taken root, and the south-side fence was now a forest of green leaves concealing small, sweet berries. One afternoon I took two plastic containers and we walked among the canes to pick the berries, just as I had with his sisters, just as his father and I had when we were children, crushing the soft red fruit in our mouths, letting them thud into our containers, one of the first sounds of summer.

At one point I looked down the row of raspberry canes and saw Graham's small blond head bent over the plastic container he was holding up to his face.

"My precious," he whispered to his collected berries. *"My precioussss . . ."*

I was used to the onslaught of fruit by now; I was prepared. When the raspberries came on I made jam and raspberry curd. I froze them. I made pie. And as soon as I made pie, I gathered friends.

One evening the kids and I took a pie down to a North Seattle park, where a wide expanse of grass sloped down toward the water. To swing on the swings there was to soar up over that expanse into an even wider sky and to feel as though you might actually be able to take flight into all that blue. Every time we went there I was glad these children were growing up in a city so tangled up in nature that it was hard to separate the two.

We met friends there, some of whom had brought desserts of their own. I was calling it a dessert picnic. How better to bring people together than in sweetness and summer? The kids raced across the grass and the grown-ups chatted and the sun slanted toward the west until everyone was bathed in a golden glow so beautiful it almost hurt.

We cut into the pie, the luscious filling staining plates, forks, small faces. Friends had brought a lemon blueberry tart, each berry elegantly arranged, and we savored that as well. When we had all eaten our fill, I pulled out the Hula-Hoops that I had, on a whim, tossed in the car as we were leaving Orchard House. The kids (and a few grown-ups) fell on them with glee, swinging around the plastic hoops, swaying with the motion of it. The niecelets might have had some practice, but no one could hold a candle to my friend's daughter. Ten-year-old Maia kept her hoop in motion seemingly without effort, her slim body rocking back and forth.

I stood there in the glow and took it all in, as if I could affix the scene in my memory for all time: the joy on the kids' faces, the laughter, the friends, the supreme silliness of it all. It was one of those moments you tuck into your pocket to sustain you through the long, dark winter.

"All you do is plan parties and picnics," my mother had once complained to me.

What I wanted to tell her—what I was coming to realize—is that you have to plan the moments, you have to make the memories. None of us knew what might come next. In September of the prior year I had been picking blueberries with my friend Kim. By November she had been diagnosed with an illness none of us had ever heard of. By April she was gone, leaving a gaping hole in the community that could never be filled. How could so much energy and fun and wisecracking wisdom suddenly be gone? None of us could understand it.

As Annie Dillard wrote: "We have less time than we knew."

I wanted my mother to understand that I didn't plan picnics and parties because life was perfect and easy—*I planned them because it wasn't.* I planned them because my friend had died, because another friend's father had been diagnosed with cancer, because none of us knew what the future held. I planned them because, on the long, difficult slog up the mountain, it's important to stop and look at the view. I planned them because what is all the work for if you cannot gather the people you love around you in a golden sunset and laugh together? I planned them because winter was coming and we needed warm memories to sustain us.

We have less time than we knew. I understood that now.

While my mother was preparing to return to Seattle at the end of the summer, I decided to throw a family dinner. Mostly our family dinners took place on birthdays or holidays. We're not like my friend Susan, whose family gathers for dinner every Sunday, rain or shine. But one of the things I dreamed about when we first found the garden was leisurely family dinners at a long table in the sunshine. We had the table and the sunshine; we just needed to gather.

I got my brother and sister-in-law to agree to the plan before I mentioned it to my mother. Maybe I was scared she would say no. Maybe I thought I could surprise her into enjoying herself. This, I soon realized, was not a good idea. She might not appreciate coming home to a house full of people, even if it were her family trying to love her. And when my mother is peeved, she does not hide it.

"What do you think about having a family dinner the day you come back from Canada?" I proposed nervously. "Everyone else has already agreed."

"I'm not coming down by myself, you know—June is coming with me."

"That's fine. The more, the merrier. I know the kids want to see you." It was a manipulative move, perhaps, but I knew my mother would do almost anything if the kids were involved.

"Okay," my mother said without great enthusiasm. "I would like to see the kids."

It wasn't much, but it was enough to go forward.

My real plan was that we would all come together to work in the garden—something that, up to then, had never happened. I had asked my brother and sister-in-law for some help in the garden and they had agreed. I could only imagine how happy my mother would be to come home at the end of the summer and see her entire family working together. But when the day came, their schedule had gotten busy and they didn't arrive until just before dinnertime.

The day was hot and sunny and I was running late. There was zucchini to be grated and herbs to chop and fresh pasta to be boiled when my brother and his family showed up, and suddenly the house was full of people and their small, energetic dog, Penny, running from room to room. When the kids had asked, I told them Penny could be included, but I assumed they would keep her outside or tied up. I hadn't imagined she would be bounding around the house, all over my mother's collection of Asian carpets where no outdoor shoes were ever allowed. I winced in anticipation of her displeasure.

When my mother arrived, however, she didn't notice the dog. The house was full of so many people, and as soon as she saw little Graham, she swept him up in her arms and sat down with him on the love seat in the entryway and the two of them gazed deeply into each other's eyes until their foreheads were touching and they both giggled, and for a moment nothing else mattered.

In the kitchen, kids were running in and out, huge pots of water were being put on to boil, and three different conversations were going simultaneously. It felt like Thanksgiving, a joyful chaos of family and friends and food. It felt like I had always wanted things to feel.

"What can I do to help?" June asked; she is the sort to smooth rough edges and take care of people. I set her to grating zucchini—three pounds of it. My brother took over pasta duty and I chopped the herbs I had picked from the garden and made sure the fruit crisp got into the oven and the frittata was taken out. For a moment we were all working together and I was reminded of how much I love being in the kitchen with my brother. After I left home for college he had taught himself to cook and later spent years working in restaurants; at one point he considered culinary school. Being in the kitchen together reminds me of our commonalities, of what we share. It reminds me that we have the same dry humor, that we finish each other's sentences.

"Penny," my mom cried plaintively as the dog bounded by her. "You haven't taken your shoes off!" The kids just laughed at her.

We gathered at the picnic table on the deck as the sun went down, and there was wine and conversation and platters of pasta and salad and frittata passed around. Graham insisted on eating only hard-boiled eggs and the girls insisted on sitting at either side of their grandmother and I don't even know what we talked about—but there was laughter and chatter and at one point I looked around the table and felt like my heart could not expand wide enough to take it all in.

After the family had gone home, and June and my mother and I had cleaned up the kitchen, I got ready to go home myself.

"Dinner was really nice tonight," my mother said. "Thank you for organizing it."

I waited for the next sentence. With my mother, I was used to there always being something wrong: the dog, the family, the chaos; too much salt in the food.

"But what?" I asked, still expecting criticism.

"But nothing," she said. "The pasta was delicious."

"There's more in the fridge."

"I noticed. I'm looking forward to eating it."

Sometimes, I thought as I drove home that night, past the houses up the hill with the beautiful views, sometimes even if things don't work out exactly as you planned, they can still be pretty wonderful.

19

. . .

TENDING THE ORCHARD

IF AN ORCHARD, TECHNICALLY, was as few as five trees, we now had an orchard four times over. There were twenty trees, most of them planted in a wide semicircle around the back meadow. There were apples, pears, Asian pears, a peach, a fig, three plums, and four cherries. My mother was a great believer in cherries.

When compared with vegetable gardening, orcharding is a sedate and relaxed pastime. There is minimal weeding or watering needed. For most of the year, the trees do their thing—and reward you with a harvest each fall. It is a satisfying effort-to-yield ratio. Tending an orchard, at least a small orchard, is almost leisurely.

This is not to say that there is no work. It's just that you could go out of town for a week or two at a time—even in summer—and your orchard would probably be fine. Growing fruit trees is like being an aunt or uncle—you need to show up for important events and give love, but you're not the parent; you don't have to be there every day.

I don't remember us doing anything to the fruit trees of my childhood. The apple trees my brother and I climbed were old and established, and the trees we planted either flourished or faltered. All we did was despair over the peach leaf curl, eat all the pears, and wrap the cherry in black netting in the hopes of foiling the birds (it never worked). In Washington, however, we soon learned that growing fruit requires a bit more effort.

In this state known for apples, there was something called an apple codling moth. These are the "worms" shown poking out of shiny red apples in children's books. Not worms at all—they are the larval state of a gray-colored moth that lays eggs in apple and pear trees. When the eggs hatch, the larvae eat the fruit for energy. Eventually they cocoon and emerge as a moth, but by then your apples are ruined.

Codling moths weren't the worst of the bunch—wormholes can be cut out if you're not too fussy. Worse were the apple maggot flies, whose larvae left the fruit laced with tiny, threadlike trails of brown. The apples might look rosy and ripe on the tree, but cut one open and disappointment waits within. The apple is useless—destined to soften and rot quickly.

"What are we supposed to do about it?" I asked my mother when we were both in the back meadow by the apple trees. She had been researching apple tree problems.

"You have to put little socks over each of the apples and pears."

"You're kidding, right? We're going to put *socks* on the trees? That's ridiculous."

"That's what you're supposed to do. They're made out of this nylon stuff—like panty hose."

"Are you serious?"

"Yup—one sock on each apple."

I remembered trees I had seen in Japan, where farmers carefully wrapped each fruit in a white paper bag. From a distance it looked like the trees were covered with large white flowers. It seemed insanely time-consuming, but I knew the Japanese desire for perfection—and how much they were willing to pay for it. Their orchards also ran small. Such attention to detail would be possible only on a limited scale.

"You're telling me those huge orchards in eastern Washington put a panty hose sock on each and every apple they grow?"

"Of course not," my mom said. "They probably use chemical sprays, but we're not going to do that."

An orchard might not be as hands-on as a vegetable garden, but it was not without its labor. Apparently socks were involved.

Ours was not the only orchard with old apple trees in Seattle. Also in the northern part of the city lay Piper's Orchard, whose history stretched much further back than ours. Planted by a German immigrant family that had run a bakery and confectionary before the turn of the century, Piper's Orchard had actually been lost for years.

When the Piper family's bakery burned down in the Great Seattle Fire of 1889, they moved north, to what was then the outskirts of the city, a wild and undeveloped place. They lived in old logging cabins and used a cookhouse built over a creek that ran down through the canyons. Butter and milk were suspended through a hole in the floor into the cold water of Piper's Creek to be kept chilled.

It was Mrs. Piper—Wilhelmina or "Minna"—who planted the orchard. There were more than thirty apple trees, in addition to a few pears and cherries. Her husband baked the fruit into his confections. The family also sold produce from the garden and water lilies they grew in a large pond. They had eleven children: One was close friends with the daughter of Chief Seattle; another started a sporting goods store later purchased by a man named Eddie Bauer.

The Pipers' land was sold in the 1920s, purchased by the Carkeek family, and given to the city as a park. It was a wild place—densely wooded canyons and steep slopes. On the sunny hillside that Minna Piper had tended, blackberry vines and ivy

quickly overcame the trees, and her orchard lay lost and forgotten for more than fifty years.

The orchard was rediscovered in 1981, by a landscape archi-
tect hired by the city to create a master plan for restoring the
wilderness park. It took more than two years of work by weekend volunteers to cut back the dense thicket that had grown over
the orchard. When asked why they would go to such effort, one
of the volunteers replied, "This is living history."

By the time I arrived in Seattle, the orchard of vintage trees
was fully restored and tended by a volunteer group called Friends
of Piper's Orchard. They planned work parties and a harvest
festival in the fall that included cider pressing, pies, and apple
tasting, and in the early summer, they put socks on the fruit to
protect against the apple maggot and the codling moth. One day
in May, I left the garden to join them in the orchard.

Piper's Orchard is not car accessible. To reach it you must
leave your car at one of two trailheads and walk into the park on
a wide dirt path that winds along Piper's Creek. Sunlight filters
down through tall trees and makes dappled patterns on the mossy
rocks and ferns by the creek. The hum of the city falls away. Suddenly, the woods open up to reveal a sunny hillside planted with
gnarled old apple trees. The day I went to the orchard, there were
two men, both perched on orchard ladders, wrapping each apple
in a beige nylon sock. Apparently my mother had been right.

One of the men came down the high ladder and introduced
himself as Don Ricks, a steward of the orchard. He set me up
with a bag of nylon socks—called footies—and showed me a few
shorter trees I could work on without need of a ladder. Orchard
ladders have steps on one side, but the other side balances on a
single pole. This allows for closer access to the trees but is less
stable than traditional ladders; they take some getting used to.

Don and the other man were both professional arborists.
This was their weekend volunteer gig. As I stood in the May
sunshine, reaching up to wrap each infant apple in its own co-

coon, I heard them bantering back and forth, talking shop, telling stories of pruning adventures and challenges.

I was thinking of Minna Piper, who had grafted these trees. Fruit trees do not grow true—if you plant the seed of your Red Delicious apple, you will not grow a Red Delicious. What you grow will be a surprise, a mix of the parent tree and some other variety—the pollen of which has been carried along to your tree. In dog terms, you'll get a mutt. Occasionally you'll get an interesting mix, but often the resulting apples will be inedible.

To grow a Red Delicious, a bud or branch from a Red Delicious tree must be grafted onto the roots of another. It's not unlike those children's books that match the bottom half of one creature to the top half of another. If you've done it right, the Red Delicious bud will grow and bear fruit.

I had learned to graft in permaculture class, fascinated by fusing together the cambium growth layers of two trees, a process that felt a little like concocting my own Frankenstein's monster. That summer, when I was on the island, I had noticed chokecherry trees scattered around my mother's cabin. Could I graft real cherries onto them? Could I seed the woods with edible fruit?

"Think of the possibility for cities," my permaculture teacher Jenny had said. "All those blooming plum trees planted along streets could be grafted into edible plums. Think of how much food we could produce."

Like most homesteaders, Minna Piper had grafted a variety of apples—orchards filled with one variety are modern industrial developments. Homesteaders chose a selection of apples that would come ripe at different times—some good for storage, some for cider, some for eating. Piper's Orchard featured a rare German variety called Bietigheimer, as well as the Albemarle Pippin, known to be a favorite apple of Thomas Jefferson.

When we stopped for a break, Don Ricks told me about the old trees in the area—the oldest apple tree in the state at Fort Vancouver, the pear tree in Edmonds thought to be more than a hundred years old. When I asked him why he was so interested in vintage trees, he rubbed his head, a sheepish half smile on his face. "As I get older myself, I care more about the older trees," he said. "If you take care of them, there can be a lot of productivity in them still."

I left that day with the business cards of both men. We needed to find someone to prune our trees, and anyone passionate enough to spend their free time doing the same work they did all week, dedicated to preserving and protecting older trees, seemed a good candidate to me.

The first year we didn't prune the trees. There was just so much to do—we planted nearly a dozen more fruit trees, hacked back the blackberries, set up the side garden, and established vegetable beds. Then my mother left for the summer, and I spent the entire season trying to keep up with the growth of a productive garden: the watering, the weeds, the produce.

A farmer I once interviewed said summer was like a train pulling out of the station, and he was the passenger running to jump on board. But the train just got faster and faster, and all he could do was keep running all summer long. Sometimes the train slowed down and he almost caught it—he almost got on top of all the work—but then it sped up again. The entire season he was sprinting, just trying to keep up.

At the end of my first summer in the garden, I knew exactly what he meant. When my mother came back from Canada, I couldn't wait to leave. I was tired of weeding and watering and trying to catch up to the train that was summer. I was sick of the garden. I hightailed it to San Francisco and stayed for nearly a month.

My mother called a few times while I was gone. Perhaps I should have picked up on the low-grade panic in her voice, but I didn't. I was busy packing up my San Francisco apartment, saying good-bye to a city I loved, panicked that I might have made the wrong decision in choosing Seattle. Garden problems were the least of my worries.

"Can I use your dehydrator?" my mom asked on the phone one day.

"Sure, it's in the garage. The instruction booklet is inside."

"Oh, good, I want to make apple chips."

"That's easy. Just make sure to cut them thin enough, or else they take forever to dry."

"Okay, I will. We have *so many apples.*"

I should have noticed—my mom doing anything with food, her tone when she said *"so many apples."* But I didn't. I often bought a case or two of apples in the fall, when prices were low and you got an extra discount for buying the box. Apple chips were easy; even my mom could manage that.

It wasn't until I came back to Seattle and found myself in my mother's kitchen that I really understood. That day I opened one of the large cupboards, and the entire thing was filled with jars of apple chips in a crazy variety of sizes. It looked like my mother had become a survivalist who stocks food in preparation for the doomsday. A very odd survivalist who planned to survive on dried fruit alone. That's when I realized: an apple tree, an orchard, can provide a lot of fruit.

We were not the only ones dealing with the generosity of an autumn fruit harvest. My friends Melinda and Brian had bought a house in the northern part of the city on a steep hill with a view of snowcapped mountains. There was a yard they were beginning to landscape, which ran long and ended at a large pear tree.

Melinda told me their first autumn in the house they had been overwhelmed with pears. These days most people are not versed in the ways of food preservation. Melinda and Brian worked full-time and could not keep up with the fruit. The pears quickly began to rot and draw flies. "We ended up digging a huge hole, piling them in there, and *burying* them," she said. "We just didn't know what to do with them all."

Seattle was dotted with fruit trees, many of which went un-tended and unharvested. In fall it was not uncommon to see apple trees in the grass parking strips between street and sidewalk surrounded by fallen and rotting fruit. This was the sight that spurred Gail Savina to start a nonprofit in Seattle called City Fruit. If you had a fruit tree you couldn't keep up with, you could call and offer your harvest. City Fruit's volunteer pickers would come and pick your fruit, which was then donated to local food banks, shelters, or senior centers. It was an elegant solution de-signed for people in the same situation as Melinda and Brian.

My friend Knox had run the fruit-harvesting program in his neighborhood. My second summer in Seattle, when I had only a P-Patch garden to look after, I occasionally spent an afternoon perched on a ladder, picking plums with Knox. The fruit smelled musty and sweet in the sun, like brown sugar, and when we dropped the crates off at the food bank and I saw people lining up to the end of the block for packages of white bread, day-old pastries, and canned food, I felt glad we had saved this food from rotting on the ground. In a city where fruit sometimes went ignored and unharvested, people were still going hungry.

"I hired someone to prune the fruit trees," my mother an-nounced one day when I was working in the garden.

"Is it one of the guys whose cards I gave you?" I looked up from the weeding I was doing.

"No," she said. "A man came to the door and said he used to prune the trees here."

"How do you know he's any good?" The recommendations I had given her were reputable—people experienced with older trees, even. This stranger I knew nothing about.

"This guy knows the trees already," my mother said. "He's worked on them before. Anyway, he's coming on Wednesday. It's all planned."

My mother has a way of shutting down a conversation, of asserting that she's in charge. I never knew how much to push back. This time I didn't. They were her trees; she would be paying for the pruning. She didn't want to hear what I had to say.

It was a week before I found myself in the garden again. My mother met me at the gate, aggrieved. "I did a terrible thing," she said.

"What is it?" I braced for bad news.

"The trees, the pruner—he did a hatchet job."

"Let me see," I said, trying not to overreact. How bad could it be?

I didn't know much about pruning myself. I had taken an afternoon class, just the basics. But even I knew you shouldn't hack back branches at the tips. Even I knew pruning too much will cause the tree to go into panic mode and produce what are called "water sprouts." These numerous thin branches grow straight upright; they do not bear fruit; they are weak, an entry point for disease. Pruning too hard is a good way to ruin the shape and productivity of a fruit tree.

That is what had happened to our trees. Instead of picking and choosing the strongest branches, instead of thinning them, the pruner had given the trees an allover haircut. He had cut too much. It was exactly the wrong thing to have done. Looking at the sawed-off branches, the open, raw cuts, I felt sick to my stomach.

More than that, I felt *angry*. Someone had come into the garden under the guise of helping and instead had harmed these trees. They were under our stewardship, and they had been savaged.

The strength of my emotion surprised me. I was angry at this man for what he had done, for misrepresenting his skill and knowledge, and angry at my mother for trusting him and not listening to me. And I was angry at myself for not pushing back, for letting her shut me down.

"Why didn't you listen to me? Why didn't you call the guys I gave you?"

"I know, *I know!*"

I took no comfort in being right. Being right wouldn't bring back the trees. Every rough cut I looked at made me want to vomit. These trees had been brutalized.

"They might die," my mom said quietly, already in mourning; the woman had no faith.

I looked at the trees—how many years had they grown here? Twenty, maybe thirty? If we had to replace them, how many years would it take to make up what had been lost? *Decades.*

I sighed. Nothing could be done.

"If the trees die, you sell the house." I didn't have it in me to start an orchard over from scratch.

My mother nodded. "Yes," she said soberly. "I think you're right."

The summer that followed, the large pear tree—the biggest tree in the garden—was covered with water sprouts growing straight up. There were few flowers that spring, and at the end of the summer, this tree that had given us baskets and baskets of fruit the summer before had exactly two pears on it.

But it did not die.

As if in penance, my mother started taking pruning classes. She came home using terms like "leader cut" and "apical dominance." It occurred to me that I should be the one taking these pruning classes. She was accumulating knowledge I would eventually need. The trees would live far longer than she would.

"Before you die, you're going to have to teach me everything you're learning about tree pruning," I told her one day.

"Sure," she said amiably. The idea of death had never bothered my mother. If anything, she was surprised to have lived this long. I had recently asked if there were things she wanted to do before she died, but she didn't seem worried.

"Mostly what I want is to live long enough for Graham to remember me," she told me. "That's the really important thing."

In the meantime, there were fruit trees to look after. Though her own knowledge was growing, my mother hired an expert to help bring the butchered trees back to life. Ingela Wanerstrand was also a steward at Piper's Orchard. In the other part of her life, she worked as a designer, teacher, and garden coach specializing in edible landscapes. She had more than twenty years of experience working with fruit trees.

Ingela began coming to the garden twice a year, training the trees, teaching us how to care for them. She was patient and good-natured, and she explained everything she did. Most of the water sprouts were gradually removed, except a few that were well placed and could be converted to productive branches.

She taught us how to look at the shape of the branches to select for the form we wanted. She showed how to weight down a young, thin branch to coax it to grow in a certain direction. And she showed us how some of the baby trees we had planted were not good specimens—too long in the trunk, with awkward branching patterns. Ordering trees from a catalog means you have no say in structure or form.

It soon became clear that Ingela was training us as much as she was training the trees. At the end of a visit, the orchard was littered with leaves and pruned-off branches to be collected and disposed of, but the trees looked healthier; they looked stronger.

It took two years for the trees to outgrow the damage that had been done to them. Some of them never quite recovered. There were two others that had never borne fruit. Every year my mother talked to them, admonished them: "If you don't get it together, you're getting yanked out." The trees seemed to ignore her nagging just as much as my brother and I had when we were teenagers. As another summer approached and there was still no fruit, we talked about replacing them, putting in apricots, or a yellow plum, or maybe an almond. An orchard, it turns out, is a work in progress.

That spring the trees were again covered in tiny white and pink blossoms, and as summer rolled onward, the flowers grew into fruit. The small peach tree we had planted had its first solid harvest—more than a dozen tiny fuzzy fruits where the previous summer had seen only three. Peaches are not common backyard trees in Seattle, but this variety had been bred to ripen with less heat and resist the cracking that rains often cause on peaches in western Washington.

The fruit was on the small side, but so plentiful I had to prop up the still-thin branches so they wouldn't break under the weight of the harvest. I should have pinched off some of the fruits early in the season—thinned them to encourage growth in the ones that would remain—but I didn't have the heart. That summer Abby, Cate, Graham, and I ate small peaches colored like a sunset and grinned at each other as the juice dripped down our chins.

The big pear tree was again loaded. Again there were basket hauls that topped out at forty pounds. I chopped up pears for the freezer, to be used in baked goods and smoothies, and made pear sauce, and gave pears to friends. The rest I lined up in the refrigerator. The pears took up three shelves—row after row of upright fruit. Every time I opened the door, it looked like an army marching in formation.

Then the apples started—first one variety and then another. We weren't sure of all the names, but we seemed to have Liberty and McIntosh. Their skins were red, and when I simmered them down into applesauce, the mixture turned a rosy pink. We stocked the freezer with it—*our applesauce*—and it tasted better than any I'd had before. This applesauce had personality, a fresh and tangy flavor.

I loved marking the jars: ORCHARD HOUSE APPLE SAUCE, ORCHARD HOUSE PEAR JAM. I already knew the pleasure of producing food, of putting up something for the cold months ahead, but when it was made with ingredients we had grown, that feeling was magnified. We never set out to be self-sufficient; this was no experiment in living off the land, but I was surprised by the sense of accomplishment. When I sent jars of apple and pear sauce home with my brother and sister-in-law, to feed my nieces and toddler nephew, I nearly glowed with pride.

The best days were the ones when the kids came over and we all ended up in the kitchen. I found an old-fashioned apple peeler at a thrift store and clamped it to one of the tall kitchen stools, just the right height for them. They took turns turning the crank, watching as the apple peels ribboned out the side and piled up into a big mound. When the apple was done, they slid the fruit off its core and displayed it for all to see: perfectly peeled and sliced. It felt like magic.

I smiled at my mother and she smiled back, both of us enjoying the children's delight.

We pulled those slices apart, and my mother arranged them on the dehydrator trays, sliding them into the black, boxy machine. When turned on it made a low humming noise, and the house slowly filled with the sunny, sweet fragrance of fruit. It took nearly a day for each batch to dry. The sound and the scent of apples and pears drifted through the house for weeks.

I looked around—at the kids happily cranking the fruit, at my mother laying out the slices to be dried—and I felt as if we were in one of my books from childhood: Mary and Laura putting up food with Ma in *Little House on the Prairie,* Marilla making jams and cordials with Anne at Green Gables. It felt like we had gone back in time.

Here we were, engaged in the ancient dance of preserving the harvest. For generations this was what had kept families and communities together—pitching in to secure the basics of life. You could not raise a barn or bring in the harvest on your own. You needed people to help you. In turn you helped them—and when the winds howled and the snows came, if things went according to plan, you would all be warm and well fed. I didn't know if my brother and sister-in-law would ever join us in the garden, in the kitchen, but I hoped someday they would. That we would all work together.

In a life increasingly filled with urgency and technology, it felt good to do something elemental. In a season when food was plentiful, we were preparing some of it to be saved, to last through the winter, until the strawberries bloomed and the raspberries colored up and we had fruit again. Throughout history this had been the role of family—to work together to gather your stores, save your seeds, and hope your harvest lasted through the winter and gave you a chance at doing it all again. These days our quest is to be happy, to be successful, but for years the goal had been just to survive.

This wasn't our one chance at survival—our apple and pear chips would serve as snacks for the kids all winter long, not the only supplies in our storehouse. But still, it felt good to be providing for ourselves and teaching this new generation. They might need it someday.

I remembered a day, a few years prior, when my mother was still living in California and the girls and I were eating winter citrus. On that day I had asked Abby if she knew where oranges came from. I wanted to tell her about orange groves in California, where her grandma lived, how they sloped down to the sea, how they smelled like heaven in full bloom. She was only four at the time, but when I asked the question, she looked at me like I was an idiot. *Where do oranges come from?*

"They come from Trader Joe's," she said. Obviously.

Now, just a few years later, here we all were. The girls would never question where apples and pears came from. They had played under blooming boughs in the springtime, wandered through the tall grasses of summer, and watched fruit grow round and ripe. These apples didn't come from the grocery store—they were *our* apples.

We had grown them ourselves.

20

. . .

HARVESTFEST

I DON'T REMEMBER HOW I got the idea, but after a few years in the garden, I decided to grow our annual Thanksgiving dinner. We had already grown so many things—lettuce, berries, tomatoes, radishes, kale, peaches, zucchini. Never mind that none of these items were *on* a traditional Thanksgiving menu; once I had the idea in my head, I couldn't shake it. Thanksgiving is a harvest festival. I wanted to celebrate with a harvest of our own.

The fact that most of my family is vegetarian made it easier—my brother and I eat meat, but no one else does. We hadn't served turkey on Thanksgiving for many years. There would be no need for a poultry harvest at Orchard House.

There would be pumpkins, however, and corn and cranberries. We'd have brussels sprouts and green beans, mashed potatoes, stuffing, and apple pie. All those things were possible. I just had to make it happen.

I was probably the only person planning my Thanksgiving menu in March, as gray drizzle fell from Seattle skies and the tulips had not yet bloomed, but this would not be a quick process. One does not decide in July or August to grow a Thanksgiving meal. It seemed odd to be thinking about apples and pumpkins when the garden was still asleep, but I needed to start in early spring, when everything was still just hope and possibility.

That spring at the plant sale, I stocked up, purchasing a container of pumpkin starts that held three small seedlings. There were four tiny brussels sprouts as well, surely enough for us all, and I ordered five cranberry vines from a fruit-tree catalog. I planted them all in the earth on a late-spring day when the sunshine had just begun to have some warmth to it, when it felt like summer might be around the corner, when the season stretched ahead full of potential.

The first surprise came with the cranberries. Five vines had sounded like a lot, but they arrived thin and wimpy looking. I knew plants sometimes start small and then take off, like teen boys who sprout up seemingly overnight. I tried not to be like my mother and assume the worst. I tried to have faith.

Despite my positive outlook, the cranberries did not fill in. As spring turned to summer, they flowered—small blossoms that would eventually turn to fruit. But here was another problem. If you counted them all up, between the five vines, there were exactly seven flowers.

If everything went well, if they didn't fall prey to bird, bug, snail, or slug—or spontaneously fall off the vine for no apparent reason (this happened with alarming regularity), we would have exactly seven berries.

Seven berries were not enough to make cranberry sauce; seven berries were not enough to garnish cocktails. I wasn't sure there was *anything* you could do with only seven cranberries. Place-card holders on the Thanksgiving table?

I told myself it would be okay. The kids didn't even like cranberry sauce.

Next came the brussels sprouts.

Growing up on the California coast, I had been used to brussels sprouts—thick, stubby stalks festooned with tiny, cabbagelike heads. I thought they were funny looking. When seen as a pile of baby cabbages in the market, they look adorable; on the stem they look like a surrealist vegetable mash-up.

That year the brussels sprouts took their revenge on me and refused to grow, remaining small and stunted even late into the summer. I didn't know then that brussels sprouts often do not thrive in the Northwest. It's hard to grow them to a decent size.

Even the pumpkins gave me a run for my money. There had been three seedlings in the pack I bought: three tender shoots, their secondary leaves already unfurling, prickly and green.

I planted them in the side garden, where the soil was excellent and they would get plenty of light. As soon as I did, one of them withered and died. I had watered them equally, and the other two were doing fine. I stood there looking blankly at the now-brown shoot.

Our statistical chance of pumpkin pie had just dropped by 33 percent. Who knew if there would be a Thanksgiving dinner at all?

My menu might have been in jeopardy, but the event itself was never in question. Of all the holidays, only Thanksgiving belonged to my family. Other secular holidays—the Fourth of July, Memorial or Labor Day—we never spent together.

The religious holidays were more complicated. My mother's family had not been observant, but in raising children, she wanted us to know the culture we had come from. So we lit Hanukkah candles, and if we were lucky, there were latkes, though my mother was never a fan of potatoes or deep frying.

But there was never any community, no gathering. The three of us sat at the kitchen table in that house in the country and spun the dreidel all alone.

What community we had came with Christmas, when the entire neighborhood gathered at the home of the family with the largest house—a huge, barnlike structure the husband had designed and built himself. They were of German descent, and their Christmas tree, which soared up to the second story, was decorated with real candles that glowed through the evening and seemed to touch everything with magic. At some point in the evening, Santa Claus would appear and pass out a gift to each and every child. One year I found a small pink diary hidden in my mother's closet, and when Santa gave it to me at the Christmas party, I realized the parents were supplying the gifts.

My mother wasn't fond of Christmas, but she wasn't sure how to avoid it. There were craft fairs in town, festive gatherings among friends and at school, decorations in stores and on houses. It's hard not to notice Christmas if you live in mainstream America.

Every year my mother swore she wouldn't fall into the Christmas trap. She didn't like the holiday, didn't believe in the commercialism, the excess. The truth is she also couldn't afford it.

Every year she held out until Christmas Eve. That was the day she could no longer be strong, the day she couldn't bear to disappoint her children.

"I always ended up buying some stupid plastic crap—just to have something to give you," she told me many years later. "You know those glitter stars? I bought them at the drugstore on Christmas Eve. I had to get *something;* they were the only things I could find."

The stars were made of clear plastic filled with water and silver glitter. When you shook them or turned them upside down, the glitter scattered to the bottom as in a snow globe, shining and sparkling. My brother and I had loved them and spent hours watching the glitter sink slowly through the water, gleaming as it fell. The stars now sit on a shelf in the bedroom my mother has for her grandchildren. They sparkle still.

It would be years before I heard the other reason my mother didn't like Christmas.

When my mother was a little girl of six or seven, the other children in her school threw rocks at her—they stoned her. They shouted and yelled at her because her family was Jewish; they told her she killed Jesus.

"What did you *do*?" I was horrified. I had been raised in a time and place that embraced diversity. I couldn't imagine such a thing.

"I was young, but I was smart," my mother said. "And I was good at history. I shouted back, 'I didn't kill him—the Romans did!' And I ran away as fast as I could."

Christmas is a complicated thing, even when you don't celebrate it.

As adults we did not spend the holiday together. My brother spent it with his children and in-laws, a flurry of wrapping paper, and a twelve-foot-tall Christmas tree. When I lived in San Francisco, I relied on the generosity of friends, glad to have it but sad I did not have a family to go to, a place where my presence was expected. The anxiety over where I was going to be for Christmas started up every fall.

My mother vanished for the holiday. She went to her cabin in Canada and retreated from the world. She read books; she slept; she ventured out only if friends invited her over. She said she was happy being alone.

I joked that she was fleeing—the country, the commercialism, the dominant religion she did not share, the excess and waste, the cheap plastic crap. It was everything she did not believe in.

She ran away, as fast as she could.

After initial disappointment with the pumpkin seedlings, the two that survived grew strong. Floppy lobed leaves sprouted from thick and prickly stems; thin tendrils reached out to grasp whatever they could to support the vines' growth. They reminded me of the decorations on Cinderella's carriage.

One of the stems shot out of the side garden and into the lilac bush nearby. It grew into the branches, threading its way through the leaves and woody stems until it was impossible to untangle the two. Perhaps we would have orange pumpkins hanging from our lilac that year.

Eventually, after much hope on my part, flowers emerged—tissue-paper thin and colored like the sun. They unfurled slowly, these big showy flowers. I eagerly checked their stems.

All squash, including pumpkins, produce male and female flowers—you can see the gender at the base. The male flowers have long, slender stems, while female flowers feature a round, slightly swollen bump. It is this bump that, once pollinated, grows larger and larger and eventually becomes a pumpkin or other squash. The first few flowers the vine produces will always be male. It is only when there is enough pollen available that a female flower is produced.

I hadn't known the excitement of that first female flower—the swollen stem that holds the potential for fruit. It's not the same strange wonder as when a friend becomes pregnant and you realize she holds future life inside her, but it's not unrelated either.

Unlike with female pregnancy, that swollen stem is just potential, not the event itself. To be expecting in the squash world requires a visit from a bee that has already visited male flowers and picked up pollen on the tiny hairs of its body. In the squash world, conception requires a middleman.

Despite my earnest attempts to be hopeful—at least more

hopeful than my mother—I was worried. It seemed such a gamble. What if a bee never came? (They had been dying off lately.) What if it was her first stop of the day, and she hadn't picked up enough pollen? What if she had the wrong pollen? Female flowers were open for only a day or two. There wasn't a lot of time to get this right.

In human fertility terms, it was akin to leaving a vial of sperm on the side of the road and hoping that someone would come along and be nice enough to deliver it to the doctor's office down the street within the required time period. Nature is exquisitely attuned and mind-blowingly intricate, but this seemed a long shot. What if it didn't work?

When the first female squash flower withered on the vine and the round, swollen bit turned soft and yellow and dropped off, I grieved. I decided I needed to do something about this. Perhaps I wasn't so hopeful after all.

One mid-August day I stood in the side garden and hand-pollinated my pumpkins. I'd heard you could do this, but I had never tried before. I picked a male flower and carefully peeled back the thin, damp petals. What I saw when I got down to the business surprised me.

The male pumpkin blossom had a center protrusion that tapered slightly and then swelled round and long, covered with golden pollen. It took me aback. I knew it was the flower part called the stamen, but it definitely looked phallic.

When I carried it over to the open female flower, things got stranger still. In the center was a circle of yellow bits—the stigma—that spouted up like a fountain and curled backward in a manner reminiscent of the paintings of Georgia O'Keeffe.

Then, in the center, was something that looked surprisingly like a hole.

What was I to do? I blushed. I looked around awkwardly to make sure no one could see me. Then I stuck the long, thick golden male stamen deep into the hole.

But first I rubbed it quickly around the outside of the opening. Because I thought the poor female flower deserved a decent chance of enjoying herself.

Growing up we usually spent Thanksgiving at home. Occasionally other people joined us, but rarely the same person twice. People came in and out of our lives like flowing water in the early years. Sometimes they were from my mother's past, or her current colleagues. A few times when I was very young, we went to someone else's home for the holiday, but that was rare.

What I remember is this: a day spent together, hanging out, cooking. There was usually a walk in late-November sunshine that was still golden even though the leaves had already turned. In the early days, we were out in the country, in the ramshackle house with the old apple trees. In my teenage years, we spent Thanksgiving in my mother's kitchen, with its big windows and the leafy yard all around, a huge maple tree flaming scarlet.

My first year of college, we had our meal there, with a teaching colleague of my mother's who had become a friend. Then we all drove out to the beach to see the small cabin my mother and this friend had begun to rent as a weekend getaway.

When we walked out on the deck and saw the view—the wide-open panorama of the Pacific stretching to the horizon—my brother said what everyone had been thinking: "Why didn't we have Thanksgiving *here*?" After that, and for all the rest of our California years, we did. I thought we always would.

Thanksgiving was important to me. It was a day based on gathering, coming together, sitting down around a large table. It celebrated food and harvest and excluded no one. If someone had made a national holiday just for me, it would look a lot like Thanksgiving.

As with so many things, I wished we had Thanksgiving traditions—a family stuffing, an apple pie recipe passed down from a grandmother. I envied those whose repeated rituals had worn grooves deep and wide; such things provide guides in life, a way to navigate, assurance that you are on the proper path. In my family, it felt like we were careening all over the place.

I tried to build us a scaffold for Thanksgiving. I researched recipes and borrowed traditions and grew fixated on the details of the day. A casual observer might have thought I was obsessed with the menu, but that wasn't it. I wanted to bind us together, to smooth the edges, to make us a family. Because I didn't know how to do that, I used what tools I had: those in the kitchen.

I suspected my family sometimes saw me as a kitchen fascist—insistent on what size to dice the onion, how long to roast the sweet potatoes. I was just trying to bring us together, trying to feed us, trying to meet my own needs. It was only a meal, but it was all I had.

My first Thanksgiving in Seattle had been my favorite ever. I had just returned from California with news of a book contract. We spent it at The Treehouse: me cooking, my brother and sister-in-law on the couch, little niecelets running into the kitchen to spank me and laugh and run away. I had been gone three months, but they hadn't forgotten me. Abby was not yet three years old, and she wanted to take her nap in my bed, wearing my T-shirt, and we whispered together under the covers. My mother presided over it all, fluttering around in her hummingbird way, and it felt good to celebrate exciting news with this family of mine that felt old and new all at the same time.

The year my mother bought Orchard House, my brother hosted Thanksgiving. When I started bugging him about menu planning weeks ahead, he was noncommittal. He didn't seem to care.

He didn't go grocery shopping until the night before Thanksgiving. Later he told us about a face-off he'd had with another man over the very last bag of brussels sprouts in the store—akin to the shoot-out at the O.K. Corral. It was a funny story, but it cut a little. This holiday mattered to me.

Instead of us all coming over early, instead of hours of hanging out and cooking and a walk in the woods, that year we didn't get together until late in the day. My brother and his family spent the day together, but my mother and I were not to arrive until shortly before the meal—like invited guests rather than family. It didn't feel like our holiday at all.

When I called my brother that day to check on details, we got in a fight. He thought I was angry about the menu, about what dishes were being served.

"I don't care about the food," he told me. "As far as I'm concerned, we could order Chinese."

I didn't know how to tell him what I really felt—maybe I didn't yet understand it myself. It wasn't about the stuffing or gravy, it was about us being together. I wanted to spend the day cooking with my brother in the kitchen, one of the few places I felt close to him. I wanted us to be a team; I wanted us to be family; I wanted it to matter to him as much as it did to me.

So I argued with him about mashed potatoes instead.

Standing on the deck of my mother's house that day as we bickered back and forth on the phone, I had a thought that stopped everything. I thought about my friend Paul.

What if my brother died? What if he were suddenly gone? How sad I would be that I had wasted this time arguing with him. We had wasted years already just trying to figure out how to love each other.

This Thanksgiving is going to be different, I thought, as I tended my pumpkins and corn and watched the apples ripen on the trees. My mother was still in Canada, my brother and his family gone to the East Coast for their annual vacation; I was the only one in Seattle. Even though it was August and the holiday months away, I was already making plans.

Really they were spring plans that were now coming to fruition. The wave that was summer had begun to crest. There were baskets of green beans and tomatoes every day, tomatillos and blackberries galore. I hurried them into bags in the freezer, into jam and salsa and blackberry curd. The end of the summer is such a busy time. One of the farmers on the island in Canada had told me, "This time of year, we put up a week's worth of food every day."

I was watching carefully as well. The pumpkins were growing larger and larger (*squash sex works!*), turning from green to orange. One of them was indeed hanging in the branches of the lilac bush. Every time I walked by and saw them, I felt a swell of parental pride, more than I normally did for the plants I grew. I had helped *create* those pumpkins (there is a high statistical probability they would have been just fine without me).

As August turned to September and October, the planning really began. We would have the roasted root vegetables my mother always makes—beets, carrots, and parsnips, a mass of jewel tones on the plate. My brother would make mashed potatoes from tubers the girls had helped harvest the week before. We had planted them in the beginning of summer. Now, digging underground, we turned up dozens of potatoes with a thin, almost yellow skin; it felt like finding buried treasure.

There would be corn pudding, rich with golden kernels and eggs from the hens. And one of the pumpkins would be stuffed with a filling of chard sautéed with garlic, caramelized onions, bread, and Gruyère cheese. When we cut the pumpkin into wedges, the stuffing would have gone all oozy with cheese, the bread swollen and silky; to me it tasted better than turkey.

My shopping list for the meal was almost all dairy: milk, butter, cheese, cream, and a few lemons. When I thought of what is usually involved in shopping for Thanksgiving, I smiled. All my purchases fit in a hand-carried basket, and I stood in the ten-items-or-less line and watched people pushing heavy carts piled high.

There were other things on our menu as well—a cheese plate with pickled green tomatoes, tangy and sour. There were pickled Asian pears with allspice, cinnamon, and Aleppo pepper. And one early fall day, Knox and I spent an entire afternoon pickling the tiny green figs on our tree that never got fully ripe.

The recipe Knox wanted to try was a traditional one, requiring us to blanch the figs in multiple changes of water to rid them of any bitterness before they were simmered in spiced sugar syrup. It was a laborious process—from an era when you worked hard to make even unripe fruit palatable. A time when food was precious, as important as the seeds in your storehouse and the chance of rain and a strong family to help you work the fields and bring in the harvest.

We had begun calling the day not Thanksgiving but Harvestfest.

The kids helped us cook the meal. I taught them to make pie the way my friend Kate taught me: without worrying about ripped dough. We chopped apples from our trees and mounded them high. When I placed the top crust, we crimped the edges, painted on an egg wash, and sprinkled the pie with sugar. Then we slipped it into the oven and watched through the window as our pie baked and browned and filled the entire house with the sweet scent of autumn.

When it was done, it joined other pies already made—a pumpkin and a mincemeat (one must do something with all those green tomatoes). Some might say three pies were too many, but I figured we'd struggled enough with the bitter; it was time for sweet.

When at last we sat down that afternoon, it was to a meal made of memories. The mashed potatoes tasted like the summer day the girls and I had slipped their brown quarters into the soil. The pudding was hot August when the corn silk tassels had waved and I had tried to construct a barrier to keep the raccoons out. The applesauce was made of days in the kitchen with the kids, their delight at cranking the apple peeler, preserving the harvest. The kale salad tasted of early, wet spring when my mother planted the greens that helped feed me what I needed. The pickled figs were the flavor of friendship, an afternoon spent in someone else's kitchen, trying something new.

I watched my family eat what I had planted and tended. These tiny seeds had already yielded so much. Here we were, so far from that little house in the country, all together, with our own harvest: a fruitful garden still out of control, my mother getting older, the kids growing as fast as the weeds, but more gentleness, more understanding between us with each season. I still had hope.

To me it felt like a beginning. There was much more I wanted—to plant currants and grapevines, and start a canning club, and host a cider-making party in the fall, and grow mushrooms on logs. Perhaps next year I would even stay on top of the weeding; I would manage to dig the dandelions out of the lawn. Maybe not.

But next year I hoped for more people at the table, more friends who felt like family. The people I leaned on and loved and let catch me were not just my relatives any longer. I felt lucky that way. The table was growing longer, year by year.

We'd need more food, of course, but that wasn't a problem. We just had to start earlier, sprout more seeds, dig another vegetable bed. It was all possible if we were willing to put in the time, the effort, to tend our crop, to care for the harvest, to care for each other.

The garden was here. We had only just begun to grow.

ACKNOWLEDGMENTS

. . .

This book owes its existence to my smart, feisty, and fierce-hearted friend Kim Ricketts, who, one night at Contigo in San Francisco, leaned over the table to where I was chattering on about the garden my mother was buying in Seattle and looked at me intently. "You *have got* to write about this," she said, "you know that." And because Kim was always right, I did.

I'm so sad Kim is not here to read the final product, but her spirit and all that she taught me about family and community and kindness are in these pages. Thank you, Kim. I'll miss you forever.

This book found its way forward thanks to my friend and agent Danielle Svetcov, who is also smart, feisty, and fierce-hearted. Thank you for championing my work, for being patient with long gestation periods, and for not killing me when I let your daughter use the kitchen knife. Chats with you are one of the highlights of this gig.

This book would not have been completed without the support, good cheer, and excellent feedback given by the women in my writing group (smart, feisty, and fierce-hearted, all of them). Erica Bauermeister, Randy Sue Coburn, and Jennie Shortridge, outstanding writers themselves, generously and gracefully helped shepherd the wayward child forward. For this, and for regular deadlines, writerly commiseration, and champagne corks out the window, I cannot thank you enough.

This book owes its final form to the support and vision of editor Pamela Cannon at Ballantine, who gave it a very soft spot to land. A finished book is always the work of many hands, the author's being only the first. To Pamela, and to Betsy Wilson, Loren Noveck, Katie Herman, Robbin Schiff, Susan Turner, and Simon M. Sullivan: Thank you for giving *Orchard House* a home, and for making it far, far better than I ever could have on my own. And thanks to Lindsey Kennedy, Quinne Rogers, and David Glenn, for helping the book out into the world.

To my readers, who have cheered me along from the start, and waited very patiently while I have been working on this project, thank you for your generosity, for your support, for saying you would wait until I was done. You have no idea how much it means.

Writers do not exist without mentors and companionship. Thanks to my teachers Barbara Owens, Elaine Johnson, Patricia Holland, and David Arehart, and in memory of John Nicholson (I have never forgotten that John Ciardi assignment). Thanks to Elmaz Abinader and Sarah Pollock, and in memory of the late, great Amanda Davis. To my Mills compatriots, Litquake, and the gang at Seattle7Writers, a grateful toast. To Anne Patchett, for saving my writer's sanity a time or two, Anne Lamott, for showing me how important it is to write truth about hard things, and Cheryl Strayed, for reminding me to be brave on the page and in life.

Thanks also to the Mesa Refuge writers' residency, for the opportunity to work on this book in a stunningly beautiful place, and deepest appreciation to Dr. Brené Brown, for giving me both an understanding of and a language to describe the concept of vulnerability. To Amanda Soule and family, for inspiration, and to Elaine Petrocelli and family at Book Passage, for giving me an extraordinary bookstore to grow up in.

I would not be here today without the support of my friends. Thank you to the Cookbook Club women (smart, feisty, and fierce-hearted, all of you), to Rebekah Denn and family, Myra Kohn, Michelle Hamilton, Knox Gardener, Paul McCann and family, Megan Gordon and Sam Schick (for telling hard truths), Sian Jones, Lian Gouw, Andrea J. Walker, Anne Livingston, Mari Osuna, Adam de Boor, Jennifer Johnson, Meg Peterson, my friends at Camp Unalayee, the community at Book Larder—and to Molly Wizenberg, Brandon Pettit, and the gang at Delancey, who make the meals that put my pieces back together.

Thanks, especially, to Ginnie and Bruce Ellingsen, who made a little girl feel at home; to Lorraine Ginter, for being the best babysitter we ever had, and for getting me curious about cooking; and to John Preston and Fawn Baron (otherwise known as June), for caring.

Thanks also to the many farmers, permaculturalists, and food folks who have inspired and helped educate me (any mistakes are very much my own). To Billy Allstot of Billy's Gardens; Adam Schick of Linnaea Farm; Casey and Eric Reeter from Wilderbee Farm; Don Ricks and Ingela Wanerstrand of Friends of Piper's Orchard; Gail Savina of City Fruit; Cole Tonnemaker of Tonnemaker Farms; Novella Carpenter of Ghost Town Farm; Dr. Stephen Jones of WSU Mt. Vernon; permaculturalists Jenny Pell, Marisha Auerbach, and Kelda Miller; Nazila Merati for #askabotanist; Jon Rowley for strawberries; Flatland Flower Farm for those first raspberry canes; Margaret Roach and Gayla Trail for inspiration and education; Michael Pollan; Seattle Tilth; and the Master Gardener program of King County. And thanks to Jill Lightner and *Edible Seattle* for giving me the opportunity to meet so many of these fine folks. And to chef Dan Barber of Blue Hill Restaurants, for a life-changing story, and Kate McDermott, for lessons in pie and graceful living.

As much as I miss my San Francisco friends (I do, I so do), I really have found a community in Seattle that I hadn't thought possible—thanks to all who are part of it (far too many to list here, a happy fact). Thank you, particularly, for putting up with my many absences and canceled camping trips while working on this project, and special thanks to Katie Briggs, for the best deadline care package ever; to Kate Vander Aa, for constant cheering, many car rides, and that amazing email; to Hsiao-Ching Chou, for wontons when needed, birthday cupcakes, and the Dimples; to Ellen Pohle for plates of dinner, mojitos, and berry picking; to Leslie Seaton for cheering cards, long talks, and camping trip organization; and to Lianne Raymond and Mary Plummer Loudon, for love and support in keeping the ship sailing forward. I couldn't have done it without you.

Finally, thanks to my family, who are dealing quite well with the trial of having a writer in their midst. To my mother, for giving me gardens, for letting me share her story, and for believing in me so much it's scary; to my brother and sister-in-law, who in their children have given me the best gift of my life; and to the kidlets, who are smart and feisty and fierce-hearted as well. You make it more fun to be on Team Weaver than I ever imagined possible. I love you all.

ABOUT THE AUTHOR

. . .

TARA AUSTEN WEAVER grew up running wild on the rocky coasts of Northern California and British Columbia. A writer focusing on travel, food, agriculture, and the environment, she is the author of *The Butcher and the Vegetarian* and *Tales from High Mountain* and writes the award-winning blog Tea & Cookies. Her work has appeared in *San Francisco Magazine, San Francisco Chronicles,* and on Apartment Therapy: The Kitchn and Chow.com. She is trained as a master gardener, master composter, and permaculture designer. Weaver lives in Seattle, Washington, where she is also the editor of *Edible Seattle* magazine.

For more information and photos of Orchard House please see:

taraweaver.com
teaandcookiesblog.com
@tea_austen

ABOUT THE TYPE

. . .

This book was set in Bembo, a typeface based on an old-style Roman face that was used for Cardinal Pietro Bembo's tract *De Aetna* in 1495. Bembo was cut by Francesco Griffo (1450–1518) in the early sixteenth century for Italian Renaissance printer and publisher Aldus Manutius (1449–1515). The Lanston Monotype Company of Philadelphia brought the well-proportioned letterforms of Bembo to the United States in the 1930s.